Kentucky's Twelve Days of Christmas

A Literary Anthology

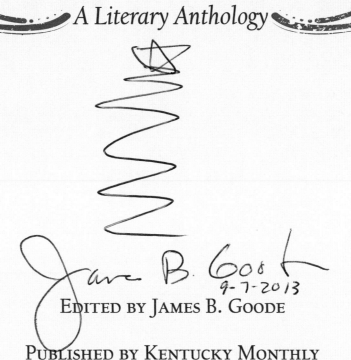

James B. Goode
9-7-2013

EDITED BY JAMES B. GOODE

PUBLISHED BY KENTUCKY MONTHLY

Kentucky's Twelve Days of Christmas is published by
Vested Interest Publications and *Kentucky Monthly*.

Edited by James B. Goode

Publisher Stephen M. Vest
Executive Editor Kim Butterweck
Associate Editor Patricia Ranft
Contributing Editor Ted Sloan

Art Director and Designer Kelli Schreiber
Designer Rebecca Redding

Director of Retail Sales Lindsey McKinney

ISBN 13: 978-0-615-67861-0
Library of Congress Control Number: 2012945981

All book order correspondence should be addressed to:

Kentucky Monthly
P.O. Box 559
Frankfort, KY 40602-0559

1-888-329-0053
www.kentuckymonthly.com

Manufactured in the United States of America
Price: $24.95

Contents

Introduction

In the February 12, 2012 issue of the *Lexington Herald-Leader* article, Neil Chethik, the director of the Carnegie Center, declared Lexington, Ky., the "... literary capital of Mid-America and the Carnegie Center as its statehouse." After completion of *Kentucky's Twelve Days of Christmas*, I could make a strong case for Kentucky being the literary capital of the United States. Tom Eblen, who authored the article, says that "... few [states] can top what writers who were born in or moved to Kentucky have produced—and are producing." A recent example is the University of Kentucky professor Nikky Finney who won the 2012 National Book Award for poetry for her book *Head Off & Split*. But there are many more examples of literary achievement from the past—most notably Robert Penn Warren who won the Pulitzer Prize in 1947, 1958, and 1979 (once in fiction and twice in poetry).

Harriette Arnow was runner-up for the Pulitzer Prize in Fiction for her novel *The Dollmaker*, falling just short of William Faulkner, who won for his *A Fable* in 1954.

With all this rich literary talent at my disposal, in December, 2011 I embarked on the mission of crafting an anthology of Christmas-themed writing by Kentucky writers, or those with a close connection to the Commonwealth. I was excited by the possibilities of what I knew could be found within this extraordinarily rich literary heritage. I was aware of two previous finely crafted publications that had focused on this theme: George Ella Lyons' *A Kentucky Christmas* (The University Press of Kentucky, 2003) and *Appalachian Christmas Stories* (The Jesse Stuart Foundation, 1997). George Ella says near the end of her book, "As the pages you have just read reveal, ours is a state eminently rich in writers. One volume cannot contain them all." This is our effort to add another volume to include some of those important missing selections.

Interestingly, Christmas stories, poems and songs were being written by Kentucky writers almost from the beginning of the Commonwealth in 1792. But there are also many examples of Christmas themed stories, poems, and songs based on much older traditions and myths. For example, Jean Ritchie recorded a version of "The Cherry Tree Carol" on her album *Kentucky Christmas: Old and New* (Greenhays, 1997) that was collected by the Harvard professor Francis James Child, and dates back to at least the 17th century Britain and possibly to the ninth century. Another older selection included here is Albery Allson Whitman's poem "One Snowy Night" from his collection *Not a Man, Yet a Man* published in 1877.

During the evolution of this manuscript, I was pleased to find that the amount of quality material not anthologized far exceeded my expectations. Robert Penn Warren's short story "The Christmas Gift," Harriette Arnow's 13th chapter of *The Dollmaker*, Irvin

S. Cobb's 1918 short story "The Exit of Anse Dugmore," John Fox, Jr.'s short story "Christmas Eve on Lonesome," Rebecca Caudill's children's story "A Certain Small Shepherd," and two Christmas sonnets by Allen Tate were among the many selections discovered along my journey.

In addition to our mission to include older material that had not been previously anthologized, we invited contemporary published writers. When we issued the call for these writers to submit selections for consideration, they responded in overwhelming numbers. Gerald R. Toner allowed us to reprint "Lipstick Like Lindsay's" (a story that appeared in *Redbook* and then was published by Penguin in a collection by the same title). Karen McElmurray contributed a chapter from her memoir *Surrendered Child*. Leatha Kendrick wrote an original short story "The Tides." Richard Taylor sent a rare and memorable creative non-fiction piece "A Wet Christmas." Joe Anthony submitted an original short story "Snow Lines" and a poem "Glomawr House." Crystal Wilkinson sent a chapter excerpt "Little Bird" from her novel *The Birds of Opulence*. James B. Goode offered two previously published short stories "A Change of Heart" and "The Christmas Snow Angel." Frank X Walker contributed a poem "Elves" from his collection *Black Box*.

Talented emerging writers sent high-quality, previously unpublished poems, short stories, and creative non-fiction pieces including Jacqueline Kohl's "The Christmas Chair," Leif Erikson's "Nativity Set," Stephen M. Vest's "One Hundred and One Christmases," and Tammy Ramsey's "Christmas in Store."

Readers will be treated to a wonderful variety of writing in this landmark anthology. These selections involve a range of themes from those that wax nostalgic to those that examine the dark side of holiday dysfunction. I hope you will sit down in front of a fireplace with a hot beverage, put your feet up, open *Kentucky's Twelve Days of Christmas* and become captivated by the superb artistry of some of the best this state has to offer.

There are many people to thank: Most of all, Vest who had the idea to begin with and fiercely supported me in my mission. Kim Butterweck, executive editor, and the entire staff of *Kentucky Monthly* who patiently listened, made wise suggestions, and served as my cheerleaders while we worked through this long tedious process. A special thanks to the dozens of Kentucky writers, both living and dead, who granted me the privilege of being able to hold their art in my hands, if albeit for a brief time. I consider it an honor to have been entrusted with their golden words.

— JAMES B. GOODE
Christmas 2012

The First Day

The Cherry-Tree Carol

JOSEPH was an old man,
an old man was he,
He married sweet Mary,
the Queen of Galilee.

As they went a walking
in the garden so gay,
Maid Mary spied cherries,
hanging over yon tree.

Mary said to Joseph,
with her sweet lips so mild,
'Pluck those cherries, Joseph,
for to give to my child.'

O then replied Joseph,
with words so unkind,
'I will pluck no cherries
for to give to thy child.'

Mary said to cherry-tree,
'Bow down to my knee,
That I may pluck cherries,
by one, two, and three.'

The uppermost sprig then
bowed down to her knee:
'Thus you may see, Joseph,
these cherries are for me.'

'O eat your cherries, Mary,
O eat your cherries now,
O eat your cherries, Mary,
that grow upon the bough.'

As Joseph was a walking
he heard angels sing,
'This night there shall be born
our heavenly king.

'He neither shall be born
in house nor in hall,
Nor in the place of Paradise,
but in an ox-stall.

'He shall not be clothed
in purple nor pall,
But all in fair linen,
as wear babies all.

'He shall not be rocked
in silver nor gold,
But in a wooden cradle,
that rocks on the mould.

'He neither shall be christened
in milk nor in wine,
But in pure spring-well water,
fresh sprung from Bethine.'

Mary took her baby,
she dressed him so sweet;
She laid him in a manger,
all there for to sleep.

As she stood over him
she heard angels sing,
'Oh bless our dear Saviour,
our heavenly king.'

COLLECTED BY FRANCIS JAMES CHILD

Christmas Gift

The big white flakes sank down from the sagging sky. A wet gray light hung over everything; and the flakes looked gray against it, then turned white as they sank toward the dark earth. The roofs of the few houses along the road looked sogged and black. The man who sat in the wagon that moved slowly up the road wore an old quilt wrapped around his shoulders and a corduroy cap pulled down over his eyes. His ears stuck out from under the cap, thin as paper and lined with purplish veins. Before him, vanishing, the flakes touched the backs of the mules, which steamed and were black like wet iron.

When the man spoke to the boy on the seat beside him, the ends of his mustache twitched the amber drops that clung to it. "You kin git off at the store," he said.

The boy nodded his head, which looked tight and small under the rusty-felt man's hat he wore.

The hoofs of the mules cracked the skim ice in the ruts, and pale yellow mud oozed up around the fetlocks. The wagon wheels turned laboriously, crackling the ice with a sound like paper.

The man pulled on the reins, and the mules stopped, their heads hanging under the sparse downward drift of flakes. "Whoa," he said, after the mules had already stopped. He pointed his thumb toward the frame building set beside the road. "You kin git off here, son," he said. "Most like they kin tell you here."

The boy climbed over the side of the wagon, set his foot on the hub, and jumped. His feet sank in the half-frozen, viscous mud. Turning, he took a step toward the building, then stopped. "Much obliged," he said, and started on. For a moment the man peered after him from small red-rimmed eyes. He jerked the reins. "Giddap," he said; and the mules lay against the traces, their hoofs crackling the skim ice.

The boy mounted the steps to the sloping boards of the porch, and put his sharp grey claw-like fingers on the latch-bar. Very quietly, he pushed the door inward a little space, slipped his body through the opening, and closed the door, letting the latch back down without a sound. He looked down the shadowy corridor of the store between the shelves of cans and boxes and the clothing hung on racks against the other wall. At the end of the corridor some men sat, their bodies in huddled outline against the red glow of a stove.

With hesitant steps, the boy approached them, stopping just behind the circle. A big man, whose belly popped the broad leather belt he wore, let his chair come forward to rest on the floor, and surveyed him. "What kin I do for you today, buddy?" he said.

The tight skin of the boy's face puckered greyly toward the lips, and his Adam's apple twitched up his throat. The

big man kept on looking at the boy, who stood dumbly beyond the circle, the over-size mackinaw hanging to his knees, and shook his head at the big man.

"You wanter git warmed up?" the big man said.

The boy shook his head again.

"Naw sir," he managed.

"You look cold," the big man said. "You come round here." He motioned to the open space in front of the stove.

Eyes fixed in question on the big man's face, the boy obeyed the gesture. He came round, carefully stepping over a man's out-thrust leg. He stood inside the circle, about six feet from the stove, and spread his hands out to it.

"Git up closter," the big man said. "Git yore bottom up to hit."

The boy moved forward, and turned his back to the stove, his hands behind him working weakly toward the warmth. The men kept looking at him. Steam from the mackinaw rose up against the stove, with the sick smell of hot, wet wool.

"Now ain't that better?" the big man demanded.

The boy nodded at him.

"Who are you, pardner?" one of the men said.

The boy turned toward him. He was a short stocky man, bald and swarthy, and he sat with his booted legs bunched under him like an animal ready to spring.

"I know who he is, I've seen him," another man said. "He's one of Milt Lancaster's kids."

Another man beyond the stove leaned forward, bucking his chair nearer to the boy. "Now ain't that nice," he said. "Pleased ter meet you. So you're one of Milt's little bastards."

The bald, swarthy man glared at him. "Shut up!" he ordered abruptly.

The other man leaned elaborately back and studied the ceiling, softly whistling between his teeth.

"In doing yore Satiday trading?" the bald swarthy one said.

The boy shook his head. Then he looked at the big man. "I wanter git the docter."

"That's what he's for," the big man admitted, and blinked at the stove.

"Yore folks sick?" the bald, swarthy man said.

"My sister," the boy said, "she's gonna have a baby."

The man who was whistling stopped. "Yore little sister, buddy?" He addressed the ceiling in mock solicitude, and shook his head. "Them Lancasters allus did calf young."

"Hit's my big sister," the boy said to the bald man. "She come up here last summer. She ain't nuthin but my sister on my ma's side."

"Well, well," said the man who was looking at the ceiling. He let his chair thump down on the front legs and spoke

to no one in particular. "So they's gonna be another little bastard out to Milt's place."

The bald swarthy man stared glumly across at the speaker.

"Bill Stover," he commented with no feeling, "you gonna make me stomp hell outer you fore sun."

The boy glanced quickly from one to the other. The bald swarthy man stared across the space, his legs bunched under him. The other man grinned, and winked sidewise.

"I oughter do hit now," the bald swarthy one said as if to himself.

The other stopped grinning.

"If you want the doc," the big man said, "you go up the road four houses on the right hand side. It ain't no piece. That's where Doc Small lives. They's a office in his front yard right smack on the road, but you go up to the house, that's where he is."

"Hit's a chicken office," one of the men said. "That's where the doc keeps his chickens now going on twenty years."

"You ain't gonna miss hit," the big man said.

The boy came out of the circle and stopped before the big man. He looked up with a quick, furtive motion of the head. "Much obliged," he said. He pulled his mackinaw about him, taking up the slack in the garment, and moved down the corridor toward the door.

"Wait a minute," the big man called after him. He got up ponderously to his feet, hitched his belt up on his belly, and went forward to the single glass showcase. The men watched him, craning their necks, all except the bald swarthy one, who crouched and stared at the red bulge of the stove.

The big man reached into the glass showcase and took out a half dozen sticks of red-striped candy. He thrust them at the boy, who, looking suspiciously at the objects, shook his head.

"Take em," the man ordered.

The boy kept his hands in the pockets of the mackinaw. "I ain't got nuthin ter pay fer it with," he said.

"Here, take em, buddy," the man said.

The boy reached out his hand uneasily, all the while studying the man's face, which was without expression. The fingers, scaled grey by cold like a bird's claw, closed on the candy, jerked back, clutching the sticks. The hand holding the candy slipped into the loose mackinaw pocket.

"Beat it," the big man said, "afore they beat hell outer you at home."

The boy slipped out the door, quick and quiet as a cat.

The big man came back to the stove and sank morosely into his chair. He tilted it back and put his arms behind his head, on which the thin brown hair was slickly parted.

"You sick, Al?" one of the men said.

He did not answer.

"You must be sick, giving something away just off-hand like that."

Bill Stover again leaned forward, wet his lips, and winked at the man who spoke. He himself seemed about to speak. Then he saw the face of the bald swarthy man, whose dark eyes burned with a kind of indolent savagery.

"You go straight to hell," the big man was wearily saying.

•••••

The snow had almost stopped. It was getting colder now. The flakes were smaller now, drawing downward breathlessly like bits of white lint. They clung to the soaked grass by the road and lay on the frozen mud. The boy's feet cracked the skim ice on the mud, then, in withdrawal, made a sucking sound.

Two hundred yards up the road he came to the place. Jutting on the road, the one-room frame building stood beside a big cedar. A tin sign, obscured by rust and weather, was nailed to the door, carrying the words: Doctor A. P. Small, Office. The boy turned up the path by the cedar, whose black boughs swooped down toward the bare ground. The house was set far back from the road, half hidden by trellises to which leafless horny vine clutched and curled. The windows of the house gave blankly, without reflection, on the yard where grass stuck stiffly up from dirty ice-curdied pools at the roots. The

door had a glass pane in it; behind the glass a lace curtain hung like a great coarse cobweb.

He tapped the paintless wood of the door.

It was a woman who, at last, opened the door.

"What do you want, boy?" she said.

"I wanter git the docter," he said.

She said, "Clean your feet and come in," and abruptly turned down the low hall. He scraped his shoes, stooped to wipe them with his fingers, and then, wringing the mud from his hands, wiped them on the mackinaw. He followed her, with quick secret glances from one side to the other. She was standing before a door, her thin arm pointing inward. "You come in here," she ordered. He stood back from the hearth while the woman thrust her hands nervously at the blaze. She was a little woman, and while she warmed her hands, she kept looking over her shoulder at him with a wry, bird-like asperity. "What's the matter?" she said.

"My sister's gonna have a baby," he said.

"Who are you, boy?"

"Sill Lancaster's my name, mam," he said, looking at her little hands that approached and jerked from the bright blaze.

"Oh," she said. She turned fully at him, inspected him sharply from head to foot. "You ought to take off your hat when you

come in the house, boy," she said.

He took the big hat off his head, and standing before her, held it tight in both hands.

She nodded at him; said, "Wait a minute"; and was gone out the door.

With a dubious, inquiring step, as on suspected ice, he went across the straw matting toward the hearth, and put his back to the fire. He looked at all the objects in the room, covertly spying on them as though they had a life of their own: the gilt-iron bed covered by a lace counterpane, the unpainted rocking chairs with colored pillows on the seats that were pulled up to the hearth, the table on which stood a basket full of socks rolled up in neat balls. The fire spat and sputtered in mild sibilance, eating at the chunks of sawn wood on the hearth. And the clock, its face supported by plump cupids of painted china, ticked with a small busy sound. The boy laid his hat on the yellow cushion of one of the chairs and put his hands to the fire. Against the plump little cushion, its color so bright, the hat was big and dirty. With hands still stretched out, the boy regarded it. It was soggy black with wet flecks of mud clinging to it; at the creases it was worn through. The boy took it quickly off the chair.

With that neat industrious sound the clock kept on ticking.

"Hello, son," the man in the door said.

The man was buttoning up a brown overcoat that dropped to his ankles. Beneath the coat his small booted feet stuck out. The woman slipped in past him and came to the fire, put her hands toward the blaze again, jerked them back, all the while looking at the boy. The man pulled a black fur cap on his head and turned down the ear-flaps. "Les go," he said.

The woman went up to him, touching his breast with a quick indecisive motion as when she spread her hands to the fire.

"Don't wait up for me," he said.

He put his face down, a sharp expressionless face that seemed inconsequential under the big fur cap; and the woman kissed his cheek. Her kiss made a neat, dry sound, like a click.

"Les go," he said.

He went into the hall, the boy following to the door of the room, where the woman stood aside to let him pass. He paused an instant at the threshhold. "Much obliged," he said to her, and slipped down the hall after the man like a shadow.

A horse and buggy, the curtains up, stood beyond the cedar at the corner of the office. The powdery flakes of snow drifted cautiously downward, were lost in the dark branches of the tree, on the road where the horse stood, head down in patience.

"You get in," the man said, and went around to the driver's side. The boy climbed into the buggy, slipping under the curtain. The man got in and bent to

fasten the curtain flap on his side. "You fix em over there," he said, and picked up the reins. The boy fumbled with the metal catch, the man, reins in hand, watching him. "Don't you know nothing, son?" he said.

"I ain't never fixed one, afore," the boy said.

The man thrust the reins into the boy's hands, leaned across his knees to latch the curtain, straightened up, and took the reins as though lifting them from a peg. "You pull that rug off the seat back of you," he said, "and give it here."

The boy obeyed, unfolding the rug. The man took an end, jabbed it under his thigh and wrapped it around the outside leg. "Now fix yourself up over there," he ordered. He shook out the reins through the slit in the curtain.

The horse swung into the road, the front wheel groaning and scraping with the short turn, the buggy jerking side-wise over the ruts. The buggy straightened out, and drew more easily. The hoofs crunched and sloshed, the wheels turning.

"That's right, ain't it," the doctor said, "we go outer the settlement this a-way?"

"Yes sir," the boy said.

"I thought I recollected it so."

They drew past the store. A man went down the steps and started to walk up the road, walking with a plunging, unsteady stride, plowing the mud. His high shoulders hunched and swayed forward.

"John Graber." The doctor jerked his mittened thumb toward the man. "He better be gitting on home, his woman sick like she is." He shook his head, the sharp features without expression. "A mighty sick woman. Kidneys," he said.

"Yes sir," the boy said.

"Graber'll be cooking his own supper fore long."

They passed the last house, a small grey house set in the open field. Yellow gullies ran across the field, bald plateaus of snow-smeared sod between gully and gully. A mule stood close to the barbed-wire fence which separated the field from the road, and the fine flakes sank in the field and the gullies. From the chimney of the house a line of smoke stood up very still amidst the descending flakes.

"Graber's house," the doctor said.

The boy sat up straight and peered through the isinglass panels at the house and the smoke and the gutted field.

"Do I turn off up the creek?" the doctor asked.

"Yes sir."

They crossed the wood bridge, where the timbers creaked and rattled loosely with the turning wheels. Beneath it the swollen water plunged between limestone rocks, sucking the yellow foam. The flakes touched the spewing foam, the water plunging with a hollow constant sound.

"What's your pappy doing now?" the doctor said.

"My pappy's croppin on a place fer Mr. Porsum, but hit ain't no good."

"Uh-huh," the man grunted. He looked through the isinglass in front. They had turned off the main road up the road by the creek. On one side, the limestone stuck out from the bluff side, thin grey icicles hanging from the grey stone among the shriveled fern fronds. The creek, below the dead growth of the gorge on the other side, made its hollow sound.

"Hit ain't worth nuthin. Cain't even grow sassafras on hit."

"Uh-huh," the man said.

"We be leaving this year. We ain't gonna have no truck no more with Mr. Porsum that ole son-of-a-bitch. He ain't done nuthin like he said. He ain't ..."

"That's what your pappy says," the man said.

"My pappy says he's a goddam sheep-snitchin son-a-bitch."

The man stared through the isinglass pane, his sharp nose and chin sticking out in front, his head wobbling with the motion of the buggy. Then he opened his mouth: "I reckon Jim Porsum's got something to say on his side."

The boy took a stolen glance at the man's face, then relapsed to the motion of the buggy. Out of the red mess of the road, limestone poked, grey and slick like wet bone, streaked with red mud. The wheels surmounted the stone, jolting down beyond on the brittle mud. On the bluff side the cedars hung. Their thick roots thrust from the rotten crevices of stone, the roots black with moss, garnished with ice; their tops cut off the light.

The man reached the reins over to the boy. "Hold em," he said.

The boy drew his hands from under the rug and held the reins. He grasped them very tight with both hands, the knuckles chapped and tight, and peered through the isinglass panel at the horse; the head of the horse, under the cedars, bobbed up and down.

Clamping his mittens between his knees, the man rolled a cigarette. His breath, as he licked the paper, came frostily out from his mouth in a thin parody of smoke. He lighted the cigarette; then, as he reached for the reins, he found the boy observing him, observing the twisted paper that hung from his lips. He did not put the tobacco sack in his pocket, but, after a moment of hesitation, held it toward the boy. "All right," he said, "go on and take it."

The boy shook his head, watching the sack.

"Aw hell," the man said, and dropped the sack on the boy's lap.

The boy took the sack without assurance, adjusted the paper, poured tobacco into it. Biting the string with his teeth, big square teeth irregularly set in the tight mouth, he pulled the sack together, and dropped it. Then he lifted the paper

to his lips; the tip of his tongue darted out between his lips, strangely quick from the stolid, pinched face, and licked the edge of the paper. With that delicacy of motion, with the sharp grey fingers bunched like claws together to hold the bit of paper to his mouth, the boy, crouching there in the dim interior, looked at that instant like a small coon intently feeding.

He took a deep drag of the smoke, the end of the cigarette shriveling with the sucking coal, and his thin chest expanded under the cloth of the mackinaw.

Balancing the sack in his mittened hand, the doctor regarded the process. The smoke drifted colorless from the boy's nostrils, which were red and flattened. "You ought not to do it," the doctor said, "and you just a kid like you are."

"I'm ten," the boy said.

"It's gonna stunt your growth all right."

"Hit never stunted my pappy's growth none, and he's been a-smokin ever since he was eight. He's big. Ain't you never seen him?"

The doctor looked at the lips, which puckered greyly to the twist of paper, the pale eyes set close together under the man-size hat. The two cigarettes, the man's and the boy's, glowed indecisively in the shadow. "I've seen him all right," the man said at length.

"He's a plenty strong son-a-bitch," the boy said.

The man pushed his cigarette through a crack in the curtain, and sank back. His torso, swathed in the heavy overcoat, rolled and jerked to the impact of rut or stone like some lifeless object in uneasy water. Down the gorge, like the sound of wind driving through woods, the creek maintained its hollow constant plunging. "I didn't know Milt Lancaster had any girl big enough to be having babies yet," the man said.

"He ain't. Not I knows anything about."

"You said your sister, didn't you?"

"She's my sister on my maw's side. That's what she says and that's what my maw says."

The live cigarette, burned almost to the very end, hung at the corner of the boy's lips, glowing fitfully and faintly with his speech. It hung there, untouched by his hands, which were thrust under the rug. He no longer drew the smoke in; it seemed to seep in without conscious effort on his part, drifting from his nostrils thinly with his breath.

"She just come up here last summer," the boy said. "I never knowed nuthin bout her afore that. Maw was glad ter see her, I reckin. At first, I reckin."

"Uh-huh," the man said absently, his sharp features fixed forward apparently without attention.

"But pappy warn't, he just raised holy hell fer sartin. She just worked round the house and never said nuthin ter nobody.

Cept ter me and the kids. Then pappy got so he didn't pay her no mind ter speak of."

The cigarette burned close to the lip, the paper untwisting so that bits of red ash slipped from it and fell toward the rug. The boy withdrew one hand from beneath the rug, and with thumb and forefinger pinched together, removed the cigarette. The paper had stuck to the flesh of the lip; he jerked it free, licking the place with that strange darting motion of the tongue tip. The tongue was pink and damp against the dry grey flesh of the lips. "Then she up and got sick and she's gonna have a baby," he said.

"So that's why she's up here," the man said.

The boy shook his head. "I dunno," he said. "She just come."

In the gloom of the buggy, their bodies, one long and lax against the back of the seat, the other short and upright, jerked and swayed.

The road climbed a little. The bluff wall lost its steepness, falling to heaps of detritus among boulders. No cedars showed here, only stalks of weeds and the wiry strands of vine showing on the broken surface. Then the road went down again, swinging away from the creek. There was no further sound of the water.

At the foot of the slight grade the bottom spread out: bare corn fields with stubble and shocks that disintegrated to the ground, rail fences lapped by the leafless undergrowth. Away to the left a log house stood black under bare black trees. From it the somnolent smoke ascended, twined white and grey against the grey sky. The snow had stopped.

Beyond the bottoms, the knobs looked cold and smoky. From them, and from the defiles, fingers of mist, white to their blackness, crooked downward toward the bare land. The horizon rim, fading, sustained a smoky wreath that faded upward to the space without sun.

They drew to the lane that led to the log house.

"You go on past here," the boy said. "Hit's up them knobs."

The boy, almost surreptitiously, took a stick of candy from his pocket, broke off half, and stuck it between his lips. He looked at the man's sharp, expressionless profile. Then he held out the piece to him. Without a word the man took it and stuck it between his lips, sucking it.

They moved forward between the empty fields.

Robert Penn Warren

"This is the Day His hour of life draws near..."

This is the day His hour of life draws near,
Let me get ready from head to foot for it
Most handily with eyes to pick the year
For small feed to reward a feathered wit.
Some men would not see it an epiphany
At ease, at food and drink, others at chase
Yet I, stung lassitude, with ecstasy
Unspent argue the season's difficult case
So: Man, dull critter of enormous head,
What would he look at in the coiling sky?
But I must kneel again unto the Dead
While Christmas bells of paper white and red,
Figured with boys and girls split from a sled,
Ring out the silence I am nourished by.

Allen Tate

ALLEN TATE

"Ah, Christ, I love you rings to the wild sky..."

Ah, Christ, I love you rings to the wild sky
And I must think a little of the past:
When I was ten I told a stinking lie
That got a black boy whipped; but now at last
The going years, caught in an accurate glow,
Reverse like balls englished upon green baize—
Let them return, let the round trumpets blow
The ancient crackle of the Christ's deep gaze.
Deafened and blind, with senses yet unfound,
Am I, untutored to the after-wit
Of knowledge, knowing a nightmare has no
Sound;
Therefore with idle hands and head I sit
In late December before the fire's daze
Punished by crimes of which I would be quit.

Allen Tate

ALLEN TATE

About The Authors

Francis James Child *was born in 1825 and by 26 was appointed as the Boylston Professor of Rhetoric and Oratory at Harvard University. He later became Harvard's first professor of English in 1876. Although he was a well-known Chaucerian scholar, he is best known for having collected 305 ballads within the British Isles in the late 19th century, which subsequently were published by Houghton-Mifflin in 10 volumes between 1882 and 1898. Some of his more notable contributions include variations of Barbara Allen, Lord Randall, The Elfin Knight, Thomas the Rhymer, three dozen that relate the story of Robin Hood, and scores of "murder ballads." According to scholars, his collection is essentially responsible for the folk-music revival beginning in the 1950s and continuing well into the 1960s when ballads became part of the repertoire of musicians such as Kentuckian Jean Ritchie, Pete Seeger, Joan Baez, Art Garfunkel, John Jacob Niles, and Bob Dylan.*

Robert Penn Warren *is the only Kentucky author to win the Pulitzer Prize three times and in two different genres. He won in 1947 for the novel* All the King's Men *and for two books of poetry, in 1948 for* Promises: Poems, 1954-1956 *and again in 1979 for* Now and Then: Poems, 1976-1978. *Warren wrote 10 novels, beginning in 1939 and ending in 1977. Two were made into movies:* All the King's Men *(twice) and* Band of Angels. *He authored and published 16 books of poetry, beginning in 1936 and ending in 1985. He also published two collections of short stories, three children's books, four textbooks, six collections of essays, three historical works, one play, and one biography. Warren was a poet, critic, novelist, and teacher. He taught at Vanderbilt University, Nashville, Tenn., Southwestern College, Memphis, Tenn., University of Minnesota, Yale University, and Louisiana State University. He was appointed the nation's first poet laureate February 26, 1986. Warren was born in Guthrie, in Todd County, Ky. He was educated at Vanderbilt University (having entered at the age of 16), graduating in 1925 summa cum laude, Phi Beta Kappa, and as a recipient of the Founder's Medal. He received his master's from the University of California in 1927, did post-graduate work at Yale University the following year, and received a B. Litt. from Oxford University in 1930. Warren died Sept. 15, 1989.*

Allen Tate *was the founding editor of the Vanderbilt University-based magazine of verse* The Fugitive, *named for the literary group of southern poets including Robert Penn Warren, John Crowe Ransom, Donald Davidson, and Merrill Moore, who were defenders of formal techniques of poetry and of the traditional values of the agrarian lifestyle of the South against the threat of the invading urban industrialization. He was one of the contributors to the famous agrarian manifesto* I'll Take My Stand *(1930). He was born in 1899 in Winchester, Ky., in Clark County. He studied violin at the Cincinnati Conservatory of Music and then went on to Vanderbilt University in 1918. He edited the prestigious* Sewanee Review *from 1944-1947 and also served as the associate editor of* The American Review. *He mentored such great poets as Robert Lowell, John Berryman, and Randall Jarrell. From 1951 until his retirement he was Professor of English at the University of Minnesota. He had also served on the faculty as poet-in-residence at Princeton University where he founded the creative writing program. He authored 13 books of poetry and 13 books of prose. His most famous poem, "Ode to the Confederate dead," appeared in his first book of poetry* Mr. Pope and Other Poems *(1928). He is also known for his biographies* Stonewall Jackson: The Good Soldier *(1928) and* Jefferson Davis: His Rise and Fall *(1929). He died in 1979 in Nashville, Tenn.*

The Second Day

The Exit of Anse Dugmore

When a Kentucky mountaineer goes to the penitentiary the chances are that he gets sore eyes from the white walls that enclose him, or quick consumption from the thick air that he breathes. It was entirely in accordance with the run of his luck that Anse Dugmore should get them both, the sore eyes first and then the consumption.

There is seldom anything that is picturesque about the man-killer of the mountain country. He is lacking sadly in the romantic aspect and the delightfully studied vernacular with which an inspired school of fiction has invested our Western gun-fighter. No alluring jingle of belted accouterment goes with him, no gift of deadly humor adorns his equally deadly gun-play. He does his killing in an unemotional, unattractive kind of way, with absolutely no regard for costume or setting. Rarely is he a fine figure of a man.

Take Anse Dugmore now. He had a short-waisted, thin body and abnormally long, thin legs, like the shadow a man casts at sunup. He didn't have that steel-gray eye of which we so often read. His eyes weren't of any particular color, and he had a straggly mustache of sandy red and no chin worth mentioning; but he could shoot off a squirrel's head, or a man's, at the distance of a considerable number of yards. Until he was past thirty he played merely an incidental part in the tribal war that had raged up and down Yellow

Banks Creek and its principal tributary, the Pigeon Roost, since long before the Big War. He was getting out timber to be floated down the river on the spring rise when word came to him of an ambuscade that made him the head of his immediate clan and the upholder of his family's honor.

"Yore paw an' yore two brothers was laywaid this mawnin' comin' 'long Yaller Banks togither," was the message brought by a breathless bearer of news. "The wimmenfolks air totin' 'em home now. Talt, he ain't dead yit."

From a dry spot behind a log Anse lifted his rifle and started over the ridge with the long, shambling gait of the born hill-climber that eats up the miles. For this emergency he had been schooled years back when he sat by a wood fire in a cabin of split boards and listened to his crippled-up father reciting the saga of the feud, with the tally of this one killed and that one maimed; for this he had been schooled when he practised with rifle and revolver until, even as a boy, his aim had become as near an infallible thing as anything human gets to be; for this he had been schooled still more when he rode, armed and watchful, to church or court or election. Its coming found him ready.

Two days he ranged the ridges, watching his chance. The Tranthams were hard to find. They were barricaded in their log-walled strongholds, well guarded in

anticipation of expected reprisals, and prepared in due season to come forth and prove by a dozen witnesses, or two dozen if so many should be needed to establish the alibi, that they had no hand in the massacre of the Dugmores.

But two days and nights of still-hunting, of patiently lying in wait behind brush fences, of noiseless, pussy-footed patrolling in likely places, brought the survivor of the decimated Dugmores his chance. He caught Pegleg Trantham riding down Red Bird Creek on a mare-mule. Pegleg was only a distant connection of the main strain of the enemy. It was probable that he had no part in the latest murdering; perhaps doubtful that he had any prior knowledge of the plot. But by his name and his blood-tie he was a Trantham, which was enough.

A writer of the Western school would have found little in this encounter that was really worthwhile to write about. Above the place of the meeting rose the flank of the mountain, scarred with washes and scantily clothed with stunted trees, so that in patches the soil showed through like the hide of a mangy hound. The creek was swollen by the April rains and ran bank-full through raw, red walls. Old Pegleg came cantering along with his rifle balanced on the sliding withers of his mare-mule, for he rode without a saddle. He was an oldish man and fat for a mountaineer. A ten-year-old nephew

rode behind him, with his short arms encircling his uncle's paunch. The old man wore a dirty white shirt with a tabbed bosom; a single shiny white china button held the neckband together at the back. Below the button the shirt billowed open, showing his naked back. His wooden leg stuck straight out to the side, its worn brass tip carrying a blob of red mud, and his good leg dangled down straight, with the trousers hitched half-way up the bare shank and a soiled white-yarn sock falling down into the wrinkled and gaping top of an ancient congress gaiter.

From out of the woods came Anse Dugmore, bareheaded, crusted to his knees with dried mud and wet from the rain that had been dripping down since daybreak. A purpose showed in all the lines of his slouchy frame.

Pegleg jerked his rifle up, but he was hampered by the boy's arms about his middle and by his insecure perch upon the peaks of the slab-sided mule. The man afoot fired before the mounted enemy could swing his gunbarrel into line. The bullet ripped away the lower part of Pegleg's face and grazed the cheek of the crouching youngster behind him. The white-eyed nephew slid head first off the buck-jumping mule and instantly scuttled on all fours into the underbrush. The rifle dropped out of Trantham's hands and he lurched forward on the mule's neck, grabbing out with blind, groping motions.

Dugmore stepped two paces forward to free his eyes of the smoke, which eddied back from his gun muzzle into his face, and fired twice rapidly. The mule was bouncing up and down, sideways, in a mild panic. Pegleg rolled off her, as inert as a sack of grits, and lay face upward in the path, with his arms wide outspread on the mud. The mule galloped off in a restrained and dignified style until she was a hundred yards away, and then, having snorted the smells of burnt powder and fresh blood out of her nostrils, she fell to cropping the young leaves off the wayside bushes, mouthing the tender green shoots on her heavy iron bit contentedly.

For a long minute Anse Dugmore stood in the narrow footpath, listening. Then he slid three new shells into his rifle, and slipping down the bank he crossed the creek on a jam of driftwood and, avoiding the roads that followed the little watercourse, made over the shoulder of the mountain for his cabin, two miles down on the opposite side. When he was gone from sight the nephew of the dead Trantham rolled out of his hiding place and fled up the road, holding one hand to his wounded cheek and whimpering. Presently a gaunt, half-wild boar pig, with his spine arched like the mountains, came sniffing slowly down the hill, pausing frequently to cock his wedge-shaped head aloft and fix a hostile eye on two turkey buzzards that began to swing in narrowing circles over one particular spot on the bank of the creek.

The following day Anse sent word to the sheriff that he would be coming in to give himself up. It would not have been etiquette for the sheriff to come for him. He came in, well guarded on the way by certain of his clan, pleaded self-defense before a friendly county judge and was locked up in a one-cell log jail. His own cousin was the jailer and ministered to him kindly. He avoided passing the single barred window of the jail in the daytime or at night when there was a light behind him, and he expected to "come clear" shortly, as was customary.

But the Tranthams broke the rules of the game. The circuit judge lived half-way across the mountains in a county on the Virginia line; he was not an active partizan of either side in the feud. These Tranthams, disregarding all the ethics, went before this circuit judge and asked him for a change of venue, and got it, which was more; so that instead of being tried in Clayton County—and promptly acquitted—Anse Dugmore was taken to Woodbine County and there lodged in a shiny new brick jail.

Things were in process of change in Woodbine. A spur of the railroad had nosed its way up from the lowlands and on through the Gap, and had made Loudon, the county-seat, a division terminal. Strangers from the North had come in,

opening up the mountains to mines and sawmills and bringing with them many swarthy foreign laborers. A young man of large hopes and an Eastern-college education had started a weekly newspaper and was talking big, in his editorial columns, of a new order of things. The foundation had even been laid for a graded school. Plainly Woodbine County was falling out of touch with the century-old traditions of her sisters to the north and west of her.

In due season, then, Anse Dugmore was brought up on a charge of homicide. The trial lasted less than a day. A jury of strangers heard the stories of Anse himself and of the dead Pegleg's white-eyed nephew. In the early afternoon they came back, a wooden toothpick in each mouth, from the new hotel where they had just had a most satisfying fifty-cent dinner at the expense of the commonwealth, and sentenced the defendant, Anderson Dugmore, to state prison at hard labor for the balance of his natural life.

The sheriff of Woodbine padlocked on Anse's ankles a set of leg irons that had been made by a mountain blacksmith out of log chains and led him to the new depot. It was Anse Dugmore's first ride on a railroad train; also it was the first ride on any train for Wyatt Trantham, head of the other clan, who, having been elected to the legislature while Anse lay in jail, had come over from Clayton, bound for the state capital, to draw his mileage and be a statesman.

It was not in the breed for the victorious Trantham to taunt his hobbled enemy or even to look his way, but he sat just across the aisle from the prisoner so that his ear might catch the jangle of the heavy irons when Dugmore moved in his seat. They all left the train together at the little blue-painted Frankfort station, Trantham turning off at the first crossroads to go where the round dome of the old capitol showed above the water-maple trees, and Dugmore clanking straight ahead, with a string of Negroes and boys and the sheriff following along behind him. Under the shadow of a quarried-out hillside a gate opened in a high stone wall to admit him into life membership with a white-and-black-striped brotherhood of shame.

Four years there did the work for the gangling, silent mountaineer. One day, just before the Christmas holidays, the new governor of the state paid a visit to the prison. Only his private secretary came with him. The warden showed them through the cell houses, the workshops, the dining hall and the walled yards. It was a Sunday afternoon; the white prisoners loafed in their stockade, the blacks in theirs. In a corner on the white side, where the thin and skimpy winter sunshine slanted over the stockade wall, Anse Dugmore was squatted; merely a rack

of bones enclosed in a shapeless covering of black-and-white stripes. On his close-cropped head and over his cheekbones the skin was stretched so tight it seemed nearly ready to split. His eyes, glassy and bleared with pain, stared ahead of him with a sick man's fixed stare. Inside his convict's cotton shirt his chest was caved away almost to nothing, and from the collarless neckband his neck rose as bony as a plucked fowl's, with great, blue cords in it. Lacking a coverlet to pick, his fingers picked at the skin on his retreating chin.

As the governor stood in an arched doorway watching, the lengthening afternoon shadow edged along and covered the hunkered-down figure by the wall. Anse tottered to his feet, moved a few inches so that he might still be in the sunshine, and settled down again. This small exertion started a cough that threatened to tear him apart. He drew his hand across his mouth and a red stain came away on the knotty knuckles. The warden was a kindly enough man in the ordinary relations of life, but nine years as a tamer of man-beasts in a great stone cage had overlaid his sympathies with a thickening callus.

"One of our lifers that we won't have with us much longer," he said casually, noting that the governor's eyes followed the sick convict. "When the con gets one of these hillbillies he goes mighty fast."

"A mountaineer, then?" said the governor. "What's his name?"

"Dugmore," answered the warden; "sent from Clayton County. One of those Clayton County feud fighters."

The governor nodded understandingly. "What sort of a record has he made here?"

"Oh, fair enough!" said the warden. "Those man-killers from the mountains generally make good prisoners. Funny thing about this fellow, though. All the time he's been here he never, so far as I know, had a message or a visitor or a line of writing from the outside. Nor wrote a letter out himself. Nor made friends with anybody, convict or guard."

"Has he applied for a pardon?" asked the governor.

"Lord, no!" said the warden. "When he was well he just took what was coming to him, the same as he's taking it now. I can look up his record, though, if you'd care to see it, sir."

"I believe I should," said the governor quietly.

A spectacled young wife-murderer, who worked in the prison office on the prison books, got down a book and looked through it until he came to a certain entry on a certain page. The warden was right—so far as the black marks of the prison discipline went, the friendless convict's record showed fair.

"I think," said the young governor to the warden and his secretary when they had moved out of hearing of the convict

bookkeeper—"I think I'll give that poor devil a pardon for a Christmas gift. It's no more than a mercy to let him die at home, if he has any home to go to."

"I could have him brought in and let you tell him yourself, sir," volunteered the warden.

"No, no," said the governor quickly. "I don't want to hear that cough again. Nor look on such a wreck," he added.

Two days before Christmas the warden sent to the hospital ward for No. 874. No. 874, that being Anse Dugmore, came shuffling in and kept himself upright by holding with one hand to the door jamb. The warden sat rotund and impressive, in a swivel chair, holding in his hands a folded-up, blue-backed document.

"Dugmore," he said in his best official manner, "when His Excellency, Governor Woodford, was here on Sunday he took notice that your general health was not good. So, of his own accord, he has sent you an unconditional pardon for a Christmas gift, and here it is."

The sick convict's eyes, between their festering lids, fixed on the warden's face and a sudden light flickered in their pale, glazed shallows; but he didn't speak. There was a little pause.

"I said the governor has given you a pardon," repeated the warden, staring hard at him.

"I heered you the fust time," croaked the prisoner in his eaten-out voice. "When kin I go?"

"Is that all you've got to say?" demanded the warden, bristling up.

"I said, when kin I go?" repeated No. 874.

"Go!—you can go now. You can't go too soon to suit me!"

The warden swung his chair around and showed him the broad of his indignant back. When he had filled out certain forms at his desk he shoved a pen into the silent consumptive's fingers and showed him crossly where to make his mark. At a signal from his bent forefinger a Negro trusty came forward and took the pardoned man away and helped him put his shrunken limbs into a suit of the prison-made slops, of cheap, black shoddy, with the taint of a jail thick and heavy on it. A deputy warden thrust into Dugmore's hands a railroad ticket and the five dollars that the law requires shall be given to a freed felon. He took them without a word and, still without a word, stepped out of the gate that swung open for him and into a light, spitty snowstorm. With the inbred instinct of the hillsman he swung about and headed for the little, light-blue station at the head of the crooked street. He went slowly, coughing often as the cold air struck into his wasted lungs, and sometimes staggering up against the fences. Through a barred window the wondering warden sourly watched the crawling, tottery figure.

"Damned savage!" he said to himself. "Didn't even say thank you. I'll bet he never had any more feelings or sentiments in his life than a moccasin snake."

Something to the same general effect was expressed a few minutes later by a brakeman who had just helped a woefully feeble passenger aboard the eastbound train and had steered him, staggering and gasping from weakness, to a seat at the forward end of an odorous red-plush day coach.

"Just a bundle of bones held together by a skin," the brakeman was saying to the conductor, "and the smell of the pen all over him. Never said a word to me—just looked at me sort of dumb. Bound for plumb up at the far end of the division, accordin' to the way his ticket reads. I doubt if he lives to get there."

The warden and the brakeman both were wrong. The freed man did live to get there. And it was an emotion which the warden had never suspected that held life in him all that afternoon and through the comfortless night in the packed and noisome day coach, while the fussy, self-sufficient little train went looping, like an overgrown measuring worm, up through the blue grass, around the outlying knobs of the foothills, on and on through the great riven chasm of the gateway into a bleak, bare clutch of undersized mountains. Anse Dugmore had two bad hemorrhages on the way, but he lived.

•••••

Under the full moon of a white and flawless night before Christmas, Shem Dugmore's squatty log cabin made a blot on the thin blanket of snow, and inside the one room of the cabin Shem Dugmore sat alone by the daubed-clay hearth, glooming. Hours passed and he hardly moved except to stir the red coals or kick back some ambitious ember of hickory that leaped out upon the uneven floor. Suddenly something heavy fell limply against the locked door, and instantly, all alertness, the shock-headed mountaineer was backed up against the farther wall, out of range of the two windows, with his weapons drawn, silent, ready for what might come. After a minute there was a feeble, faint pecking sound—half knock, half scratch—at the lower part of the door. It might have been a worn-out dog or any spent wild creature, but no line of Shem Dugmore's figure relaxed, and under his thick, sandy brows his eyes, in the flickering light, had the greenish shine of an angry cat-animal's.

"Whut is it?" he called. "And whut do you want? Speak out peartly!"

The answer came through the thick planking thinly, in a sort of gasping whine that ended in a chattering cough; but even after Shem's ear caught the words, and even after he recognized the changed but still familiar cadence of the voice, he abated none of his caution. Carefully he unbolted the door, and, drawing it inch by

inch slowly ajar, he reached out, exposing only his hand and arm, and drew bodily inside the shell of a man that was fallen, huddled up, against the log door jamb. He dropped the wooden crossbar back into its sockets before he looked a second time at the intruder, who had crawled across the floor and now lay before the wide mouth of the hearth in a choking spell. Shem Dugmore made no move until the fit was over and the sufferer lay quiet.

"How did you git out, Anse?" were the first words he spoke. The consumptive rolled his head weakly from side to side and swallowed desperately. "Pardoned out—in writin'—yistiddy."

"You air in purty bad shape," said Shem.

"Yes,"—the words came very slowly—"my lungs give out on me ... and my eyes. But—but I got here."

"You come jist in time," said his cousin; "this time tomorrer and you wouldn't a' never found me here. I'd 'a' been gone."

"Gone!—gone whar?"

"Well," said Shem slowly, "after you was sent away it seemed like them Tranthams got the upper hand complete. All of our side whut ain't dead—and that's powerful few—is moved off out of the mountings to Winchester, down in the settlemints. I'm 'bout the last, and I'm a-purposin' to slip out tomorrer night while the Tranthams is at their Christmas rackets—they'd layway me too ef ..."

"But my wife—did she ..."

"I thought maybe you'd heered tell about that whilst you was down yon," said Shem in a dulled wonder. "The fall after you was took away yore woman she went over to the Tranthams. Yes, sir; she took up with the head devil of 'em all—old Wyatt Trantham hisself—and she went to live at his house up on the Yaller Banks."

"Is she ...Did she ..."

The ex-convict was struggling to his knees. His groping skeletons of hands were right in the hot ashes. The heat cooked the moisture from his sodden garments in little films of vapor and filled the cabin with the reek of the prison dye.

"Did she—did she ..."

"Oh, she's been dead quite a spell now," stated Shem. "I would have s'posed you'd 'a' heered that, too, somewhars. She had a kind of a risin' in the breast."

"But my young uns—little Anderson and—and Elviry?"

The sick man was clear up on his knees now, his long arms hanging and his eyes, behind their matted lids, fixed on Shem's impassive face. Could the warden have seen him now, and marked his attitude and his words, he would have known what it was that had brought this dying man back to his own mountain valley with the breath of life still in him. A dumb, unuttered love for the two shock-headed babies he had left behind in the split-board cabin was the one big thing in Anse

Dugmore's whole being—bigger even than his sense of allegiance to the feud.

"My young uns, Shem?"

"Wyatt Trantham took 'em and he kep' 'em—he's got 'em both now."

"Does he—does he use 'em kindly?"

"I ain't never heered," said Shem simply. "He never had no young uns of his own, and it mout be he uses 'em well. He's the high sheriff now."

"I was countin' on gittin' to see 'em agin—an buyin 'em some little Chrismus fixin's," the father wheezed. Hopelessness was coming into his rasping whisper. "I reckon it ain't no use to—to be thinkin'—of that there now?"

"No 'arthly use at all," said Shem, with brutal directness. "Ef you had the strength to git thar, the Tranthams would shoot you down like a fice dog."

Anse nodded weakly. He sank down again on the floor, face to the boards, coughing hard. It was the droning voice of his cousin that brought him back from the borders of the coma he had been fighting off for hours.

For, to Shem, the best hater and the poorest fighter of all his cleaned-out clan, had come a great thought. He shook the drowsing man and roused him, and plied him with sips from a dipper of the unhallowed white corn whisky of a mountain still-house. And as he worked over him he told of the tally of the last four years: of the uneven, unmerciful war,

ticking off on his blunt finger ends the grim totals of this one ambushed and that one killed in the open, overpowered and beaten under by weight of odds. He told such details as he knew of the theft of the young wife and the young ones, Elvira and little Anderson.

"Anse, did ary Trantham see you a-gittin' here tonight?"

"Nobody—that knowed me—seed me."

"Old Wyatt Trantham, he rid into Manchester this evenin' 'bout fo' o'clock—I seed him passin' over the ridge," went on Shem. "He'll be ridin' back 'long Pigeon Roost some time before mawnin'. He done you a heap o' dirt, Anse."

The prostrate man was listening hard.

"Anse, I got yore old rifle right here in the house. Ef you could git up thar on the mounting, somewhar's alongside the Pigeon Roost trail, you could git him shore. He'll be full of licker comin' back."

And now a seeming marvel was coming to pass, for the caved-in trunk was rising on the pipestem legs and the shaking fingers were outstretched, reaching for something.

Shem stepped lightly to a corner of the cabin and brought forth a rifle and began reloading it afresh from a box of shells.

·····

A wavering figure crept across the small stump-dotted "dead'ning"—Anse Dugmore was upon his errand. He dragged the rifle by the barrel, so that its butt made

a crooked, broken furrow in the new snow like the trail of a crippled snake. He fell and got up, and fell and rose again. He coughed and up the ridge a ranging dog-fox barked back an answer to his cough.

From out of the slitted door Shem watched him until the scrub oaks at the edge of the clearing swallowed him up. Then Shem fastened himself in and made ready to start his flight to the lowlands that very night.

•••••

Just below the forks of Pigeon Roost Creek the trail that followed its banks widened into a track wide enough for wagon wheels. On one side lay the diminished creek, now filmed over with a glaze of young ice. On the other the mountain rose steeply. Fifteen feet up the bluff side a fallen dead tree projected its rotted, broken roots, like snaggled teeth, from the clayey bank. Behind this tree's trunk, in the snow and half-frozen, half-melted yellow mire, Anse Dugmore was stretched on his face. The barrel of the rifle barely showed itself through the interlacing root ends. It pointed downward and northward toward the broad, moonlit place in the road. Its stock was pressed tightly against Anse Dugmore's fallen-in cheek; the trigger finger of his right hand, fleshless as a joint of cane, was crooked about the trigger guard. A thin stream of blood ran from his mouth and dribbled down his chin and coagulated in a sticky smear upon the gun stock. His lungs, what was left of them, were draining away.

He lay without motion, saving up the last ounce of his life. The cold had crawled up his legs to his hips; he was dead already from the waist down. He no longer coughed, only gasped thickly. He knew that he was about gone; but he knew, too, that he would last, clear-minded and clear-eyed, until High Sheriff Wyatt Trantham came. His brain would last—and his trigger finger.

Then he heard him coming. Up the trail sounded the muffled music of a pacer's hoofs single-footing through the snow, and after that, almost instantly Trantham rode out into sight and loomed larger and larger as he drew steadily near the open place under the bank. He was wavering in the saddle. He drew nearer and nearer, and as he came out on the wide patch of moonlit snow, he pulled the single-footer down to a walk and halted him and began fumbling in the right-hand side of the saddlebags that draped his horse's shoulder.

Up in its covert the rifle barrel moved an inch or two, then steadied and stopped, the bone-sight at its tip resting full on the broad of the drunken rider's breast. The boney finger moved inward from the trigger guard and closed ever so gently about the touchy, hair-filed trigger—then waited.

For the uncertain hand of Trantham,

every movement showing plain in the crystal, hard, white moon, was slowly bringing from under the flap of the right-side saddlebag something that was round and smooth and shone with a yellowish glassy light, like a fat flask filled with spirits. And Anse Dugmore waited, being minded now to shoot him as he put the bottle to his lips, and so cheat Trantham of his last drink on earth, as Trantham had cheated him of his liberty and his babies—as Trantham had cheated those babies of the Christmas fixings which the state's five dollars might have bought.

He waited, waited …

•••••

This was not the first time the high sheriff had stopped that night on his homeward ride from the tiny county seat, as his befuddlement proclaimed; but halting there in the open, just past the forks of the Pigeon Roost, he was moved by a new idea. He fumbled in the right-hand flap of his saddlebags and brought out a toy drum, round and smooth, with shiny yellow sides. A cheap china doll with painted black ringlets and painted blue eyes followed the drum, and then a torn paper bag, from which small pieces of cheap red-and-green dyed candy sifted out between the sheriff's fumbling fingers and fell into the snow.

Thirty feet away, in the dead leaves matted under the roots of an up torn dead tree, something moved—something moved; and then there was a sound like a long, deep, gurgling sigh, and another sound like some heavy, lengthy object settling itself down flat upon the snow and the leaves.

The first faint rustle cleared Trantham's brain of the liquor fumes. He jammed the toys and the candy back into the saddlebags and jerked his horse sidewise into the protecting shadow of the bluff, reaching at the same time to the shoulder holster buckled about his body under the unbuttoned overcoat. For a long minute he listened keenly, the drawn pistol in his hand. There was nothing to hear except his own breathing and the breathing of his horse.

"Sho! Some old hawg turnin' over in her bed," he said to the horse, and holstering the pistol he went racking on down Pigeon Roost Creek, with Christmas for Elviry and little Anderson in his saddlebags.

•••••

When they found Anse Dugmore in his ambush, another snow had fallen on his back and he was slightly more of a skeleton than ever; but the bony finger was still crooked about the trigger, the rusted hammer was back at full cock and there was a dried brownish stain on the gun stock. So, from these facts, his finders were moved to conclude that the freed convict must have bled to death from his lungs before the sheriff ever passed, which they

held to be a good thing all round and a
lucky thing for the sheriff.

December

From Songs of the Month (1904)

Winter now has fully come
With its heavy frost and snow;
Frozen over is the brooklet,
Ceased now is its rippling flow.

All the pretty little flowers
That went to sleep so long ago,
Are snugly covered over
With the pretty, shielding snow.

But the outside is forgot,
By the cheerful hearth-fire's light,
Where merry games are going on
'Mong the group so gay and bright.

Snowy, icy, cold December,
Oh, how much we love you, dear,
For you bring dear Christmas with you,
Merriest day of all the year.

EFFIE WALLER SMITH

Christmas Card: For Edward

All out of shepherds, angel, wise men,
even painted on velvet or appliquéd,
we would like to send you something
more than two words we always say:
MERRY JOYOUS, the computed words.

We would like, at least, to decorate some letters
M or C, in tempera and gold on vellum,
were we are not vague about handling gold,
even about the nature of vellum;
few stores stock either, even in this season.

A holly cart? A friendship quilt?
A wassail bowl? Winter flowers? Berries?
Disney figures under mistletoe?
Something, something, cooked, forged, carved
from our remembered community of Christmas?

What will you accept?
A picture of your house, or ours? In snow?
Better, a flake of snow, immaculate.
We wish your merry joyous Christmas tranquil,
complete as a flake of snow.

Hollis Summers

HOLLIS SUMMERS

In Memory of Hollis Summers

From *The Wick of Memory*

Christmas Eve. Wild Turkey in my glass,
my country's finest drink, I sit remembering
the poet, plump, tall, bald, wisps of
smoke coiled from a cigarette holder.
I offer my poetry thesis. He laughs, says
"I'm a prissy man." He might have said
exact, or strict, as Allen Tate often did.
Later, as if bruised, he'd scowl, "Must you say
beautiful eyes?" And years later,
as if by accident, after my graduation,
he meets me in the hall, his hand out,
so I accept his almost last manuscript
of poems, many speckled and moled
as his forehead, veined by hours
of burning tobacco, ash-dark as coffee
each with scars of excisions, connections
looping word to word like metastasized
disease, but his steady strong heart
still visible, and what he wanted heard.
"Mr. Summers, I'd begin, despite quick
sputters of protest, refusing still to give
the Hollis *he asked me many times to say*
against the decades between us, being
in his view countrymen, Virginia
and Kentucky joined in that Ohio room
always bare, bright as the northern snow
we'd met in that first day. Like pioneers
with dangers in common. Now this one
came, I handed him his manuscript, not

wanting the grim words I had to give also,
circling like a scout back and forth at
the obvious, his love for her, the boys,
an old dog, a man's ways. But I knew
I'd been taught his truths, and now
fumbling to address what shadowed
what he was I made my clumsy cuts
and watched him stiffen bit by bit, who
every Christmas had a poem to send
I don't know how many students in the end.
Handwritten, the same long fingers
sharp as an aunt's needling memory as he
pointed and rasped. "Say the poem
as if it matters, David," he once groaned,
so I feel that distant hurt close in again,
being alone with these cold walls,
the chill that's in my hand as I try to find
today a heat that summered in his words,
beginning with Hollis, *then reading from*
the posthumous backward to the start
where I must shake his hand and say Sir.

DAVE SMITH

About The Authors

Irvin S. Cobb, *humorist, journalist, short story writer, novelist, screenwriter, and actor who was known as the "Duke of Paducah," published newspaper columns, more than 60 books, and more than 300 short stories in national magazines and book collections. When he was promoted to managing editor at the* Paducah Daily News, *he was the nation's youngest at 19. He later became a columnist for* New York Evening World, New York Evening Sun, Louisville Evening Post, *and* Cincinnati Post. *Cobb covered World War I for* The Saturday Evening Post. *He was born June 23, 1876 at his grandfather Saunders' home in Paducah. Irvin was a dyed-in-the-wool Kentuckian. Several of Cobb's stories were made into silent films and later adapted for sound films. Cobb also had an acting career, appearing in 10 films between 1932 and 1938, starring in* Pepper: Everybody's Old Man *(1936), and* Hawaii Calls *(1938). He was host of the 1935 Academy Awards. Joel Harris said of Cobb's Judge Priest tales "Cobb created a South peopled with honorable citizens, charming eccentrics, and loyal, subservient blacks, but at their best the Judge Priest stories are dramatic and compelling." He died in New York on March 10, 1944.*

Effie Waller Smith *was born in 1879 to former slaves in Pike County, Ky. She began writing at 16 and preferred the traditional poetic styles of Tennyson and Longfellow. She attended Kentucky Normal School for Colored Persons in Frankfort, Ky., in the early 1900s (now Kentucky State University). She published three volumes of verse including:* Songs of the Months *(1904),* Rhymes from the Cumberland *(1909), and* Rosemary and Pansies *(1909). Seven of her poems were published in major American literary magazines between 1908 and 1917. She published the poem "Autumn Winds" in the September 1917 edition of* Harper's Monthly *and then promptly quit publishing. She died in 1960 in Wisconsin. In the introduction to Effie Waller Smith's book of poetry* Songs of the Months *is written: "Miss Waller's poems, as all who read them will observe, are possessed of much pathos and beauty, having an originality all their own."*

Hollis Summers *turned down his inheritance by refusing to become the Baptist minister his family wanted him to become. Instead, he pursued an bachelor's in English from Georgetown College (1937), earned a master's degree from Bread Loaf Middlebury College (1943), and a doctorate at the State University of Iowa (1948). He had a long teaching career, beginning at Holmes High School, Covington, Ky., then Georgetown College (1944–'49), the University of Kentucky (1949–'59), and joined the faculty of the Department of English at Ohio University, Athens in September 1959, where he remained until his retirement in 1985. His most famous student there was Dave Smith. Summers published widely in fiction, non-fiction, and poetry. Among his books were* City Limit *(Houghton Mifflin, 1948),* The Weather of February *(Harper, 1957),* The Walk Near Athens *(Harper, 1959),* Someone Else: Sixteen Poems About Other Children *(Lippincott, 1962), and* Start from Home *(Rutgers U P, 1972), among many others. His magazine credits include:* Atlantic, Saturday Review, Southern Poetry Review, Paris Review, Sewanee Review *and* Hudson Review. *He edited the first significant collection of Kentucky short stories:* Kentucky Story: A Collection of Short Stories *(U of Kentucky P, 1954). In 1978, Summers was a Fulbright lecturer at the University of Canterbury, Christchurch, New Zealand. He died Nov. 14, 1987.*

Dave Smith *is a poet, novelist, critic, and editor, born in Portsmouth, Va. The first member of his family to graduate from college, Smith received a bachelor's from the University of Virginia, a master's from Southern Illinois University, and a doctorate from Ohio University, where he was a student of Hollis Summers. Smith has published dozens of volumes of poetry, including* Little Boats, Unsalvaged: Poems 1992–2004 *and* The Wick of Memory: New and Selected Poems, 1970–2000, *which was chosen as the Dictionary of Literary Biography's Book of the Year in Poetry. Smith's prose includes the novel* Onliness *(1981),* Southern Delights *(1984), and* Hunting Men: Reflections on a Life in American Poetry *(2006). He has been an editor of the* Southern Review *and the* New Virginia Review. *He edited* The Essential Poe *(1991). He has twice been a finalist for the Pulitzer Prize. Smith has taught at Johns Hopkins University, Louisiana State University, and Virginia Commonwealth University. He lives in Baltimore.*

The Third Day

Now that it is Christmas

From Brickdust and Buttermilk

Now *that it is Christmas*
You might try to weave
A wreath around me,
Just to prove to me
That you do love me.
The wreath might be made from sprigs of yew
Or holly or rosa multiflora
Or frost-tinged blueberry leaves.
Any of these would serve so admirably
If you would do the weaving
And if I be permitted
To stand by and torment you
With suggestions
And little pats and sweet pinches
And endless declarations of my love.
Now that it is Christmas,
You might try to weave
A wreath around me,
One that would never wither.

JOHN JACOB NILES

Christmas Card Poem: 1947

When the white stars talk together like sisters
And when the winter hills
Raise their grand semblance in the freezing night,
Somewhere one window
Bleeds like the brown eye of an open force.

Hills, stars,
White stars that stand above the eastern stable.
Look down and offer Him.
The dim adoring light of your belief.
Whose small Heart bleeds with infinite fire.

Shall not this Child
(When we shall hear the bells of His amazing voice)
Conquer the winter of our hateful century?

And when His Lady Mother leans upon the crib,
Lo, with what rapiers
Those two loves fence and flame their brillancy!

Here in this straw lie planned the fires
That will melt all our sufferings:
He is our Lamb, our holocaust!

And one by one the shepherds, with their snowy feet,
Stamp and shake out their hats upon the stable dirt,
And one by one kneel down to look upon their Life.

Thomas
Merton

THOMAS MERTON

Christmas Eve on Lonesome

It was Christmas Eve on Lonesome. But nobody on Lonesome knew that it was Christmas Eve, although a child of the outer world could have guessed it, even out in those wilds where Lonesome slipped from one lone log cabin high up the steeps, down through a stretch of jungled darkness to another lone cabin at the mouth of the stream.

There was the holy hush in the gray twilight that comes only on Christmas Eve. There were the big flakes of snow that fell as they never fall except on Christmas Eve. There was a snowy man on horseback in a big coat, and with saddle-pockets that might have been bursting with toys for children in the little cabin at the head of the stream.

But not even he knew that it was Christmas Eve. He was thinking of Christmas Eve, but it was of the Christmas Eve of the year before, when he sat in prison with a hundred other men in stripes, and listened to the chaplain talk of peace and good will to all men upon earth, when he had forgotten all men upon earth but one, and had only hatred in his heart for him.

"Vengeance is mine! saith the Lord."

That was what the chaplain had thundered at him. And then, as now, he thought of the enemy who had betrayed him to the law, and had sworn away his liberty, and had robbed him of everything in life except a fierce longing for the day when he could strike back and strike to kill. And then, while he looked back hard into the chaplain's eyes, and now, while he splashed through the yellow mud thinking of that Christmas Eve, Buck shook his head; and then, as now, his sullen heart answered:

"Mine!"

The big flakes drifted to crotch and twig and limb. They gathered on the brim of Buck's slouch hat, filled out the wrinkles in his big coat, whitened his hair and his long mustache, and sifted into the yellow, twisting path that guided his horse's feet.

High above he could see through the whirling snow now and then the gleam of a red star. He knew it was the light from his enemy's window; but somehow the chaplain's voice kept ringing in his ears, and every time he saw the light he couldn't help thinking of the story of the Star that the chaplain told that Christmas Eve, and he dropped his eyes by and by, so as not to see it again, and rode on until the light shone in his face.

Then he led his horse up a little ravine and hitched it among the snowy holly and rhododendrons, and slipped toward the light. There was a dog somewhere, of course; and like a thief he climbed over the low rail-fence and stole through the tall snow-wet grass until he leaned against an apple-tree with the sill of the window two feet above the level of his eyes.

Reaching above him, he caught a stout

limb and dragged himself up to a crotch of the tree. A mass of snow slipped softly to the earth. The branch creaked above the light wind; around the corner of the house a dog growled and he sat still.

He had waited three long years and he had ridden two hard nights and lain out two cold days in the woods for this.

And presently he reached out very carefully, and noiselessly broke leaf and branch and twig until a passage was cleared for his eye and for the point of the pistol that was gripped in his right hand.

A woman was just disappearing through the kitchen door, and he peered cautiously and saw nothing but darting shadows. From one corner a shadow loomed suddenly out in human shape. Buck saw the shadowed gesture of an arm, and he cocked his pistol. That shadow was his man, and in a moment he would be in a chair in the chimney corner to smoke his pipe, maybe—his last pipe.

Buck smiled—pure hatred made him smile—but it was mean, a mean and sorry thing to shoot this man in the back, dog though he was; and now that the moment had come a wave of sickening shame ran through Buck. No one of his name had ever done that before; but this man and his people had, and with their own lips they had framed palliation for him. What was fair for one was fair for the other they always said. A poor man couldn't fight money in the courts; and so they had shot from the brush, and that was why they were rich now and Buck was poor—why his enemy was safe at home, and he was out here, homeless, in the apple-tree.

Buck thought of all this, but it was no use. The shadow slouched suddenly and disappeared; and Buck was glad. With a gritting oath between his chattering teeth he pulled his pistol in and thrust one leg down to swing from the tree—he would meet him face to face next day and kill him like a man—and there he hung as rigid as though the cold had suddenly turned him, blood, bones, and marrow, into ice.

The door had opened, and full in the firelight stood the girl who he had heard was dead. He knew now how and why that word was sent him. And now she who had been his sweetheart stood before him—the wife of the man he meant to kill.

Her lips moved—he thought he could tell what she said: "Git up, Jim, git up!" Then she went back.

A flame flared up within him now that must have come straight from the devil's forge. Again the shadows played over the ceiling. His teeth grated as he cocked his pistol, and pointed it down the beam of light that shot into the heart of the apple-tree, and waited.

The shadow of a head shot along the rafters and over the fireplace. It was a madman clutching the butt of the pistol now, and as his eye caught the glinting sight and his heart thumped, there stepped

into the square light of the window—a child!

It was a boy with yellow tumbled hair, and he had a puppy in his arms. In front of the fire the little fellow dropped the dog, and they began to play.

"Yap! yap! yap!"

Buck could hear the shrill barking of the fat little dog, and the joyous shrieks of the child as he made his playfellow chase his tail round and round or tumbled him head over heels on the floor. It was the first child Buck had seen for three years; it was "his" child and "hers"; and, in the apple-tree, Buck watched fixedly.

They were down on the floor now, rolling over and over together; and he watched them until the child grew tired and turned his face to the fire and lay still—looking into it. Buck could see his eyes close presently, and then the puppy crept closer, put his head on his playmate's chest, and the two lay thus asleep.

And still Buck looked—his clasp loosening on his pistol and his lips loosening under his stiff mustache—and kept looking until the door opened again and the woman crossed the floor. A flood of light flashed suddenly on the snow, barely touching the snow-hung tips of the apple-tree, and he saw her in the doorway—saw her look anxiously into the darkness—look and listen a long while.

Buck dropped noiselessly to the snow when she closed the door. He wondered what they would think when they saw his tracks in the snow next morning; and then he realized that they would be covered before morning.

As he started up the ravine where his horse was he heard the clink of metal down the road and the splash of a horse's hoofs in the soft mud, and he sank down behind a holly-bush.

Again the light from the cabin flashed out on the snow.

"That you, Jim?"

"Yep!"

And then the child's voice: "Has oo dot thum tandy?"

"Yep!"

The cheery answer rang out almost at Buck's ear, and Jim passed death waiting for him behind the bush which his left foot brushed, shaking the snow from the red berries down on the crouching figure beneath.

Once only, far down the dark jungled way, with the underlying streak of yellow that was leading him whither, God only knew—once only Buck looked back. There was the red light gleaming faintly through the moonlit flakes of snow. Once more he thought of the Star, and once more the chaplain's voice came back to him.

"Mine!" saith the Lord.

Just how, Buck could not see with himself in the snow and him back there for life with her and the child, but some strange impulse made him bare his head.

"Yourn," said Buck grimly.

But nobody on Lonesome—not even Buck—knew that it was Christmas Eve.

Johnny, Jr.

JOHN FOX, JR.

One Snowy Night

The laughter of sleigh bells was heard on the lips of the snow storm
All day long, and passers were scarcely seen thro' the falling flakes
Hurriedly going, wrapped close, and one not speaking to another.
'Twas bitter cold, and the stiffened forests tossed in the northern blast;
And the great old pines, as the gale smote their snowy heads, grumbled,
And seemed in their anguish to mutter: 'Let loose our hair and our whiskers!'
The slow wreathes of smoke curled dreamily thro' the still branches
That burdened with snow, stooped down and were sad-hearted and silent.
All sounds of the barn-yard were hushed in the chill breath of Winter.
The cottage was still, and within doors the cotter kept quiet.

The nightfall came, and still the flakes were coming thickly down.
'How it snows,' said Leeona, as she shut the neat door of her cottage.
Then she drew her chair near Rodney, and sat before a warm fire of logs.
This night the little green cottage was unusually cozy;
The cat on the rug sung low to the slumbering puppy,
Who yelped in a dream, and nipped at the heels of a rabbit.
The light of the fire-place, streaming across the clean hearth,
Glared on the walls, and flashed from the chairs and the tables,
Like the recollections of childhood flinging their cheer across life's path.

Now thus to her lord spoke the heroine of the Savannas:
'The approaching Christmas throws the shadows of mirth into Sussex.
Never before was there such buying of presents among us;
Never before such love without dissimulation.'
Of a sudden Leeona hushed and fixed her eyes upon Rodney.
'Whoa!' cried a voice at the door, as rough as the oaths of a seaman,
'Still, Sorrel!' and a sleigh had stopped at the door of the cottage.
Leeona rose up quickly, but Rodney sat still and listened

Till she had opened the door and looked out in the darkness.
A dim lamp in the driver's hand streamed thro' the falling flakes
And discovered two men in the sleigh and one woman.
The men in their great coats wrapped dismounted, and then the woman,
Muffled in heavy furs, and veiled, stepped down between them;
When the driver reined his horses and dashed away in the silence.
The strangers entered the door and Father Eppinck before them,
And bowing, he said: 'These are my friends of whom I spoke aforetime.'

Rodney arose and stood erect in speechless wonder and silence,
As the tall and lovely form of Dora, the heroine of Saville,
Stood in the midst of the floor of his humble dwelling, and reached
The white hand of recognition, saying, with the sweetness of other days:
'Do mine eyes behold thee, oh Rodney, my dearest benefactor!
I have heard of you here and have come to remove you to Montreal.
My home is a home for you, and the days of your toil are ended.'
For the tears of gladness and gratitude the manly hero
Of a thousand trials hard could not speak, but he seized the small hand
Extended, and wept a benediction of tears upon it, and kissed it.

His great stern face of simple fidelity and manhood brave,
Was now lighted up with a glow exceeding portrayal,
And in its effulgence approaching those who stand in white robes
Ever, within the tidal glory of the Throne Eternal.
There were greetings then, and the joy of all hearts was running over;
And there countenances all shone with the light of the Kingdom of Heaven.

ALBERRY ALLSON WHITMAN

About The Authors

John Jacob Niles *was a Louisville native, born there in 1892. Niles developed an early interest in music which led him to start collecting songs at 12 and to write and publish his first song* "Go 'way From My Window" *in 1907, which he based on a line of song collected from an African-American farm worker. Bob Dylan quoted the song some 60 years later in his song* "It Ain't Me Babe." *Niles graduated from DuPont Manual High School and, after a brief employment by the Burroughs Adding Machine Company, enlisted in the U.S. Army Signal Corps, where he served as a reconnaissance pilot during World War I. There he collected songs from his fellow soldiers which later resulted in his publishing collections such as* Singing Soldiers (Charles Scribner's Sons, 1927), Hell on Wheels (1928) *and* Songs My Mother Never Taught Me (Gold Label Books, 1929). *His collaboration with photographer Doris Ullman, with whom he traveled to Appalachia in the 1930s, resulted in a strong influence of Appalachian folksongs in his repertoire. His discography includes albums such as* The Tradition Years: I Wonder as I Wander (1958, Tradition Records; 2006, Empire Musicwerks), American Folk & Gambling Songs (1956, Camden Record LP), An Evening With John Jacob Niles (1959, Tradition Records LP; 2002, Empire Musicwerks), *and* John Jacob Niles Sings Folk Songs (1964, Folkways Records LP). *He published his only book of poetry,* Brick Dust and Buttermilk *in 1977. Niles maintained an active performance, composition, and recording career until his death March 1, 1980 at Boothill Farm near Lexington, Ky. He is buried next to his wife, Rena, in the graveyard of St. Hubert's Episcopal Church in Clark County, Ky.*

Thomas Merton *wrote more than 70 books covering a wide range of genres including autobiography, biography, essays, poetry, novels, and letters. He authored numerous poems and articles about religious spirituality, non-violence, social justice, interfaith understanding, comparative religion and nuclear proliferation. Most notable of his publications were his best-selling autobiography* The Seven Storey Mountain (1948), Seeds of Contemplation (New Directions, 1949), *and* The Sign of Jonas (Harcourt Brace and Company, 1953). *He published more than 2,000 poems during his career. He attended Cambridge University for one year in 1933. He entered Columbia University in January 1935 and received a bachelor's in English in 1938. In late 1938, he made a religious conversion and was received into the Catholic Church. He stayed at Columbia, taking graduate courses toward his master's. In 1940, he completed his master's thesis* On Nature and Art in William Blake. *From 1940-'41 he taught English at St. Bonaventure College in Allegany, N.Y. In 1941, he entered the Abbey of Our Lady of Gethsemani near Bardstown, Ky., as a Trappist Monk and remained there until his accidental death from electrocution in 1968 in Bangkok, Thailand, where he was attending a conference.*

John Fox, Jr. *is best known for his Civil War-based novel* The Little Shepherd of Kingdom Come (1903), *the first American book to sell a million copies. His novel* The Trail of the Lonesome Pine (1908) *was also a best seller. He wrote 14 novels and 45 short stories. Fox was born in Bourbon County, Ky., in 1862. He was educated at his father's Stony Point Academy, entered Transylvania University at 14, Harvard at 16, and graduated cum laude with a degree in English when he was 19. After graduation, he practiced journalism with the* New York Times *and the* New York Sun. Harper's Weekly *sent Fox to Cuba to report on the Spanish-American War. In 1886, he moved to Big Stone Gap, Va., to join his brother in the real estate business and to be involved with his family's mining ventures. His first creative work was serialized in* Century Magazine. *He died July 8, 1919 in Big Stone Gap. He was buried in the Paris Cemetery in Bourbon County, Ky.*

Albery Allson Whitman *was known as the* "Poet Laureate of the Negro Race." *Born into slavery in 1851 in Hart County, Ky., he was orphaned at 12. He became a farmer, worked in a plough shop and in railroad construction, and was a school teacher before attending Wilberforce University for a short time. He served as a financial agent for Wilberforce before becoming a pastor in Ohio, Kansas, Texas, and Georgia. He published seven collections of poetry including:* Not a Man, and Yet a Man (1877), The Rape of Florida (1884—republished as Twasinta's Seminoles *in 1885),* The World's Fair Poem (1893), *and* An Idyl of the South: An Epic Poem in Two Parts (1901). *Whitman's works were well received by African American readers and critics. Whitman used complex rhyme and metrical schemes. He died in Atlanta in 1901.*

The Fourth Day

The Dollmaker: Chapter Eighteen

Gertie stood with her head thrust out the partly opened kitchen door, and watched the gray brown sparrows feed on the coal-shed roof. Twice she had spread crumbs for them, but once a gray alley cat had chased the birds and licked the crumbs, and when they were back again Tony Bommarita had covered their food with handfuls of freshly fallen snow. The birds were ugly-voiced and dirty looking, but standing so, with the inside door shut behind her, there was for the moment a feeling of being alone with them, the way it had used to be back home, like the day she'd cut the hickory tree down on the Tipton Place. She had stood then, and watched two red birds. She closed her eyes. If she shut out the alley, she could smell cold creek water and cedar, the cedar smell strong and clean, like on a still, misty morning.

"Mom, Mom, make Amos gimme my auto! He got a big red wagin, an now he wants my little ole toy auto."

Gertie turned back into the kitchen slowly, for in turning the red birds flew away, the smell of cedar faded, and there was the closeness, the noise, the overcrowding of all her family at home on Christmas Day. The radio could not cry again of so many shopping days until Christmas. Everything was sold that could be sold. Millions and millions of women would be happy to have a man like Clovis.

"Enoch, hand me that wrench on the table." Clovis, taking the wrench from the angry Enoch, smiled up at her from where he worked flat on his back under a large secondhand but bright washing machine. "I'll have this thing a worken pretty soon. An you can do a washen, old woman, with no work atall."

She tried to smile. All morning that had been the hardest part, the trying to smile in the heat and the steam of the oven baking the turkey Clovis had bought. But she had smiled on everything, even on the dried-out Christmas tree that had no smell except one that make her think of shoe polish, for Clytie had sprayed it with artificial snow. It held no memory of earth or wind or sun or sky; a tree grown in a field, Clovis had said, just for Christmas. Lifeless it was, as the ugly paper wreath Clytie had bought. But still she had to smile, for the big gifts were for her. "Mom, Mom, Cassie climbed up an got the scissors. She knows she ain't supposed to have 'em," Clytie quarreled from the passway. Then, with no permission from Gertie, she whirled and jerked the scissors from Cassie.

"Cassie Marie," Gertie began, "you know, you oughtn't—"

Cassie had suddenly dissolved into a heartbroken weeping. She quickly checked her sobs, but then, just as unusual for her as the crying, she tried to argue with her mother. "I need um, Mom. I'll be real careful with them scissors," she begged.

She came into the kitchen and looked hopefully up at Gertie, the new fancy doll that Santa had bought clutched upside down in her arms.

"You'd ruin them sharp scissors, an they'd ruin you, mebbe," Gertie said.

Cassie turned away, weeping again. She sounded so sorrowful that Gertie turned to pick her up and baby her a bit. But when Cassie went away to the block of wood, Gertie stopped by the kitchen table. Getting out of the kitchen seemed, for the moment at least, too much trouble. Never again could she walk straight into the passway, even with the table against the wall. The new washing machine took up so much room she could hardly slip her big body sidewise between it and the table. Amos began screaming again for the red plastic car, and Clovis shook his head in weariness.

"A body ud think them youngens got nothen. I thought Cassie was crazy over that new doll, an she did keep a talken about how pretty it was dressed." He sighed, resting on his elbows by the washing machine. "I allus hoped Clytie could have a nice store-bought doll like that—an now she's too old, an Cassie she ain't so pleased. An th money I've spent. What did she want?"

"Mebbe," Gertie said, looking again at the hopping sparrows, "she don't know. Lots a grown people never git an never know what they want. They spend money, hopen it'll satisfy em, like a man a hunten matches in a strange dark house."

She nodded toward the alley where Sophronie's Wheateye was running down the steps. She wore a new pink rayon dress, and had an oversized doll on one arm and the box of red plastic dishes cradled in the other. Gertie watched a little saucer fall from a corner of the flimsy crumpling box and lie, a bright spot of red in the snow. She ought to call and tell the child that she had lost a dish, but she only shook her head. Did it matter? In a few days the box would be gone, the dishes broken, and nothing left but their price. Sophronie would pay that off at so much a week. $2.75 they had cost. How much was $2.75?

Clovis said, "There," in the pleased voice which meant that something he had meant to fit was fitted.

The sparrows flew away as Mrs. Anderson, wearing her coat and boots, came down her steps carrying a bright red tricycle, and followed by a snow-suited Georgie. Then the Daly door opened and out poured the Daly boys. All seemed to have either fancy wheeled toys or new sleds, though soon she saw that two were on hockey skates fastened to special shoes, the kind Enoch had wanted. Even Reuben, who would have little to do with the alley games, had somewhat sheepishly said the other day that he would like to learn to skate.

Mrs. Daly, steamy-faced, straggeldy-headed, her apron damp with dishwater, the least one in her arms, stood in the door and watched, smiling. Her glance leaped from child to child; each broadened the smile so that when she was at last able to tear her eyes away and look at Mrs. Anderson, struggling to get Georgie face forward on the seat of the tricycle, her face was so full of smiles it broke into joyful laughter as she called, "Merry Christmas!"

She flipped her apron about the baby and came on down the alley. "Such a fine Christmas," she said, beaming up at the plainly unhappy Mrs. Anderson. "Fresh snow. Nobody sick." She glanced at the Bommarita door, then at Mr. Anderson behind his storm door, and spoke more loudly. "Our father home sleepen. He went last night wit Maggie tudu midnight mass. My, ain't she pretty? What's her name?" She was talking now to Wheateye, coming from the Miller door where she had been to show her doll.

"Sally Marie," and Wheateye held up the great doll, demonstrated its powers of going to sleep and saying, "Mama," then ran to get the new doll buggy.

"That Santa Claus, he's sure got a failen fu kids." Mrs. Daly smiled on Wheateye as she had smiled on her own. Her joy even touched Mrs. Anderson, who for a moment seemed what she was, a young pretty woman, hardly 30. Her voice was gay when she called to Gertie, now on her stoop:

"Your turkey smells good, sage in the stuffing like we always had at home. You almost never smell it here." And after a wary glance at Georgie, still sitting backward on his tricycle, she came over and stood by Gertie's stoop, smiling up at her. "If I shut my eyes here by your door, I can think I'm back home."

"I'll give you some a mine I brung frum home."

"Homer doesn't care for sage and red pepper," Mrs. Anderson said in the weary, talking-to-herself voice she often used, so that it seemed she was not the same woman who a moment ago had laughed in the alley. "Homer doesn't care for fruit cake, either. The pediatrician would faint at the idea of letting Georgie taste it. I made fruit cakes mostly—I guess because I ... " She reached for a pinch of fresh snow from the porch rail, watched the snow disappear, then looked at her empty fingers, ... "I wanted something that wasn't sensible and vitamic, just once, for Christmas," she confessed all in a breath.

Wheateye was rolling new and shining doll buggy, large enough for a live baby, down the Meanwell steps. She was being helped by a yawning Sophronie in a new housecoat, shinier and flouncier than the old had been. Sophronie nodded sleepily, but smiled as she returned the Christmas greetings the women called to her. No sooner had she gone back into her kitchen than Mrs. Anderson began in a low,

worried voice, her disapproving glance on Wheateye's doll carriage, "Isn't it awful how they work at terrible jobs—have you seen Sophronie's hands lately—and then waste their money. That housecoat: what in the world does a factory worker with three children need with a flimsy rayon housecoat? And all that foolishness for the children. It makes it hard on the others with sensible parents."

"'Man cannot live by bread alone,'" Gertie suddenly said in a surprised voice.

Mrs. Anderson nodded. "'But by every word that proceedeth out of the mouth of God.' I went to Sunday school too, when I was little. But a flimsy doll buggy given by a mother who can't afford it to a child who won't take care of it has nothing to do with bread and God's word."

Gertie was silent, her thoughts on bubble gum and shoestrings. She wished she'd got skates for Reuben—and maybe Enoch too.

The sound of a through train rushing by silenced Mrs. Anderson. The smoke rolled and the cinders rattled down. Christmas seemed gone, sped with the train to some quieter, cleaner place. The smoke was still falling when Enoch's friend, Mike Turbovitch, came plunging and staggering on hockey skates, clumsy in the snow. He stopped at the bottom step and called: "Oh Enoch, come on out. Yu gitchu hockey skates?"

Enoch came running to the call, but

stopped, his head around the storm door when he saw Mike's skates. He looked past him to the Dalys and their toys, and then saw Tony Bommarita pulling a long new sled. He turned quickly away. His choked mumble, "I'd ruther listen to th radio an play with my builden set," was cut off by the slamming door.

Mike looked after him with a shrewd but pitying glance, then turned to Gertie with a sharp, accusing look. "Didn't he git his hockey skates nor nothen?"

Gertie, conscious of Mrs. Anderson's watching, listening face, said, "Oh, sure, a builden set an stuff," but Mike looked suspicious still, and after a moment's waiting and another call he staggered away.

When he had gone, Gertie called into the house and suggested to Enoch that he and Amos come out and play with the new wagon, but Enoch's answer was tearful and resentful. "Wagins is baby stuff, Mom."

Amos, roused from his boats in the bathroom, cried, "I ain't no baby," but an instant later he was in the living room, screaming because Enoch had the wagon.

There was a thumping and bumping of the wagon while Enoch yelled: "You wasn't usen it. You an Cassie allatime play with my things." There were more screams and thumps, and Clovis finally scolded. Though his voice was loud, it held the absent-minded tone of one taken up with

some beloved pastime, so that his, "Behave yerselves youngens, fore I git a hick'ry limb," had no effect at all.

Gertie, embarrassed by the poor showing of her family on Christmas, turned to chide the boys, but Clytie screamed: "Mom, make em quit! They're tearen th place up, an I cain't hardly try on my new dress."

"Merry Christmas." It was Mrs. Daly, who had at last managed to tear herself away from the sight of her children, going now into the next alley.

"We ain't so merry," Gertie said.

"Sick on Christmas day?" Mrs. Daly asked, coming up the walk. Gertie shook her head. The screaming of Amos, the bumping of the fought-over wagon, and Clytie's shrill cries that they'd knock the Christmas tree over told Mrs. Daly enough of the Christmas in her house without her adding words to it. The sounds proclaimed to any listening ears that Santie had brought to all the children only one real toy fit for showing up and down the alleys.

Mrs. Daly listened and nodded as Clovis listened and nodded over the car's motor on a cold morning. She shook her head. "Yu gotta git um all a big present apiece. Once I tried one sled between Chris an Joe." She sighed at the memory, then winked at Gertie and whispered, "Yu least kid's Amos, ain't he?"

When Gertie had nodded, Mrs. Daly stuck her face close to the broken-out pane in the storm door, and called above the tumult: "Amos, it's too bad youse is too little to steer an don't know how. You could steer outside. Du kids is haven a kind a Christmas parade. An let youse brudder push." She opened the storm door invitingly.

Another fight threatened over who should pull the wagon to the door. "Now, now," Mrs. Daly cried, going into the kitchen. "I ginerally git all th big toys tudu door myself. S'job in a crowded place. My, my, youse gotta big Christmas." Her voice was warm with genuine pleasure as she went on: "A refrigerator—such a big one an so fine—linoleum anu washing machine. An ina war when stuff's so hard to git." As soon as she had put the wagon through the door, she must turn back and examine the great white icebox. It rose higher than her head and blocked most of the kitchen window, but her eyes were worshipful, pleased, Gertie thought, as if the thing had been her own.

Enoch forgot his quarrel with Amos and sprang to show Mrs. Daly the wonders of the icebox. As soon as he was out of bed, he had put water into the trays. Then, it had seemed to Gertie, trying to get breakfast in the sharply contracted kitchen, that he had opened the thing at least a hundred times to see if the water was freezing. Now, trying as before to catch the light going on, he opened its door with a quick hard pull, calling to

Mrs. Daly: "Lookee. Lookee. It's got a place fer butter an meat an vegetables an everything. He opened little doors and pulled out trays and drawers. The Icy Heart, as if trying to impress the little woman, flung out air so cold it made a fog in the hot kitchen. Next there came a soft purring, as if some strange kind of polar cat were curled in the heart of it.

"It's one of th finest I've ever seen," Mrs. Daly said.

"A 1942 Icy Heart with nine and three-tenths cubic feet," Enoch said, putting his ear close the better to hear the white cat. "Pop was real lucky to git it: no black market, taxes, nothen. He got it off'n a man he knows in th shop that got TB an is a goen to Arizona. He sold it an th washing machine—cheap."

"His wife was sure a good housekeeper, not a nick on it," Mrs. Daly said, running a gentle finger down the blue and silver handle. "Youse's lucky."

Clovis warmed to her praise. "The man gimme time an sold it some under OPA. Thataway, he said, them secondhand dealers wouldn't make a pile on him."

Gertie carried the wagon down the steps. Conscious of Mrs. Anderson's questioning glance, she tried to smile the way a woman with an almost new ten-cubic-foot Icy Heart should smile. "I know you're awfully proud of your new things?" Mrs. Anderson asked.

Last night, when she had learned what Clovis had done with the Henley money he had asked for a few days before, telling her then he only wanted to borrow it to pay more on his car debts, she had somehow kept down the bitter-tongued anger that seemed always rising in her of late. She had smiled last night for the children, all gay and excited with surprise for her. It had been so hard then, it ought to be easy now. Cassie, gay again and singing one of her own songs, ran past her down the walk. Enoch next, and then Amos. Gerite turned away from Mrs. Anderson on the pretext of getting the children started off with the wagon.

A plane went over, but too high to kill conversation with its sounds. The children were beginning to squabble now, especially Wheateye, who was screaming at some of the Daly boys for ruining her doll buggy with snowballs. Behind Mrs. Bommarita, watching her children from her doorway, a radio was crying out the news of great slaughter in Germany. Somewhere another radio was singing Peace on Earth. Mrs. Anderson noticed none of these things. She continued to watch Gertie and wait for her comment.

"I've lived a long time with sich," Gertie said at last. "An when we go back we'll have to sell em, mebbe fer less than we paid, an—it's more debts."

"I'll betcha never asked fer one of them damn' big things. I seen it last night when they was moving it in." It was

Max on her steps, dressed in her Sunday best in a long coat with fur on the collar. The dark fur and a dark hat made Max's face seem gentle as some early spring flower blooming out of last year's snow-blackened leaves. The bluish rings under her eyes made them seem bigger and softer, her lips redder, kinder. "Victor's mother," she went on, coming over to Gertie's stoop, "she buys th best—has got one exactly like it, only bigger. Always loaded down with enough damn' junk to start a delicatessen. All them drawers an shelves an trays to fiddle with an keep clean. An now Victor wants one."

Mrs. Anderson smiled. "You're just jealous. Don't you know, Max, that every woman, that is, every American woman, dreams of the day when she'll own—"

"Yu mean have in her kitchen," Max said, lighting a cigarette. "Nobody in this alley owns nothen. When they get most a th payments made on something, it breaks down an they hafta trade it in on some more crap."

"Now, Max," Mrs. Anderson said, still smiling a strange Whit-like smile, "you're un-American—or else you don't listen to the radio. Every woman dreams of a ten-cubic-foot Icy Heart in her kitchen—Icy Heart power—Icy Heart. We must hurry up and win the war so we can all go out and buy Icy Hearts." She had stopped, trying to remember. "Last summer I knew it by heart; Mrs. Bommarita had the Icy

Heart program on every day."

"I hope she's not listening to th news today," Max interrupted. "It's awful. A couple a them generals must have went on a drunk in Paris an left th war to run itself. Her man, he's a waist gunner."

"It's the infantry that's so hard hit," Mrs. Anderson said. "Sophronie has a brother somewhere over there in the infantry. I hope she isn't listening."

"She ain't got time," Max said. "I hope Whit got her what she wanted. She'd set her heart on a housecoat she seen ina window at American Credit."

"With flounces and lots of gold?" Mrs. Anderson asked.

Max nodded, glad. "He must a got it. Full-skirted, swishy?"

"You mean," Mrs. Anderson asked, "she actually wants the kind of housecoat he gives her? But what in the world does a woman in her … station …"

Max dropped her arms from a long child-like yawn, smiled at Mrs. Anderson. "You've got me, kid, but she wears it, not me. Why did Jesus change water into wine? Water is a lot more healthful. Besides, you can wash your face in it, and it's cheaper, my pop used to say when Mom would quarrel a little because he'd brought home wine in th middle a th week stead just on Saturday night."

"Was your father a minister?" Mrs. Anderson asked.

"I don't remember that he ever

called himself that but once or twice. I remember once somewhere down in North Carolina—it was spring and he wanted to stop awhile on the way north so he turned off on a gravel road. And somehow he said something to a farmer made the man think Pop could castrate pigs. The farmer begged him and begged him. He thought Pop wouldn't do it on account he didn't have no money. So Pop castrated. He'd never done it, and Mom fussed and said he oughtn't to do it, for after he'd done the first pigs a lot a other farmers come. They paid us in hams, the best hams, an eggs an dried apples, and fresh-caught trout. Did you ever eat fresh-caught, fresh-fried trout with real young tender ..."

"But, Max, what did your father say or do?" Mrs. Anderson cried in an agony of curiosity.

"Why, he said, 'Thank you,' I guess."

"I mean about being a minister or something."

"Oh. When Mom complained because he castrated pigs when he'd hardly ever been close to a pig, he said, 'Good lady, I minister to th wants and needs of all mankind.' Yu want it for Homer?"

Mrs. Anderson shook her head, and was suddenly interested in the whereabouts of Georgie, while Gertie asked, "Did his pigs do all right?"

Max nodded, and Mrs. Anderson sighed heavily. "But Max, was he a preacher, like in a church?"

"I don't remember but once or twice, when we was real hard up. Once in West Virginia, by a mining town—th mines was running, but Pop couldn't mine—we'd even run outa gas, so he preached onu rich man going to heaven through that needle's eye. It made them pore miners feel good, I recken. Th money come rollen in, but he didn't like to take it; he said ..."

Her words were drowned by Mrs. Daly's calling from Gertie's doorway. "It works—he fixed a motor. Can yu imagine?"

Clytie behind her, all in a jiggle of excitement, was begging: "Come an see it, Mom. It's worken. Can I do a washen?"

Enoch, who had been pushing the wagon with Amos in it, heard and ran back to the house screaming, "Lemme see! Lemme see!"

Wheateye, who had overturned her doll buggy in the snow while fleeing from snowballs, took up the cry of, "Lemme see, lemme see," and came running, as did the other children, who had by now marched down the other alley, around, and home again. Gertie got as far as the second step, but got stopped by the crowding children, and when Sophronie's Gilbert came running, his skate blade striking her shoe, she came down again and stood with Max and Mrs. Anderson. The three women by the house wall made an island of stillness among the eddying children, running now from distant alleys, drawn by the cries of,

"Lemme see." "What is ut?" "Somethen for free?" Still others heard Mrs. Daly call across the alley to Mrs. Bommarita, "Come and seedu Icy Heart."

"Don't let it freeze the eggs an frostbite th lettuce," Max said with a shiver. "They're powerful things, them Icy Hearts."

"Maybe I'm jealous," Mrs. Anderson said, "but I don't like stuff so cold. Casimir does wake the baby and track in dirt, but an ice box was all we had in Muncie," and her voice grew warm, warmer than when she spoke of her children. "It stays on the back porch. I guess it is inconvenient, but we have the nicest back porch. There's a big maple—we have a big old frame house on the edge of town—right by the porch, too close, Homer thinks; he plans to have it pruned when we go back. But in summer the porch is always cool and shady, and in the fall, when you go out for the milk, the red and yellow leaves are all plastered on the floor, and it smells a little like the woods."

"Mornens last fall when I'd go to th spring, th poplar leaves they'd be plastered thick," Gertie said in a low voice.

We seen th poplars yellow once up in West Virginia hills," Max said. "But once in October, in Ohio someplace—I know Cleveland wasn't so far away—oh, them maples then. I remember Pop got us right in under one. Th leaves fell all over th roof—an he set ina door drinking coffee an watched um fall half th mornin."

"Max," Mrs. Anderson asked, after a polite pause to make certain the girl was finished, "I was wondering the other day, where is—or was—your home and people?"

Max dropped her cigarette, clasped her gloved hands in front of her, and, like a child relating a thing learned so well there can never be a forgetting, said: "From Earth, Lord, I come. That's one of the smaller planets; you would know it as a sister of Venus." She choked and turned toward her door, remembered, whirled back, and looked at Gertie as she asked, her voice hoarse: "A dream? I gotta have a dream; that's what I came out for."

"Cedar," Gertie said, realizing that through all the hubbub she'd heard a small child's troubled weeping. She found it on the other side of her stoop step, apparently lost. She picked it up and held it on her hip. It at once left off crying and began licking a purple sucker that had been stuck to the red plastic fish it carried.

Max was repeating, questioning the word, "Cedar?"

Gertie explained. "A little peaked cedar like grows by th creek on a limestone ledge. You know how they look fore sunrise on a summer mornen, with mebbe a little spider web er two, all white with dew."

Max's gum was still between her front teeth while she considered. "Yeah? Kinda.

I'll take it. Seems like it was cedars we saw so much in Arkansas—but I don't remember any dew. Cedar's enough, though. I've gotta scram. Victor might wake up 'fore I'm gone. I gotta be at work by two o'clock, an I want Christmas dinner first."

Mrs. Anderson clucked in sympathy. "What a shame they make you work on Christmas day—and not get to eat at home."

Max was hoarse again as she turned away. "It wouldn't seem like home, dinner at home on Christmas day. Victor's mom's gonna have a fit when I don't show up. But I couldn't take it—all them Poles together, knowen one another, talken u same lingo. I *would* be lonesome then." She looked back, her eyes lingering on Gertie like one lonesome now. "I found a girl that wanted to be off—claims she's got kids. But I figger she wants to give her boy friend—her man's inu marines—a real good Christmas—present. Cedar, cedar," and she went running up her steps.

Gertie looked about for someone who knew the child, though on her hip it seemed contented enough. There were plenty of children. Some satisfied with seeing, ran down the steps, bumping into others running up. There was a great deal of shoving, joggling, and good-humored pitching of soft snowballs, while others pounded drums or blew horns. Most were also eating—candy, bananas,

cookies, apples, oranges, and raw carrots. Wheateye, holding a bottle of pop in one hand, a horn in the other, the horn cradling her doll and one long spear of celery, divided her attention between blowing, taking little bites of celery and offering the doll the strings, and drinking, then handing the doll dainty nips from the bottle. At times she would wave the bottle and the horn and cry, "Da biggest ice box ya ever seed—13 cubic feet an it costed a thousand dollars."

The tide was thinning, the cries of "Lemme see," and "What's cooken?" were giving place to comments, many admiring, some belittling. "We've got a bigger one dan dat." "Who'd want a old secondhand junk heap?" "We're gonna buy a brand-new one soon's the war's over." And a jeering voice from a strange alley, "Dem hillbillies, dey come up here an get all da money in Detroit."

Mrs. Anderson, listening, nodded as over a page in a book. "That interests Homer a lot. He's working on his Ph.D. thesis in sociology, you know: The Patterns of Racial and Religious Prejudice and Persecution in Industrial Detroit." Gertie blinked, and Mrs. Anderson went on more rapidly. "That," and she nodded toward Mrs. Daly coming out the door, "interests him a lot. Almost nothing has been written about the hatred of the foreigner for many of our native-born Americans whose religion and social customs are different

from his own. He's always finding evidence of it; it's interesting."

"*Bein* th evidence ain't so interesten," Gertie said, smoothing back the child's hair. She had such pretty hair, black and curly, soft, curly as Callie Lou's. She looked up as Max's door opened and Max hurried away, calling over her shoulder, "Come out good; no sevens."

Mrs. Daly heard and asked, "Does she still pick her numbers from da dream book?"

Timmy Daly looked up, wonderingly. "Where'd her getta slip? Casimir ain't sellen ice today."

And Mrs. Anderson, with the puzzled look of a woman stepping into a fog at noon of a bright sunny day, asked her sharp, breathless questions: "Why did she want a number? Oh, dear, I wasn't listening. Why did she want a dream? And what does Casimir …"

"Such a fine icebox, Mrs. Nevels. I hope to be getting a bigger one soon. But it's like I tell Maggie, if I don't never save a down payment maybe du old can do till u war's over and dey'll take it fudu down payment. And Maggie, when she's married, will have a fine new one with a freezer chest all u way acrost u top like one I seen in u magazine." She caught the mouth-open, wanting to ask questions glance of Mrs. Anderson, and hurried on: "Oh, how come I could forget it. I wanta tell youse about Maggie's Christmas present—two towels, pure linen, hand-monogrammed for her hope chest." She picked up the baby's sucker, fallen into the snow, and put it back into its mouth, saying, "Du snow was clean." She turned again to Mrs. Anderson, emphasizing her words with nods: "Nobody, but nobody, can never say to my Maggie, 'Yu had no dowry; yu've brought not one stich u linen tuyu marriage.' She'll have it. Linen, all pure linen, Christmas, birthdays since she was born—always one piece, two this Christmas, u linen, pure linen. Such …"

Georgie screamed from somewhere down the alley. Mrs. Anderson had to hurry away, but Mrs. Daly lingered a moment, looking after her. "Books and schooling, nutten all her life but books and schooling—no wonder she don't know nutten. Does she think Casimir make his liven out u ice?"

Mrs. Daly, afraid her baby would get chilled, hurried home. Gertie started down the alley to hunt the owner of the child, a dark eyed little girl about two years old. She knew that she had never until now seen the child, yet she seemed strangely familiar. She was standing hesitant near the end of the alley, when Cassie came running, laughing, one hand outstretched. But instead of the witch child's hand she held an envelope smudged with licorice candy. "Lookee, Mom, what that nice bubble-gum boy gimme, a Christmas card all for me." She opened the envelope to

show the wonders of a fat red-cheeked Santa Claus with big-eyed reindeer that looked like horned calves.

Gertie admired the card, held it up for the little child to see. She made a sound and held out her hand for it. Cassie, really looking at her for the first time, asked, "Mom, how come you've got Mable?"

"Mable?"

"Uhuh, her's th bubble-gum boy's kid sister. His mom hadda work today. He's hunten her now. Lemme take her home. She walks good."

Mable wanted down, and went away with Cassie while Cassie talked to her of Santa Claus and reindeer. Gertie stood a moment, smiling as she watched them go. At last she turned slowly back to her own door. She saw, at the foot of her sidewalk, the red wagon, no good for playing in the snow, and so deserted by her boys. She tried not to think of the twelve dollars the flimsy thing had cost as she walked past it. On the stoop she lingered a moment, hand on the storm-door knob. The alley was deserted for the moment, even by the sparrows. Still, her searching glance went over it; maybe behind some other door she might find the things not found behind her own.

Standing so, she heard the whirrity glug of the washing machine, Bing Nolan gargling away on "Silent Night" on the radio, and then, more loudly, Clytie's outraged quarreling. Gertie hurried into the kitchen when she heard enough to learn that whatever it was it had been done by "that mean, mean Cassie." She saw then the bit of shiny blue rayon in Clytie's hands as she held it up for her father to see. "Look, Pop, what that mean youngen's went an done. She's cut up th dress off'n that fine new Christmas doll and stuck it on a little ole makeshift doll Mom whittled fer her 'fore we left home."

Gertie saw that the fine blue cloth was draped about the little hickory doll, the "golden child" she had whittled by the Tipton Spring. She stood a moment looking, her eyes warm as if a sparrow had pecked a crumb from her hand. Both Clytie and Clovis, she realized, were looking at her with disapproval. Tightening her apron about her, she turned resolutely toward the Icy Heart to begin the last part of the Christmas dinner preparations.

While Clovis quarreled about the ravished doll, her own thoughts of Cassie demanding scissors helped her through the dinner getting. She felt sorry for Clovis. He looked so bleary-eyed and tired. He'd been getting less overtime since going on the midnight shift. But he was slow about learning to sleep in the daytime, and he'd spent a lot of his sleep time pushing his way through the hot, overcrowded, smelly department-store basements hunting Christmas for them all.

She kept her silence, but lost the warm-eyed look when, during the dinner that

had cost so much, Clovis upbraided her ignorance of turkey cookery. Hemmed as it had been in the too small oven, the turkey had burned on the outside, scorching the breast meat, but they all came near gagging when Clovis cut into a thigh joint and blood ran out.

The real butter, that was to have been a Christmas treat with hot biscuit, had got so hard and cold from its stay in the Icy Heart that it refused to melt even on the hottest of biscuit, and butter and biscuit were chilled together. Clytie had the lettuce in the wrong place, and it was frozen. Reuben complained the milk was so cold it hurt his teeth. Clytie blamed it on Enoch, who'd turned down the cold controls; Enoch was angry; and Clovis turned sorrowful because the Icy Heart, like Cassie's new doll and the other things he'd bought, was unappreciated.

Harriette Simpson Arnow

HARRIETTE ARNOW

Ode to a Purple Aluminum Christmas Tree

Last year when residential streets
with their strings of colored lights
resembled filling stations
and the glitter of shop windows
hurt my eyes
a woman met in the course of an errand
said:
"Oh, you must go to Mike's
out on Stadium;
you can't imagine the Christmas trees
they have for sale;
all aluminum
but in different colors,
a whole row of big purple ones;
I could stand all day
and just look at them."
I wanted to cry;
instead went home and tried to write
Ode to a Purple Aluminum Christmas Tree.
Trying
was as far as I ever got.

Harriette Simpson Arnow

HARRIETTE ARNOW

Gathering Christmas

This poor family
Had nothing but the land,
The rocky hillside
Full of pines,
Birds huddled
In those snowbound times …
But every year
With faith
They went with axe and saw
To bring the Christmas home,
And every year,
They heard
And smelled
The forest in their house,
Saw the maker in the design
And in their humble way
Filled their desperate lives
With the hope
Of something
Most divine.

James B. Goode

JAMES B. GOODE

About The Authors

Harriette Simpson Arnow *is the author of* The Dollmaker, *perhaps one of the most famous Appalachian novels of the 20th century. Published in 1954,* The Dollmaker *remained on the best-seller list for 31 weeks, won the Friends of American Writers Award, and placed second in the National Book Awards. Her first published works were short stories published in* Esquire, *sent there with the pseudonym "H.L. Simpson" and with a photograph of her brother to disguise her gender. She was born in Monticello in Wayne County, Ky., on July 7, 1908, but grew up in Pulaski County, Ky. Both her parents were teachers and she tried, unsuccessfully, to follow in their footsteps. She had two other successful novels,* Mountain Path *(1936) and* Hunter's Horn *(1949), which was a best seller and a Fiction Book Club selection and finished close to William Faulkner's* A Fable *in that year's voting for the Pulitzer Prize. She also published two historical studies:* Seedtime on the Cumberland *(1960) and* The Flowering of the Cumberland *(1963). Her final books were novels:* The Weedkiller's Daughter *(1970),* The Kentucky Trace *(1974), and* Between The Flowers *(written in the 1930s and published posthumously in 1999), a memoir,* Old Burnside *(1977), and a collection of short stories,* The Collected Short Stories of Harriette Simpson Arnow *(published posthumously in 2005). She died March 22, 1986.*

James B. Goode, *editor of* Kentucky's Twelve Days of Christmas, *is a Professor of English on the faculty of Bluegrass Community & Technical College in Lexington, Ky., Goode holds undergraduate and graduate degrees from the University of Kentucky and a Master of Fine Arts Degree in Creative Writing: Fiction from Murray State University. He has been a visiting Professor of English at The University of Wales at Swansea, Changsha University in China, and Maseno University in Kenya. He is an award-winning author of six books and has published numerous poems, short stories and essays in magazines such as* South Carolina Review, Huron Review, Ball State University Forum, Journal of Appalachian Studies, Appalachian Heritage, Journal of Kentucky Studies, *and* Kentucky Monthly.

The
Fifth
Day

"Remembering that it Happened Once"

From *A Timbered Choir*

VI

Remembering that it happened once,
We cannot turn away the thought,
As we go out, cold, to our barns
Toward the long night's end, that we
Ourselves are living in the world
It happened in when it first happened,
That we ourselves, opening a stall
(A latch thrown open countless times
Before), might find them breathing there,
Foreknown: the Child bedded in straw,
The mother kneeling over Him,
The husband standing in belief
He scarcely can believe, in light
That lights them from no source we see,
An April morning's light, the air
Around them joyful as a choir.
We stand with one hand on the door,
Looking into another world
That is this world, the pale daylight
Coming just as before, our chores
To do, the cattle all awake,
Our own white frozen breath hanging
In front of us; and we are here
As we have never been before,
Sighted as not before, our place
Holy, although we knew it not.

Wendell Berry

A Change of Heart

When the coal camp awoke in December, the sounds of coal being shoveled into scarred scoop buckets and the clanging of stove doors inside the wood-frame houses carried across the valley, almost gliding above the frozen grass. Soon, the acrid, sulfur smoke twisted upward from the brick chimneys and hung in a yellow fog over the glistening roofs. The smells of boiling coffee, fried smoked hog jowl, baking buttermilk cathead biscuits, and bubbling flour gravy made every stomach come alive.

Orin snuggled under six quilts, dreading getting out of the bed and placing his warm feet on the cold, wood floor. He needed to go to the outhouse, but the thought of the journey made him sink farther into the mattress and pull the quilts in tighter against his slender frame. He hadn't slept much. The excitement of going Christmas shopping in Harlan with Mom, Daddy, and his three sisters made him feel fretful inside. The county seat would be bustling with people. They would stop to see the big Christmas tree on the courthouse square, with its large multi-colored bulbs, giant candy canes, and shimmering tinsel before Daddy found a parking place and they headed to the center of town where the dime and department stores were located.

"Orin, Nelda, Sara, Leah ... time to get up and wash. Breakfast is pert near ready," his Mom, Ora Mae, said from the kitchen.

Orin looked over to the bed that held his three sisters. They were huddled like mice, with all three of their heads on the same pillow, their hair cascading like overlapping fans. They began to stir, moaning and stretching.

Orin wiggled until his feet were at the edge of the mattress, slowly pulled himself upright, and pivoted until he scooted across the edge and onto the floor. He hopped to the ladder-backed chair that held his jeans and shirt, pulling them on quickly.

His mom, Ora Mae, stirred the gravy in the iron skillet on the cook stove and glanced around to watch Orin pull on his blanket-lined jump jacket.

"Take a coal bucket with you and bring me some egg coal," she said.

Orin grasped the bail of a coal bucket, pushed open the door, and headed out the rock walkway leading from the back of the house to where the outhouse and coal bin sat on the alley dividing two rows of coal camp houses. He held his breath, to guard against the cold and smoke, and then let it out in a whirling, steamy mist. He looked upward to the mountains, now capped with a crown of white trees. He could hear a hawk whistling somewhere up a hollow, its voice bouncing from one hill to the next. He ducked into the outhouse, came out, and took the few steps to where the coal lay frosted and glistening in the

bin. He shoveled the coal scuttle full and carried it to the house, swinging it in time with his gait.

When he came into the kitchen, the girls were dressed and sitting around the metal table. Eldon, his daddy, stood with his back to the heating stove, drinking his black coffee from a white ironstone mug. Ora Mae was pouring steaming, browned gravy into a crockery bowl. Her biscuits, jowl, and fried eggs were already on the table.

"Mornin' boy," Eldon said. "How cold is it out there?" he asked.

"I saw a rabbit with jumper cables tryin' to get another started," Orin joked. "Looks like its goin' to be a beautiful day. Not a cloud in the sky—clear as a bell..."

Eldon smiled. That boy is cut right out of my skin, he thought.

"Let's eat," Ora Mae said. She set the bowl of gravy on the table.

"When are we leavin' for Harlan?" Nelda asked. She spooned the thick gravy on her crumbled biscuits.

"As soon as we get done eatin' and can get in the car," Eldon said. "Sometimes you all is like tryin' to herd cats!"

Sara wrinkled her nose at that. She didn't like being lumped in with the rest of the kids. She was always the first in the car, any time they went anywhere. Nelda and Leah were the two who dragged their feet like they were walking in cold molasses. Orin wasn't much better. He was

weird. He had a habit of coming outside, patting his pockets, and then going back into the house to retrieve his pocket knife, billfold or some comic book he wanted to read while they traveled.

"I'm a givin' you all five dollars apiece to spend on gifts, so make it go as fer as you can!" Eldon said. He dropped a chunk of butter into a big tablespoon of dark molasses, stirred it, and sopped a big biscuit in the mixture. The girls stared at him with their blue eyes. Leah, the youngest, had egg dribbled on her chin. A partially toothless grin spread across her face.

"I got dibs on the rear-passenger window!" she declared. She didn't like sitting behind her Dad. He chewed tobacco, and every time he wanted to spit, he rolled down the window and let it go. In the summer, the tobacco juice came in the rear window; in the winter, it splattered on the window, making a disgusting, gooey mess that ran down like a wind-blown glacier.

After the table was cleared, dishes washed and dried, and food put in the warming oven above the cook stove, they loaded into the old Plymouth and turned down U.S. 119 toward Harlan. The curving, twisting road was a harrowing ride through Chad, Hiram, Nolansburg, Totz, and dozens of other small whistle-stop railroad stations long since disappeared. Orin watched carefully for the landmarks

he recognized. When they passed the Bassham farm where a big Angus bull was painted on the side of the barn facing the highway, he knew they were close to the city limits of Harlan.

Harlan was the county seat of Harlan County, one of the largest counties in Kentucky. It was built in a narrow valley and at the meeting of three tributaries to the Cumberland River—Cloverfork, Martin's Fork, and the Upper Cumberland River all came together there. Small corporate and family-owned coal camps dotted the surrounding area with names like High Splint, Kitts, Game Cock, Crummies, Koppers, Black Joe, Mary Helen, Chevrolet, Wallins Creek, and Lenarue.

Eldon turned the sluggish Plymouth onto Mound Street. "Up flew a gang of birds!" he yelled out suddenly, startling everyone. "You all wake up back there!" he said. "We're real close to the courthouse. I'll let you 'uns out there and take the car down to park in the A&P parking lot." He handed four five-dollar bills to Ora Mae who turned in her seat and gave them one each. Orin studied his intently. Abraham Lincoln stared off to his left, as if he were in some trance. His face was full with the burden of the Civil War, but determined. He needed a haircut, Orin thought as he examined Lincoln's short-cropped beard and the bump on his right jaw. Orin began to fret over what gifts he was going to buy with his money. Should he buy Dad a billfold? A tie? Some Old Spice shaving lotion? What about Mom? What would she like? She had a near-empty, small blue bottle of Midnight in Paris cologne that she loved. Maybe he could get a new one on sale. The girls were less of a problem. They always liked something for their baby dolls. The dime stores sold all kinds of little blankets, miniature toboggans, doll baby bottles, and cloth diapers.

The sidewalks were filled with people. Coal miners and their families drifted in and out of the stores. A large-flake snow began to fall. The feathers of it sailed downward and stuck momentarily to the windshield, then dissolved to clear droplets that ran in small rivers down the glass. They got out of the car on the sidewalk in front of the courthouse, where a bronze statue of the World War I soldier had his bayonet thrust menacingly forward. They all craned their necks to see the tortured face beneath the helmet. Leah didn't stop. Her eyes were fixed on the tree as she walked toward it like a zombie.

"Leah, don't touch the tree!" Ora Mae grabbed her by the coattail. "That thing is plugged into juice and you might get 'lectrocuted," she warned.

They walked all around the tree, admiring the glass ornaments and cobalt blue lights. The tree smelled of the forest. The musty pine smell made them all want Christmas to hurry up and get there.

"Let's head to Woolworth's," Ora Mae said. "We're supposed to meet your daddy there. He'll be a' wonderin' where we got to."

They passed the many law offices around the courthouse; they were brightly decorated with nativity scenes, Santa Clauses, strands of multi-colored lights, and fake snow. Just before they turned the corner at Woolworth's, they passed Helton's News Stand. All of a sudden, something sprung from the shadows. A man with no legs scurried across the sidewalk, using his hands like crutches. He stopped quickly at the curb and pivoted to face them by swinging around on his well-calloused knuckles. Laced-leather sheaths covered each of the stumps of his legs.

"Won't you help a fellow soldier in God's army?" he said from the slit in the heavy beard stubble on his face. He held a battered tin cup forward, grasping it between the index and middle finger of his right hand, while the other hand balanced his torso. Ora Mae gathered in her children like a hen collects her chicks when they are in danger. She hurried them toward the street corner, cradling Leah close to her bosom. The man pivoted again, following them with his deep-set eyes and yelling, "God would have it that we have mercy on those of his children who are misfit and poor. Remember 1 John 3:17: 'But whoever has the world's goods, and beholds his brother in need and closes his heart

against him, how does the love of God abide in him?'"

Orin couldn't take his eyes from the man as he sped toward them holding out the dirty cup. Drool ran down the man's chin and his creased brow was filled with old pain—pain that would not go away.

Ora Mae dashed through the silver metal doors of Woolworth's and straight into the arms of Eldon who was standing at the lunch counter. She was shaking as she described the man on the street. Eldon patted her shoulder.

"That's just Elmer Sizemore," he said. "He got his legs cut off in a rock fall at the Cranks Creek mine. He's a beggar, just a beggar." After he got her calmed, they sat at the soda-fountain counter and had tuna-salad sandwiches on toast and cherry Cokes, but Orin couldn't erase Elmer from his mind. *How does the love abide in him who doesn't help someone in need?* he thought. After a while, he got up from his seat and excused himself to go to the bathroom. When he got out of his family's sight, he dashed through the side door to Woolworth's and down the street to where Elmer was leaning against the building. Elmer didn't move this time. He stared at Orin with his beady eyes.

"Had a change of heart?" he asked. Orin took the now-crumpled five-dollar bill from his coat pocket and placed it in the cup. He looked down at Elmer and his tattered coat. "Merry Christmas," he said.

Elmer wiped his cold nose on his dirty sleeve and a toothless grin appeared from the same slit in the heavy beard stubble on his face. "The Bible says in Luke 6:38: 'For if you give, you will get! Your gift will return to you in full and overflowing measure, pressed down, shaken together to make room for more, and running over. Whatever measure you use to give—large or small— will be used to measure what is given back to you.'"

Orin turned back toward Woolworth's. His heart was full and overflowing, pressed down, shaken, and running over.

James B. Goode

JAMES B. GOODE

Two Births

Mine was a poor place
in an eastern Kentucky
coal camp
but at least
I had a bed
a grandmother
to help me from my mother
two loving, wrinkled hands
to catch me
to wipe my tender feet
and kind wrinkled ears
to hear my baby breaths
once I settled in the crib.

His was a humble place
filled with hay
and cattle,
restless
under the full moon
and brightness of the star
a radiant new mother
bent over a manger
an anxious
wide-eyed father
standing in the shadows.
His lasting presence
a hushed gliding
of a winter air
bringing shifts of snow

in twisting waves
the message
and the miracle
in the twirled
rusty oak leaves
still clinging
to dark branches
despite
the fierceness
of the winds.

James B. Goode

About The Authors

Wendell Berry is an internationally known, prolific Kentucky author of novels, short stories, poems, and essays. He is also a farmer, environmentalist, and conservationist who has lived in sight of the Kentucky River near where it flows into the Ohio River for more than 40 years, in a landscape where generations of his family have farmed since the early 1800s. His home is at Lane's Landing near Port Royal, Ky., where has parents were born. Berry's fiction to date consists of 14 books including eight novels and six collections of short fiction including the 23 short stories collected in That Distant Land (2004), which, when read as a whole, form a chronicle of the fictional small Kentucky town of Port William. His non-fiction (mainly collections of essays) consists of 32 works published between 1970 and 2011; his poetic works include 26 books published between 1964 and 2012, many of which engage citizenship and everlasting truth for mankind in his journey through life and is the mainstream closest to his heart. He was selected to deliver the 41st Jefferson Lecture in Humanities in April 2012. This is the highest honor that the United States government bestows in the humanities. He was named Kentucky Monthly's Kentuckian of the Year in 2005.

James B. Goode's biography can be seen on page 69.

The Sixth Day

Maria Milagrosa
from *Surrendered Child*

At her moment of quickening, your mother is trying to learn to drive. She's sitting in the car's front seat and your father's hand is on hers, guiding her along unfamiliar streets, taking her through the motions. There's no real chance she'll learn to drive, or keep her waitress job at a local diner, or be anything besides what the highschool yearbook predicted—in a nice little home in the West, right beside the one she loves best. This is Kansas, a whole new world, and it's all she can do to navigate, to see through the dust and down the highways, ones so much straighter than the road up Abbott Mountain. At night, she dreams planes from the Air Force base. She dreams your father, moving across her body. And now you, the shadow of that plane moving forward into her life. Already the pear-shaped uterus contains you. The buttonlike mouth that will open to spew you out already speaks your name.

She wants to be part of this miracle, as your father calls it. He places his hand on her stomach night after night, touching this earth that will bear his name. He says, "Listen." And she can hear it too, the way the sac that holds you is growing. By day she watches herself in the mirror in the apartment hall, how she is and isn't the girl she was before. Perky, they called her in school. She was the lightest one on her feet at the drive-in where she met him, your father. Now, her middle blossoms out. She uses safety pins to fasten her pedal pushers, pulls a sweater down over a little belly she sucks in. She writes her mother letters, in desperation. She wants to go home again, wants to hoe down row after row of beans in the hot sun. She feels that earth pull her back, but this earth holds her down, this round globe of her body.

She is larger than she could ever have believed. She wobbles now when she walks, sloshes, feels the ocean in her gut, the ocean she's never seen. She is fluid. All of her is floating out, reaching for one memory of who she used to be. She is 12 and she is drawing water by a chain from the deep, deep well. She is 19 and she dreams of far away and she writes letters to a boy who says he loves her and buys her a diamond wedding ring from Morocco. At 20, she is far away. She peers over herself, barely sees the pointy toes of her little slippers sticking out.

She wishes, most days, she still knew her own heart. She is alone a lot, in the apartment they call home. She washes the pink-and-black dishes, the colors she picked for Elvis. She switches the radio on in the hall and tries to find love songs, ones to remind her of why she is here, married at 20 and living in a foreign land. She wants to put your father's hand over her chest, hold her heart still, but she feels herself shifting. Feels the placenta blossom, grow minute branches, feels it reaching out, drinking her in. She is afraid. Her heart is different, is rising inside her, pushing against her ribs, even if the doctor holds the stethoscope and says no. Her heart is nearer than it has ever been, and she touches it, just beneath her breast, feels the beating rising to her mouth. Taste is bitter.

And then, two days before the birth, she lightens. In reality, she is heavier than she has ever been. It's the end of summer and her ankles are swollen and she changes from one of her maternity tops to another, one, two, and the buttons will hardly fasten. Her back is wet with sweat, but she is floating. She is so light she could drift out through the still windows of the apartment. She could float

on the Kansas air, a hundred miles, more and more, settle at her own mother's doorstep in time for water to boil in a metal pan. Hands she knows could ease you out of the flesh between her legs.

Is that when you first think of each other? Do you open your eyes then and look up with hope into her face? Is that when she names you, middle name after a star she's loved at drive-in movies, first name one the baby book promises means "purity" and "truth"? Your worlds are crashing, one into another. Her uterus is light, grown thin and hollow. You are ready to be born, already a little girl dreaming of her mother.

•••••

Winter 1998 . Winter, and not just a time of dark after five o'clock and snowless, frozen yards, but almost Christmas. I'm living in a medium-sized southern town with a reputation for evangelical faith and a church or a bridal boutique or an estate-sale specialist around every corner. This winter, I am in love, long-distance, with a photographer and teacher of traditional dance who plucks broken teeth from his mouth after years of nighttime grinding and calls himself a wounded man. This winter, yard upon yard of my town is decorated with Santas and Jesuses, mangers and sleighs, flashing rooftop stars. One house two blocks over boasts enough red bulbs to light the way to redemption. This holiday, like I always do, I'll travel to Kentucky. But not yet.

Redemption and the holiday both feel undesirable, brittle as foil. I have put up a Christmas tree, laden it with glass balls and blue lights. I have wrapped gifts and sent cards portraying silver foxes in a snowy woods. And each night for 12 nights, I have lit a candle to the Virgin of Guadalupe. "Merciful Virgin," I read from the back of the candle, "show clemency, love, and compassion to those who love you and search for your protection. May the sweet fragrance of roses reach your divine son, that he may hear our prayers, wipe our tears, and give us love and assistance." Prayer, too, is mere holiday decoration, and I fall asleep at night with the tree lights on, holding my small, black dog. We breathe together into sleep and I am lonely and full of self-pity. I change my answering-machine message to a blues song ... "I want a Sunday kind of love." I call all my friends until there is no one left to call and ask them to tell me that I am loveable, that someone, somehow, will love me.

There has been an unexpected ice storm and so I have hibernated, inclined to influenza and isolation. The streets of my town shimmer, frozen and cold, and I go out only after the second morning, to chisel away at my truck's doors and windows. I'm later than I have ever been for my journey home, with Christmas one day away, but still I hold back, relishing cold and lethargy and my tree's blue lights at night.

I stay an extra day, make a trip 15 miles outside of town, with a friend, to test the roads. We have chili dogs and root beer at her father's country store. I stock up on homemade country sausage, ostensibly a gift for my mother, although I know that this gift will waste away in my own refrigerator while I am gone, or in hers; she fears the erratic nature of frying foods, their sizzle and splatter. My friend and I drive home slowly, before dark, on roads now ice free, and as I watch the stars and angels and mangers glitter from roadside houses, I feel lethargy turn, widen in my gut. We stop at a grocery on the outskirts and I buy jars of jam for last-minute gifts and cheap champagne for myself. I tell myself I'll celebrate New Year's now, since Kentucky will be sin-free, Southern Baptist-dry. At home, alone, I drink too much, then call my dancer lover.

"Christmas Eve," I say and I pause, waiting for him to acknowledge me and the season both. "It's Christmas," I say again. "I wanted to wish you a merry one."

"You, too, gal," he says. His voice, his most seductive quality, is low, sleep-filled.

I know, from this endearment, this gal, that he's all right with me at the moment, safe enough in his own home, six hours away. At times of less security, there are long pauses on the phone, or he won't answer at all and I leave message after message, counting, later, the rings before the machine takes over, four rings or two

or a variety, a sign, I believe, of whether or not he's checking messages, then ignoring me.

He tells me about his Christmas Eve, the movie he went to see, how cold it is, how he plans to make contact sheets later on, pictures of this dance or that or of last fall's road tour of northern California. I read beneath these words, looking for signs, symbols. Does cold mean he wishes for me, my body heat, my warm mouth? Does his reference to the ice storm mean he wants me there, in the relative safety of his desire? I read the story underneath, the one I know about from times he's let me glimpse his past—the Christmas, years ago, when his former wife left, and how beautiful his two daughters were, looking back at him from the rear window of their car. Or is it all a way to put me in my place, tell me my Christmas is here, his there?

He asks where I'm sitting, what I've done with this day, and I ease, just like that, into a familiar territory, a slick, transparent surface of only certain words, certain thoughts, a surface where we circle and glide, dance away from anything too real. But it's Christmas Eve and I'm giddy, drunk on champagne and my two-days' worth of lethargy, a heady mix that makes me want to dance faster and faster, skate at a dizzying rate until these usual words, words that make me think *polite, distant, cold,* shatter and I can look, make him look,

beneath who we are. Show me, I want to tell him, show me who you really are.

Instead I say, "Do you?"

"Do what?" he asks.

I know he is fond of Appalachian ways of knowing and speaking, and that *do what* falls into this category as an interrogative, but I also feel him hedging my real question, which I myself have not yet expressed.

"Do you love me?" I ask.

I have already known, for a long time, the answer to this question. He loves me, as a human being, as a fellow artist, as a dear old friend. That isn't what I want, even if I don't know, entirely, what I want.

"Do you love me?" I repeat.

"Gal," he calls me again, more softly this time. "How can you love anybody," he asks, his voice not unkind, "when you don't even love yourself?"

Through the spin and shiver of champagne, I feel hurt. I feel hurt and so empty I do nothing but sit with the receiver for a long while. I touch my lips to it, as if it is his mouth, any mouth. "What do you know about it," I say at last. "What do you know about love?"

"You're just a girl," he says, "a lonely girl at Christmas time wanting her mother."

•••••

I remember being almost 20 when I visited my mother again, the first true visit in almost five years. Before that I had seen her only sporadically, for hours at best, or in passing, like a stranger with whom I am somewhat friendly. Once with Joe at a holiday, before our divorce. Once for an afternoon visit in the public library at a table near the paperback romances. Another time on the streets of the small town near where she lives, near a shop where she worked for a time selling women's clothing. My father had long urged our connection with surreptitious letters and phone calls my mother would later tell me about. "She's been sick now and then, he wrote, "but she's strong." "She's not done well in school, but you can't tell her much," another letter said. This visit will be for real. I'll eat supper, greens and cornbread and beans and fatback cooked 12 hours. I imagine I'll answer questions. Fill in blanks. I'll build a bridge between the life I've been living, which she knows nothing about, and the life she's been living, about which I believe I know everything. She has gone home again and never left and I believe I have it memorized, the house of brick and concrete that is her life.

My visit is in late summer, close to my 20th birthday. In my memory it is my father who takes me to see her, parks down the road to let me out, far enough away so she won't see his Oldsmobile, or my stepmother in the passenger seat. In my memory the short stretch of road is hot and the asphalt burns my feet through the thin soles of my Chinese slippers. I hurry, climbing the steep driveway toward the house so quickly I almost don't see the drapes fall back into place. I knock and wait and knock and there's my grandmother at the storm door. At first, she just smiles at me with her gold-toothed smile, wipes her hands on the front of her housedress. Five years, I think, have made me that unfamiliar.

Before I know it I am standing in the living room of that house and looking at my mother's face as if I have never seen it before. I am studying her cheekbones, their angle, and I am trying to meet her green eyes. I'm thinking, Do you remember me? Have you missed me? Aren't you going to ask where I've been? Her eyes are beautiful, as they have always been, and they are ringed with just a hint of soft lines. She has not, I think, changed at all, not her dark brown hair, its peaks and wings of hairspray and curls, not her dry hands that snag on my sweater as she hugs me, her back straight and wary. She is wearing, I could swear it, the same thicksoled house shoes she had always worn in our house.

"Well," she says, and she laughs and I laugh and I think somehow of slivers of glass. Behind her I hear a radio playing country songs and I see a coffee table with an arrangement of plastic roses and an open Bible on a stand. My grandmother hovers in the background, then hurries back to the kitchen, which smells of soup beans and salty ham and something sweet. From his green chair my grandfather says, "Don't you just look like butter on toast?" As I hug him, his whitish old-man eyes seem pleased, and I forget for a while that this man, so I've heard, once wanted to hold me down and cut off all my hippie hair. Behind me I hear the rattle of coal trucks on the highway past this house and shift from foot to foot and see my grandfather stare at my moccasins and my bell-bottom pants. "Well," my mother says, and brings two kitchen chairs for us. "We'll sit for a while," she tells me, "just us girls."

We are girls in my memory of that reunion day. My grandmother and my grandfather listen as we talk about candy and lipstick. We talk about how my father didn't love her enough, as if he is a boyfriend who has jilted her and asked for his football jersey and his ring. We talk about how hot July has been and how she's been doing nothing in the afternoons but run a cool washcloth over her face. We talk about how, on Wednesday afternoons, she meets her two sisters in town at the drugstore, where her favorite thing is a Coke with lemon and just a little bit of ice. She has had, I am surprised to hear, small adventures. She's seen Loretta Lynn at a concert at a local high school. She's gone back to eating her mother's cooking, complete with things that fry and sizzle, and her hands, I notice, have no cracks or bleeding knuckles. A girl. She is a girl again in her mother's house, and they are girls' stories she has to tell me, this day.

We talk about long-ago events, as if they are the only present that exists. There's the story of the drive-in where she met my father, the girlfriends she's now sure he had. Goldie, she says, is the one he never got over. The fast one, the one with tight sweaters and a rinse on her hair. She herself, she says, was always a good girl. Never let my father or anyone else put his hand on her knee or anywhere else. She was a good girl and her friends were good. There was her friend Mary Katherine, the one she took Home Ec with that time they made dresses and the teacher made her rip out every seam. There was Bonnie Burchfield, the one who wore rhinestone glasses, how she died in a car wreck, went through a guardrail and over a mountainside, and how they found her glasses later, lying in the middle of the road.

They were good girls, all of them, though

goodness, she says while she files her nails, is not to be counted on. Not in this world. She whitens her nails with an orange stick. She smoothes her hair and tells me about her last permanent wave, how it's been almost six weeks. "I'm almost the same as I was back in high school," she says. Her weight, she means. And she talks of this weight, its own goodness, the one hundred pounds she's maintained, one hundred two at most. She does laps every day, she says. She walks the circle of rooms that is the house, and she watches what she eats, too, she says. But it isn't easy. Ice cream, she says, that's mostly what she has for lunch, though her mommy bakes biscuits and eggs and cornbread and all that fattening food. The mess and fuss, she says, but she's kept herself small. She can wear the same clothes she did in high school, even. The very same ones.

After a while I go into the kitchen for a glass of water. My grandmother is there frying cornbread and I look at her ankles, their rolled-down socks and her tiny feet in their tennis shoes. I look at the radio sitting on a windowsill, next to a hand mirror I'm sure my mother uses to make up her face. "The Kitchen," a plaque says, "The Room Closest to Heaven." As I sip refrigerator water I walk past the back door and into the room that is my mother's bedroom, where I stand for a while.

Her bed, covered by a polyester throw, is so neatly made a coin could bounce from its center, and at the head of the bed, on a little shelf, are the icons of my mother's life. There's a Billy Graham reader called Reflections on Today and Tomorrow. *There's a candle, rose scented, that has never been lit. There's a photograph of me in a tiny frame. I'm small and I'm walking down a sidewalk and I'm holding my mother's hand. I touch each of these things, put them back carefully in their individual, dustless spots. A spy, a covert daughter, I then inch open the dresser drawers. There are neat rows of white cotton panties, and beside those, equally neat boxes of makeup and polish remover and hand lotion. In a closet beside this dresser, there are more boxes, larger cardboard ones. "Bedroom," one says. "Living-room knickknacks," another says. "Garage storage," still another says, and I realize, with a start, that I'm reading my own father's writing. This tall stack of boxes, still taped, never opened, are boxes from my mother's other life, the one she led with us. I close the door to this closet as soundlessly as I can, then slide open the door of a free-standing wardrobe. My mother's clothes are here. Some are veiled by plastic dry-cleaning bags, each bag carefully knotted at the bottom. I imagine pedal pushers and three-quarter-sleeve sweaters. I imagine the full-skirted dress she wore at her wedding.*

I wonder, briefly, how such clothes can breathe, and then I stand for a long while, staring down at the bathroom scale at the foot of my mother's bed. I stare down and wonder about my own weight, about the tiny pouch that is my belly, the place the son she knows nothing about once lived. Then I hear a kitchen chair slide back in the living room, my mother's footsteps. One, two. Her voice, asking me where I am. I swallow the rest of my cold water, fast, and ask myself which piece of evidence I should remember longest. Which small fact that will tell me, for years to come, how it is that my mother leads her life.

•••••

Home. At the holidays, 1998, I am in one, a house I call home. It's a house with two dogs and a festive tree and a kitchen sink, although holidays take me elsewhere. At Christmas, sometimes at Thanksgiving, and for a week in the summer, I take Interstate 64 through West Virginia, via Beckley and Charleston and Huntington, then on from there to eastern Kentucky, to the little town where my mother lives, to my mother's house and to the house of her sister. Both their houses I have by this time come to call places of secrets.

I, too, inhabit a house of secrets, lead a life my mother only suspects. I am by 1998 a writer and a reader of books she vaguely calls novels, a category that for her includes romances and old movies and one long letter she reads to me again and again, one my father wrote her before their divorce. "Long enough to be a novel," she says of these 10 pages, itemized reasons my father wanted out. I am a college teacher, and she imagines me in a school yard with a bell, ringing in classes for children after recess. My growth, this body turned from girl to woman, is a mystery to her, its breasts and desires.

This winter, this Christmas of 1998, I am determined to shed my greatest secret, shed it like a snakeskin, like an undesirable and heavy coat. *I'll tell the truth*, I say. *I'll come as clean as spring water.* I'll go forth, I tell myself, having sinned and confessed. I will be absolved forever at the feet of the Mother. I will tell her I have a son and that hidden piece of myself, that fragment sharp as a sliver of glass, will be plucked out and I will then, I tell myself, be whole at last.

I hit the West Virginia Turnpike by midafternoon, a time at which everything seems rhetorical. Bare wires and bulbs from Christmas lights drape over everything. Houses and churches and barns advertising Mail Pouch Tobacco, transformed by night, are now nothing but dispirited Santa's workshops and unresplendent roofs. Every roadside diner and gas station is a testament to those of us who are part of this holiday, and not.

I stop at a BP in Marmet for a bear claw and coffee and talk for a while to the man at the counter. He has small, red eyes and a nervous way of sucking at his lower lip. He offers me free soft peppermints and tells me he's worked every Christmas, New Year's, and Fourth of July for the past 14 years. He smells like sweet wine and winks as I pay for my coffee and a pack of cigarettes. I'm not a smoker, and he's maybe not a drinker, but we're celebratory, high energy, and it's nearing the zenith of this holiday—one o'clock, time for turkey and dressing and another broadcast of *It's a Wonderful Life*.

I'm late, and I know it. But I drive slowly, thinking of my mother and her sisters. Of Ruby, who died in an auto accident a number of years ago. Ruby

had secrets, the greatest of which was the exact nature of her illness. Seizures? Manic depression? She was on her way home the night she died. I imagine her in the car on her way back to her apartment in that concrete block building with a guardrail along the halls and a persistent smell of something medicinal and sanitary. My grandfather was driving. I imagine how they came to a stop sign. Ruby might have looked off to the right, to a field and sign with praying hands and a promise, "Jesus Saves." Or maybe she closed her eyes in those last seconds before the other car crashed through, striking just as they pulled ahead. It was she who died, not my grandfather. Was that death like her dreams of a Holy Ghost with her own face?

Ruthie, the youngest sister, lives up the winding stretch of asphalt called Mining Hollow, outside of town. She also leaves home less and less, since her son shot himself in the back room of their mobile home. That was a dozen years ago. Now, she spends her days tending house and the grave of her son, which she can see from the trailer's kitchen window. When I went to visit there one August, Ruth's husband was leaving to go squirrel hunting. Just joking, he waved his rifle in the air, pointed it at us. From the couch, Ruth said, "I can't stand it when you do that." She didn't get up. I remain unsure why my cousin killed himself. Depression, they all hint darkly. And drugs, too, ones that sent

him once to an unnamed hospital, *one of those places*, they called it. The night of the shooting is called *when that happened to him, or the night that happened*, and no mention is made of death itself. It is at Ruth's house that there'll be Christmas dinner, if I'm in time.

I reach my aunt Ruth's by four o'clock, having missed this traditional dinner. My lateness has thrown everything off, their 12:30 dinnertime. They waited, a half hour, an hour, before giving in, feasting without me. Now, my dead cousin's daughter sits in the post-ice-storm warmth of the patio, rocking in the porch glider, her patent-leathered feet scooting up and back. The rest of them are inside the trailer, where there are still pots of green beans and sweet potatoes on the stove, and the refrigerator is packed with foiled pans of turkey and ham. But I can see that it's over. My uncle has already stripped the Christmas tree, an artificial one, and I can see it lying naked in the living room, a few icicles straggling on its branches. Dishes have been washed. Pa sits in his usual spot by the door.

"Hello stranger," he says, his whitish bird eyes looking me up and down.

The television is blaring football and the mother of my dead cousin's child is lounging with her second husband, sock footed, with their other three kids, one of whom is short necked and crippled, son of his own grandfather. My uncle, who is

loud and white-haired and a former radio rock 'n' roll performer, welcomes me.

"Well," he says, "look who the cat drug in. Were the roads bad?"

I tell him the ice was still around, a little, back in Virginia, but that here the roads were good. My mother is at the table in the adjoining dining room with my aunt. They're talking bloodsugar levels and hairdos, but they stop and my aunt gets up and hugs me. She's wearing a negligee, and she smells like hair spray and White Diamonds cologne.

"Were you careful on those roads?" she asks.

I've brought her a flavored-coffee selection for Christmas, but I can smell Maxwell House from the kitchen, and my gift suddenly seems off, the hazelnut and cinnamon dwarfed by the plethora of things in this trailer. To the side, along the floor of the dining room, are plaster statues—angels, dalmatians, chickens, rabbits, a windup monkey that plays reggae. Most of these were gifts from my uncle to my aunt, who seldom leaves the trailer to buy herself things. A table by the back wall displays a Bible, open, and photos—my long-dead cousin, the aunt killed in the auto accident, my grandmother, who died a few years ago from complications of pneumonia.

"Were the roads bad?" my mother asks.

"Them roads weren't a bit bad," my uncle calls from the other room.

I mention the ice and Virginia and the warm spell and as always, I am struck, when I first see my mother, by her smallness. She has a delicate face, large green eyes with the same darkness beneath I'm getting, at 42, and the knuckles of her small hands are swollen with arthritis and housework.

As I take my place at the dining-room table, my aunt offers me leftovers. "Ruthie," my mother says, "has been up since 2:30 a.m., basting the turkey and peeling 10 pounds of potatoes for her potato salad and you wouldn't believe the dishes they've washed." Soon I'm sitting with a paper plate of turkey and dressing, the potato salad, and the cranberry sauce I've liked since childhood, sliced, garnet-colored jelly, edged with tiny ridges from the can.

While I eat, my mother has a second helping of dessert, her favorite. She piles her own paper plate with vanilla cream pie and chocolate cake, cheesecake with strawberry sauce on top, all the while telling me she's lost some, that she was at 101 when she weighed this morning, as she does every morning.

"I believe you've gained a little," she says. She looks at me speculatively, takes a bite of pie, her mouth open wide, to save her lipstick. "How were the roads?" she asks. "They looked good over this way."

I tell her about the ice storm and how I chiseled open my truck, and the warming

trend since yesterday. I eat slowly, tasting fatback in the green beans, viscous marshmallow in the sweet potatoes, pickle, mustard, and Miracle Whip in the potato salad. I feel my stomach widening, my hips expanding, the untimeliness, ungainliness of me, eating, late.

"Now, she ain't fat," my uncle says. He bends behind my chair. "Just getting some of that middle-age spread," he says, nuzzling my cheek with his beard.

He whispers into my ear. "Don't you have a little sugar for your uncle?"

This is the way of this afternoon, five o'clock now, Christmas ebbing. We talk of lipstick brands and permanent waves and innovative eye creams, and after my mother finishes her cake, my aunt goes to get her blood-sugar test kit. I decline, but they solemnly poke each other's fingers, testing the rightness of their blood. Soon it will be dark outside, and I will drive my mother and Pa home along Mining Hollow, then head home along Highway 23. I think of roads, iceless roads, connecting house to house, aunt's, mother's, my own, my own house now devoid of blue tree lights, softly dark, waiting for the certainty of my return.

•••••

Absolution, that's what I really want when I say I want love. I am a lost soul, waiting to be cleansed. I absolve thee, the waters say, and I am a girl again. I am seven years old again and I am at the house of my great-grandmother and I am standing in a backyard listening to the sound of an underground spring. Its waters are pure and sweet and I know that if I taste them, my soul, if it departed right then, could ascend, full of loving-kindness. I am a girl standing on the boards of a covered well, and I dance, my feet drumming time on the hollow board. The hollow sound makes me afraid, and under my feet the well is deep, a black mouth in the earth that could drink me in. The well is forever and I'm afraid of its waters, afraid of the waters of forgiveness. Why didn't she come, my mother, and lift me into her arms and comfort me?

Fear. All of us suffer from it, my mother and her family and I. My aunt Ruth suffers from relentless dreams and memory, a grief that won't let go. And Pa, some part of himself is lost forever down a bottomless hole in the floor of his very own house. And there are cousins: The one who is a product of incest. Another who weighs three hundred pounds, insulated from the sad, outside world. Of course, the one who put a gun in his mouth is released from fear, unless hellfire and the aftermath of sin have made that impossible. My mother suffers from fear, from what diagnostic manuals would call obsessive-compulsive disorder. Or I believe this, based on my own conjectures, my own limited knowledge. I know that the illness manifests in the mid-thirties, and I have looked, again and again, at a photograph of my mother standing near our car in the drive of the house we lived in until I was 14. I am a shoulder, a glimpse of hair in this photograph, and I live her obsessions vicariously. I am them. Already, in this photograph, I know about hand washing. I know about fear of the body, of sex, of love.

Suffering. This. A winter night, 1998. Christmas

night, following food and family conversation, following discussions of beauty and the purity of our blood. Five-thirty and dusk, and we're heading along the narrow road called Mining Hollow, past trailers and debris and dogs worrying turkey bones and paper sacks, past the Church of the Pentecost and the ghost of my cousin, which follows us, taps at my window, wondering where I'm from, where we're going, if he can go too, hitch a ride, find his way out of ghostdom, forever. Where we're going is home.

•••••

I've always written about home. When I was nine, an eastern-Kentucky friend played guitar and we wrote songs and poems—pretty ones about transparent moonlight and wind in poplars and hollows. Now I write prose, less pretty, but no less filled with the ghosts of eastern Kentucky. Some years ago when I visited home, I'd go running up a road called Lick Fork. I'd pass someone's family cemetery and occasionally stop on my way back to look at the gravestones. I used to imagine the ghost of my great-grandmother, Beck, who was grandmother to my mother and Ruby and Ruth. This ghost wears a cotton dress and she smells like face powder. In real life this great-grandmother spent the last 10 years of her life in one bedroom off a gas station that, in an unpublished collection of stories of mine, became the Black Cat Diner. Her daughter, my great-aunt Della, dressed her up like a doll baby, and she died without much protest, having

almost never left that room.

"It's the Lord's will," Beck said about most everything.

My great-grandmother is only one of the ghosts, now, in the boxes in my mother's bedroom closet. In a photograph she sits in a booth at the gas-station diner, the pop machine and the cigarette shelf at her back. She is wearing a loose, apricot housedress, she is holding her favorite pipe, and her face, wistful and strong, is already a spirit between mountains and heaven. The boxes hold other ghosts—announcements of weddings and funerals, pictures of anniversary cakes. There are photos of births and of graves and of high-school graduations. The boxes themselves are ghosts, never-unpacked ghosts of my mother's move back home, after her divorce from my father, more than 25 years ago. I too am a ghost in these boxes, many ghosts. I am a baby. I am an 11-year-old in an orange dress, my expression both absent and sad.

We are both ghosts this Christmas night as we unlock the door, enter this house. It is the same house as always, this house my mother almost never leaves. It is where my mother once daily put rouge on her mother's cheeks, set her hair, clipped her nails, where now she still decorates my dead grandmother's walker with plastic flowers and does 40 minutes of laps through the immaculate rooms past an enlarged photo of my aunt Ruby, her

dead sister. It's 6:30 or 7 and I think, *Four hours until I can lose myself in silence.* At first the house is quiet as it settles for the night, floor furnace popping, breathing, in and out, of the paneled walls. She goes from window to window, plugging in the single blue candles she's set out for the holidays. Soon the quiet will dissipate, filled with voices of then and now, words said, unsaid.

On television tonight is my mother's favorite movie. Doris Day is in a hotel room, deciding between twin beds. She wears shorty pajamas and brush curlers, but she is cute, perky, alert to the least sound, the coy knock on the door to the adjoining room. She knows Rock is in there, bare-chested, dark hair slicked back with butch wax. They are antilovers, pure as vanilla-cake icing. They are destined for twin gold bands and a honeymoon at Niagara Falls.

They remind me of the twin pictures in the back room of this house—a teenaged boy and girl, both in blue, with giant eyes and bell-bottom pants. Throughout this house are other pairs, other couples. On a shelf in the kitchen are little china puppies, joined by a chain to their china mother. Two glass chipmunks have fake fur tails. On the coffee table are two plaster hands, offering up the prayer inscribed at their base. "Set me as a seal upon thine heart, as a seal upon thine arm: for love is as strong as death."

"I don't believe in this stuff," she says to me. She's sitting in the same kitchen chair she always sits in, on the other side of the end table from where I'm sitting. She's filing her nails to soft, white rounds. "This love stuff," she says. She peers at me, waiting for my answer.

"What do you mean?" I ask.

"You just can't trust people, that's all," she says.

"How?" I ask. "Why can't you trust them?"

I know the answer to this, the same answer as always, but I ask anyway. It's part of the ritual, as traditional as mistletoe or candy canes, and I can tell she's waited for this part, the retelling of the past.

As the movie unfolds, she recites for me, as she always does, a litany of loss. There was the Christmas, she says, when my father went to work at his office, when he took me and left her home alone, and the two of us, without her, ate cornbread stuffing and chess pie at a cafeteria and didn't come back until five o'clock. Don't I remember that?

Don't I remember the time he gave her nothing but a cheap bottle of cologne, nothing but a pin made of metal and gold paint that flaked off on her palm, nothing but a coat too big or pants too small or a nightgown no decent woman would wear, no less her. Don't I remember? I don't know who is remembering, she or I, but

there is winter upon winter, Christmas upon Christmas, our subdivision home, a Christmas crèche with no holy family inside, home with no Christmas tree, no Santa in the night. I remember the cold under covers and the sounds of voices, theirs, quarrel words rising like heat and I tried to catch hold, warm myself on their anger. And it was winter, too, when he left her, made her leave, she says. At gunpoint.

I listen, as I have listened for almost thirty years, to her stories of the past gone wrong, her stories of what might have been and never will be, now. While I listen, I feel inside the collar of my sweater, count the beads of my necklace—of her necklace of jet-black beads. On impulse, I reach back, unfasten the clasp.

"Do you remember this?" I ask. I place the necklace on the end table.

She's finished her nails by now and she's been peering into her hand mirror. She's been touching the lines underneath her eyes, and when she's not looking, I watch this small act, her look of inexpressible sadness. "Where did you get this old thing?" she asks as she scoops up the necklace, studies it under the lamp light.

"It's yours," I say, so softly she can't have heard me.

"Well," she says as she touches them one by one, like a rosary. "So it is."

We're quiet for a while as Doris sings, voice clear as wedding crystal. My mother sighs.

"They don't make these like they used to," she says, and I wonder if she means movies or beads.

"Don't they?" I ask, but she doesn't answer. She's staring into her hand mirror again. She's busy planning her nightly routine of soap and water and creams for her skin.

"There isn't any such thing," she says at last.

"What thing?" I ask, though I know, like always, she means love.

•••••

Some women, I know, die in childbirth. The life expectancy for women of childbearing age in some third-world nations is 37 years. I can recite a litany of possible outcomes, the mortality rate for women over 45 who bear children, for girls under 15 who give birth, for women predisposed to complications, women with particular sexual histories, women not inclined to follow all the rules of pregnancy, its foods and prohibitions and monthly sessions of listening to the fetal heartbeat. And what about women who simply fear birth?

My own mother. She grew up fearing sex in the first place, the dubious nature of men, the inexplicable ways of hands and unmentionables. No self-examinations in a hand mirror for her. The region of birth is down there, far away from the averted eye. The Bible, she knows, begins with darkness on the face of the deep, the sin that lieth at the door. The womb and its darkness are the deepest place of all, unpredictable, full of gushing blood month after month and the possibility of pain so

great women whisper about it, one to another.

This is why, I have come to know, we need rituals. Don't let a pregnant woman look into a mirror after her sixth month. Don't let a pregnant woman go walking, in the rain or the forest or up any steep hill. Pay attention to her dreams, to the shape of her handwriting, to the way the color of her eyes shifts. We need rituals, the lighted candle at the graveside of an ordinary woman, the rosaries before the likeness of the Sacred Mother. We need cemeteries and their plastic roses. We need plaques and cups and hand-embroidered samplers. Mothers, they say, light the way in this dark world. It is rituals that keep these mothers safe.

·····

Since love is no seal upon our hearts, my mother has made other seals, written other songs, rituals that carry her, smooth as a sleigh on snow. Carry her through days and months and years. Tonight she brushes her teeth, 30 minutes, while old films give way to sitcoms, happy ones about families and dogs and streets with trees. Eight o'clock, 8:30, and she talks to me through paste and cleansing. Sometimes, she tells me, she falls asleep while she is cleaning her teeth, wakes when the brush hits the floor. There are other rituals. At our feet, the torn linoleum gleams, cleaner than clean.

Tonight I will sleep beneath sheets washed tissue thin, sheets from the beginning of her marriage days, while others, warmer, thicker, Christmas gifts from me in years past, stay unopened in their new packages. Hers, the litanies of clean, of folded, of the spotless plate, the unblemished cheek. Tonight I will hear her, for an hour or two after I myself have gone to bed. She will cleanse herself, the small face, the delicate face. She will enter her own sleep pure as ice.

Nine o'clock, 9:30, and we unwrap our Christmas gifts, saved for the very last. Mine, an envelope, 20 dollars, a card that says, "Love, Mother and Pa," and "In Loving Memory," with the names of my dead grandmother and cousin. Hers, earrings, dangling gold ones with small, inset pieces of red glass. I take them from their box, point out their best feature— they're hypo-allergenic, with stainless-steel wires.

"I need your help," she says.

I push back her short hair, look at her small ears and the tiny holes. She's talking again, about the roads from Virginia, about last Christmas, the next one, about how faithless my father was. She's happy enough with this gift, this evening, but I can tell she wanted more, the necklace of freshwater pearls she has said my father never gave her, some new cologne from Estée Lauder. But I stand behind her chair, bend down, ready to guide the wires into her soft lobes. I'm gauging how hard this will be, to put earrings in someone else's ears. I'm gauging whether the moment is now, to tell the truth.

"Do you ever wonder?" I ask.

She's looking into a compact, examining her front teeth, which she fears have chipped at their edges. She touches an imperfection on her nose.

I prod with the first earring wire, searching for the other side of the hole.

"Do you wonder," I start again, "why I married when I did?"

"I'll never be able to get those in by myself," she says. She reaches up, dabs at her ear with toilet paper. It comes away clean.

I try again, more gently, and the wire slides through.

"What did you think," I say, "when you didn't hear from me for so long?"

The second earring is harder. I try once, again, a third time, and there it is, a pinpoint of red when she blots with the tissue. I hand her the alcohol bottle, watch as she dabs and examines.

"Do you want me to stop now," I say. It's not a question, but an affirmation of what I really, already know.

She looks anxious, and she peers closely into the mirror, turning her head this way and that, watching the way the earring dangles.

"I don't know," she says. "Do they make me look too young?"

She glances up at me and our eyes meet and I know, for just that long, that it's not the earrings or the mirror image of herself she's questioning at all. I see her, just a glimpse, but I see her. She's frightened of the way it could be, the words I could say. She shifts in her seat, a girl who became this sad woman, ready to hear a truth she may have suspected all along.

"We've gone this far," she says, and she tilts her head, poised, waiting for the next earring.

I have gone far, farther than I ever have, inside myself. I've seen how easy it would be to say them, those few words. *I have a son*, I could say, and it would be finished, as easy as happy-everafter. Truth, that sinuous wonder, could wind its way through this safe house, could pull long-unread letters from envelopes, could open drawers and boxes, rattle the bones and blood of secrets never told. Could open the door to this house forever and let in the cold, cold Christmas air. This house. One as safe as she has been able to make it against the way her life has gone. How hard it is to tell some truths and feel them settle with ease into someone else's life.

I do not tell her. Not now. Instead I tell her how beautiful she is, tell her how these earrings sparkle. I tell her they are like garnets or rubies, that they are a namesake for her sister, a sign the past can be kept alive. I tell her they are like real jewels and that they add color to her cheeks and, even though she won't understand, I tell her that they are a metaphor, that they are like this season, this winter and others, lovely, full of fire and remembrances, beautiful remembrances, at the heart of ice.

Someday, I will reveal my secret. It will be summer, and roses will be blooming on the graves of sons and mothers. I will be sitting with her doing the customary things, the cleansing of teeth and hands, the rites of evening, of before-bed. In the background will be the sounds of television comedies, ones she's seen a million times. She knows them by heart, Lucy in Hollywood, Buffy and Jody in the park, sentimental versions of the past. In the midst of such ordinariness, I will not intend to tell her the truth. I will have accepted the necessity for discretion by then, but nonetheless I will speak.

"Don't you realize," I will say.

And I will fill in the blank of years with the name of my son, the reason I married so young. I'll speak words she's never heard. Adoption. Relinquish. Surrender.

At that moment I will believe. I will believe in the Good Witch of the North, descending from the sky. I will believe in the long enchantment's end. In miracles and revelations. My mother and I, released from silence, will be transformed. Presto. The cost of years, redeemed. Forgiveness at the feet of the only mother who counts.

But that isn't how it will happen at all. I will watch her, at the moment the truth spills out. I will see it, what I most expect, the shadow that crosses her sad green eyes. She will tell me how her heart aches. She will tell me of her disbelief. She will give me an itemized account of my father's past sins, the way they made her life and mine. And that will be it. Except for the script I could write, if you wanted.

One in which music swells in the background, lyrics from a musical with a carousel. In this script the heroine drives away on a morning after Christmas, oblivious to ice and the wonder of sunlight over the mountains. Tragedy strikes, a desolate chord, a sultry blues song from beyond the next curve in the road. There is an accident, an unmistakable sound of metal on metal. And the ending? A rescue, perhaps. The sound of an ambulance, the cavalry, a lover's song. A lover kneels at the heroine's side, gives her breath, gives her manna in the wilderness. Later on, the heroine is miraculously healed of all injuries, of all past sins. There are afternoon walks in a civilized setting, reunions with a long-lost son, interviews on talk shows. Time, that video camera, rolls back, and mother and daughter walk in the park with a baby carriage. There is forgiveness and a family reunion. A sequel. An unlimited number of possibilities.

None of this is more true than anything else, no less true than any other revelation from a past that never ends. The truth will be told, someday. It's inevitable. The truth will be told and it will fall back into my own open hands.

• • • • •

Eleven o'clock and one hour left of this holiday. My mother and I lock the doors, front and back, turn back the covers to our respective beds. Outside my mother's house, night is here and Highway 1492 is still, waiting for after-Christmas, for loaded coal trucks, for cars laden with after-the-holiday returns. One last time, I look out the living-room window, down to the road I'll take in the morning, the highway out.

I haven't told her what I never tell,

about my own secret past, mysterious
as the boxes in her bedroom closet. I
don't tell how it felt, that winter of her
disappearance from my life, how I sat for
days with my grandmother, my father's
mother, working jigsaw puzzles of the
lakes and snow and wondering how it
would be, in two weeks, in a month, when
I went home, alone with my father, my
choice, since the law gave me that power
at 14, the power to choose a parent. I don't
tell her about the next five years, those
missing pieces between me and her, how
I grew to despise her, her clean hands and
floors, her purification of me. How I gave
birth to a son neither of us has known.

There is a river on the other side of this
highway, and down the road is a swinging
bridge. My mother used to walk there,
early mornings. I think of her in 1954,
unmarried, in pleated skirts and bobby
socks, waiting for the school bus. I think of
her now in the back room, readying herself
for sleep, her dry hands laden with lotions,
her permanent wave safe in a netted cap.
She will sleep on her back, hands folded
across her chest, covers neat, unkicked,
this sleep an inconvenience, a temporary
stay against wakefulness.

Karen S. McElmurray
KAREN McELMURRAY

What Lies Beneath

There is little reason to doubt
what lies beneath the muscled oak
within the winter wind
ticking its leaves
in the fundamental voice
soaked in every thread
in the bird singing
from the curving branches
its melody floating across the concert hall
of sky and clouds
brushing the vast canvas below
in transient shadows
changing the shades of green
that change the light that changes ...
there is little doubt
what lies beneath
it all.

James B. Goode

JAMES B. GOODE

Heartichoke

Lila Lesperance woke up on Christmas morning and thought she would like to lick something. In a different marriage, with a different man, she would lean over and lick her husband's ear until he woke, tingling and excited. Instead she lay in the stillness of the house. Peace is what she loved instead. She fashioned her family in her mind's eye under the gauze of sleep. Dwight, her husband, on his back, his sharp nose a peak above the covers, filtering air in a soft steady wheeze beside her. In the next room, teenaged Rob was face down in his pillow, with Fuzz, a warm little heart pumping dog love, wrapped tight in a ball at the back of his head. Nine-year-old Trevor angelic, his fine features purified by the light shining through the window, and Rocky, five, burrowed beneath a zoo of stuffed animals, temporarily at ease.

The curtains glowed, beckoning her from the bed.

This is Christmas cheer, she thought, as she peered through the blinds at the white snow in the yard and the round humps that were bushes and cars. White chocolate coating a mint jelly candy—that was snow on Christmas, blanketing the chaos of red and green on the inside of the house.

Later when Dwight awoke to the smell of the coffee Lila placed on his nightstand, she said, "Your parents are already downstairs."

"Jesus," he said.

"Which reminds me. I've never understood why your family, atheists ..."

"Agnostics," he corrected.

"People who have no religion actually practice Christmas. That seems hypocritical."

"Please," he said. "Not now."

"Right," she said. Never now.

Though Lila's mother, who lived across town in a nice, historic apartment and was taking the holiday on the East Coast, had graciously offered her place to the in-laws for the holidays, they spent all their waking time with Lila and Dwight. The night before, Christmas Eve, the in-laws stayed past a decent bedtime, keeping the real Santas at bay, with their long pointless stories of Christmases past, mostly tales that Lila and Dwight had screened many times on Bob Wye's 8mm films. She wondered if the in-laws really remembered the Christmases or if they remembered the films of the Christmases. She felt she had actually been present when baby Dwight had eaten wrapping paper and was there a few years later as he crashed his two-wheeler into the Christmas tree, shattering heirloom ornaments that Bob Wye never failed to say were his lost fortune. Bob Wye never mentioned the actual fortune he had gambled away one summer on pork bellies. As a result, the in-laws had lost their house near Presidio Park, in San Diego, which today would have been

worth several million.

Dwight drank his coffee. Lila led him down the stairs to the living room where the tree was festooned with ribbons and lights, and the boys were comparing their piles of still-wrapped presents. Rocky, the designated Santa, handed one to his grandmother.

Bob Wye's gift to Janet, his wife of 51 years, was two artichokes in a shoe box.

Janet's hands froze, fingers splayed, above the open box as if they were cartoon indications of a bomb exploding. Janet hadn't put on make-up yet, except for bright red lipstick, so the chromatic shift in her face from yellow-white to gray-white was perceptible. Lila wondered if Janet wore foundation to hide routine flare-ups of distress.

"Jesus, Dad," Dwight said, rescuing his mother from saying anything honest to her husband.

"They're up to 99 cents apiece," Bob Wye said. "They're a delicacy."

Dwight reached under the tree and presented his mother a gift that had been in Lila's pile. The box was wrapped in pretty silver paper embossed with pale white bells. Lila hoped Janet would, at least, spare the paper. Janet moved the artichokes to the floor and pushed them away with her slippered foot. She ripped the pretty paper off the box, then shredded it, her one show of emotion, and beamed. The present was lilac-scented bubble bath,

a soft sponge, and scented powder. "My favorite kind," she said. "Thank you. Who gets a present next?"

"That was in Mom's pile," said Rocky who had arranged the presents into stacks for each person, so he could see who got the most. He and Trevor had the same count, nine.

In years past, Lila would have made an appropriate smoothing comment. Something to suggest that perhaps the present had been mislabeled. But she was tired of being the EMT response for the slightest mood crash. She was especially annoyed that Bob Wye's cheapness should be tolerated without an outburst from Janet. What if she pitched a fit about her bubble bath going to her mother-in-law? She, instead of Old Bob Wye, would wreck the day. Should she go without a Christmas present from her husband because his dad was a boor and the family tolerated it?

"Mom, this one's from Grandma Tina, for you." Rocky rattled a square green package marked with black hieroglyphics.

Lila's mother often went on mission trips around the world and surprised them with unusual items. Lila opened the box and was startled to see Actonel calcium tablets.

"How nice," said Janet. "Those are normally prescription. Your mother knows you're getting to the age of bone loss."

"Merry Christmas to you, too, Janet,"

said Lila, a little stung by her mother's parsimonious care. She'd hoped for a dried gourd she could shake right now to accompany her desire to shout JU-BA Ju-BA as "Sweet Honey in the Rock" was on Rocky's new CD. "A gift as healthy as an artichoke," she said instead.

"Dad, here's your present from us." Dwight held out a long narrow box wrapped in shiny bronze.

Bob Wye's palsied hands shook as they clawed at the paper. Janet reached over and slid her red fingernail under the tape and lifted it. Bob Wye handed her the box. She unwrapped it and handed it back to him.

It was a pair of rabbit fur-lined kid gloves, as he had specifically requested, described, and provided the URL for. They were the most expensive present under the tree. "I hope they fit," Bob Wye snorted. As he struggled to put them on, Lila retreated to the kitchen for more coffee. She still didn't know why he needed fur-lined gloves in southern California. Though this was likely one of Bob Wye's last Christmases, she couldn't pull up any pleasant thoughts and she couldn't fake it any more. Her Christmas spirit was ruined.

The backyard looked cold. She blew on the glass and wished to walk outside, for it to snow and cover her footprints so she could abandon all the adults in her house and leave no trace. She'd find a safe place and take her children there, to a winter wonderland, perhaps a cave or an igloo with a warm cracking fire inside. Hot chocolate and sticky peppermint scenting the air when they snuggled together at night in cozy sleeping bags.

Inside the house, this life was turning her into a murderess in thought, and a suicide in soul. So why was she in it? Because she was like the winter, bare, cold, hopeful that spring would return. The one sustaining thing this season was an indoor soccer game, she thought, the one situation where she could yell with the ferocity threatening to flare in any given situation. To scream away the pressure of the day, oh, she loved her children—they were what saved her. She wanted to go hug them to her and kiss them all over but she knew they would pull away, more interested in their new toys. The coffee burned. She poured the thick liquid into the sink. She automatically made more, forgetting to measure the grounds before adding water to the brim.

Children, she thought, save us from our marriages and in turn we stay in marriages to give them stability, the veneer of normality, two incomes, two grown-ups invested in them. Can we ever love them enough?

Lila needed to be loved like that and never had been.

Fuzz, a black-and-white terrier with an under bite, came into the kitchen, wagging her curly tail, holding something green,

like a hand grenade, in her mouth. Lila reached for it. "What you got?"

Fuzz growled.

It was one of the artichokes.

"Give that to me." She lunged, laughing. Fuzz ran to the living room into the pile of torn wrapping paper and thrashed around in it.

"Look," said Rocky. "Fuzzy's burying Grandma's heartichoke."

Aroused, Bob Wye hop hop hopped to his feet from the couch and leaned on his cane, his long lock of white hair falling in his face. "Damned dog!" He beat at the agitated pile of wrappings with the stick.

"Stop it," said Lila and grabbed the cane. "Leave Fuzz alone."

They stood at either ends of the cane, combatants, her ferocity throbbing in her jaw. His silky gloves slipped their grip and she was tempted to jerk the cane out of his hands and rap him across his back, errant child that he was. He pulled hard and his robe opened. He was wearing plain white jockeys. She let the cane loose and he pulled it away and thumped the floor and chuckled, as if she had gotten what she had wanted to see. "Stupid dog," he said. "I'm going to kill it if it comes close to me."

"If you do," Lila breathed hard for she believed him capable of it. "You won't see the new year."

Dwight arrived in the room, a mug of weak coffee in his hand. He grabbed her arm and hissed. "Come here." In the dining room he said, "Don't say that in front of the boys. He is an old man. Leave him alone."

"He is not going to abuse our dog or our children or me. If he wants to abuse your mother, fine."

"This could be his last Christmas."

"Then he ought to be making a better effort."

"I am ashamed of you."

"Where's my Christmas present from you?"

"I'm getting you something else."

"Don't bother," she said. "I'll ask your mother for her martyr crown."

She left him standing in the dining room, lunch looming, everyone hungry, and went upstairs to their bedroom. She dressed for a walk, wool socks, boots, silk undershirt, cotton sweater, snow pants, red gloves, purple coat and a blue head scarf, and out she went past them all, through the yellow warmth of the house into the blank white world. She glanced back and only Fuzz was at the window, the lace curtain pulled to the side of the glass by a paw, anxiety palpitating from her wet dark eyes.

The cemetery was a mile away, but on a snowy day it was a long mile. Lila was sweating when she squeezed through the closed iron gates. Her breath was visible. She paused, watching it float and disappear, conscious of the stone eyes

and still lips around her. Her breath was what made her different from the forms of arrest, the figures above the dead, she thought. The statues, usually white and clean, were grayed by the snow's purer color. Dappled with washes of lichens and shadows, they were transformed into peculiar abstract sculptures. Lila breathed in the invisible cold and smiled.

If somebody else came here she would scream. She wanted the whole cemetery to herself, with its crop of stones, the rises and loops, the bare trees, rough black bark she would like to bite or rub her cheek and neck against, the heavy powder. All of it. For herself.

She trudged down the bank below Raphael King Solomon's grave to a glade where in the spring the tall herons often posed. She stood with a clear view of the sky and one stone angel, a woman with broad wings, near the frozen pond.

She licked the snow from her gloves and she licked the angel—she tasted the earth and ice and the cold stone.

She lay down in the snow.

Cold diffused along her back and legs and butt and neck, her neck felt coldest of all. She moved her arms through the powder. Tufts of snow blew up and dusted her arms and chest, pricked her skin. The flakes melted and froze, covering her with ice sparkles. I wonder what color I am, she asked the cold white eye of the sky.

Crystals glistened on her jeans, on her boot laces like strings of pearls. I love where I am, she told the sky. I am a warrior on a white horse, she thought, my arms are strong as wings and I can fly. She seemed to levitate from the ground to be above the icy shape of the angel I am an angel—how funny that the bite of chill was hot ...

She turned her head and took in a mouthful of snow. It formed a solid wafer across her tongue. She crunched it, cold rain to her stomach, and she shivered and felt deeply, dangerously cold. She stood up, her legs locked like lampposts. Lurching along, she passed the statues, their eyes bland, their gestures yearning for the other side, a judgment on her for feeling that tug, too, and for walking away. But away she went, walking in the footprints she had made earlier, giddy with escape, flushed with her boldness, with knowing her life was her own.

She waited for the light at Midland to turn green even though there were no cars. Was her flagging energy the result of fatigue or was it the return to her heavy duties at home? Up ahead a small gray blob, a car, her car, their car, was coming toward her. She squinted to see how many heads were inside it and could only see Dwight's, a relief of sorts. She felt a delicious shiver of guilt. It gave her an icy supreme confidence, she was still the warrior on the horse—he seemed so small, so squirrelly she almost laughed.

So magnanimous she felt that when he skidded near her and she had to jump out of the way, catching her foot against the hidden curb and falling back in the snow, she just lay there happily, protected by the white blanket.

He hopped out of the car. "Jesus! Are you okay?"

"Holy, Holy, Holy, Lord God Almighty." She laughed.

"You scared me. I thought I'd hit you." His gray scarf was wrapped tightly around his neck, lifting the extra neck folds up under his chin like mumps. "Get in the car."

She realized he hadn't known she'd been gone a long time. "What's the rush? I can walk home from here."

"No, no," he said. "Get in the car."

"Did your dad have a heart attack?"

"No, just get in the car!" Dwight's red jowls shook.

She opened the passenger side and was greeted with her boys' shouts from the back seat. They bounced up. Trevor chanted, "Don't tell, don't tell, don't tell." Rob smacked him, "Shut up, Trevor." Rocky beamed at her, the right side of his face still raw from the scrape he'd gotten the day before when Dwight had tossed him in the air and dropped him on the ice.

The car was as warm as a friendly fire and if she could join the jumble of boys in the backseat, she'd have all she wanted for Christmas.

"Quit looking at us," said Rocky, so she turned around and then two wet cold mittens were pressed against her eyes.

"I can't see." She tried to free her head but she felt more strength added, Rob's hands she guessed. "Wait, the mitten's scratching me. I need to blink."

"Mama, you're going to mess up the surprise."

"Rocky! Don't tell."

She squinched her eyes shut and held her breath. "Are we going home?" She hoped so. The car flung the sludge from the wheel tracks and skimmed a corner without any extra skid. She almost relaxed.

"We're here," Dwight said.

The mittens stayed glued to her eyes.

"Promise to keep your eyes closed until you get out," Rob said.

"Promise." She swiveled her head and showed them her closed eyes.

Trevor and Rocky pushed out of the car. She heard their happy voices in the yard.

"Nobody better hit me with a snowball when I'm not looking," said Lila as she felt for the ground with her right foot. She hoped the surprise didn't involve her in-laws. She suspected Bob Wye had rigged up some sort of camera and was filming this great moment in Lesperance history.

She stood in the snow. It was a comfort, ankle weights to keep her from slipping.

"Look, Mom!" shouted Rocky. "It's your Christmas present!"

She swung her head, getting a panoramic view of the family, Bob Wye on the porch leaning on his cane, Janet hovering next to him, the boys sliding in the yard, and Dwight extending an open palm toward a brand-new minivan with a giant red bow on the top.

As her heart plunged, the corners of her mouth went up and she said, "Wow!"

She knew she was supposed to jump into Dwight's arms and shower him with kisses for his perfect, expensive, necessary, and unexpected gift. Her feet moved forward despite the granite weight of her soul. *Shit.* The last thing she wanted was a minivan. She needed a steed.

She walked over to the large green rolling box capped with its red bow. "Wow!" she said again. Dwight was moving near, expecting the kisses, and so when he was close, she hugged him. He slipped. She scatter-stepped with speed as she grappled with his torso and used all her strength to balance him.

"Mom's dancing with Dad," said Trevor. "She likes it."

"It's a great present for all of us." She stepped away from Dwight but kept a hand on his chest to prevent him from falling. She opened the side door and the boys bounded in, Rob's coat bulging strangely and Fuzz's black nose quivering at its collar.

"No, no, you boys'll get snow inside it!" Dwight said.

"Of course they will." She shut the door and climbed into the front passenger seat. "Would you drive? I'd rather take it out after the roads are cleared."

"Mom, Dad, come on," shouted Dwight. "There's room for seven."

Oh shit shit shit, thought Lila, *shit shit shit*.

"Your dad needs help." Lila sighed through the fume of new car smell. "We don't want him to fall on the steps"—but as she spoke Bob Wye managed to stomp down two steps without his cane—and for this she blamed him—he had to do it on purpose she was sure—so what if he cracked his head on the steps, anything to take the attention away from anyone else, to crash into Dwight's moment of triumph.

"I love this van," she said to Dwight, as they watched Janet steady the flailing Bob Wye.

"We won't be going," Janet called, and steered him toward the steps, though Bob Wye resisted, jerking his arm away from hers as if he would bolt after them when free.

"Let's get out of here," said Trevor.

They watched Janet wave with one hand and tug at Bob Wye with the other. He lifted a fist, the spiky fur of his glove shaking like a rabid hand puppet.

"It's cold in the van," Trevor said.

"I'm freezing." Rob added.

"You can't be," Dwight said. "The

heat's on."

Lila felt the vent behind her head. Cold air streamed out. She shut it and opened the owner's manual.

Fuzz barked.

"What's that dog doing in here?" Dwight said.

"Taking a ride," said Rob.

"No dogs, no mess, no eating in this van," he shouted and turned the corner, a nice smooth gliding arc on the ice.

"You must have the A/C on." Lila turned the air conditioner off at the dash and told Rob to move the rear temperature control to red. "The heat comes up from the floor," she read.

"Just like Hell," Rob said.

Lila loosened her coat in preparation for the coming heat.

Lynn Pruett

LYNN PRUETT

About The Authors

Karen Salyer McElmurray's *newest novel is* The Motel of the Stars, *part of the Linda Bruckheirmer Series (Sarabande Books, 2008). The novel was nominated for The Weatherford Prize in Fiction, was a Lit Life Novel of the Year and was named Editor's Pick by Oxford American. She is also the author of* Surrendered Child: A Birth Mother's Journey *(University of Georgia Press, 2004), recipient of the AWP Award for Creative Nonfiction, as well as* Strange Birds in the Tree of Heaven *(Hill Street Press, 1999), winner of the Chaffin Award for Appalachian Writing. Her work has received numerous awards, including grants from the National Endowment for the Arts, the North Carolina Arts Council, and the Kentucky Foundation for Women. She has a MFA degree in fiction writing from the University of Virginia, a Master's in Creative Writing from Hollins University, and a doctorate from the University of Georgia, where she studied American Literature and Fiction Writing. She currently is an Associate Professor of creative writing at Georgia College and State University and is creative nonfiction editor for* Arts and Letters: A Journal of Contemporary Culture. *She is also on the faculty at Murray State University Creative Writing Limited Residency Program, where she mentors and teaches creative non-fiction students. She is frequently visiting writer and lecturer at a variety of programs and reading series including, the Appalachian Writer's Workshop at Hindman Settlement School and at Indiana University, Bloomington.*

James B. Goode's *biography can be seen on page 69*

Lynn Pruett *is a graduate of Mount Holyoke College and the University of Alabama where she received her MFA in Creative Writing. She is the author of the novel* Ruby River *(Grove/Atlantic Press, 2002) and recently contributed to the anthologies* When the Bough Breaks *and* An Angle of Vision. *Her work has also appeared in* Louisville Review, Arts & Letters, American Voice, Southern Exposure, *and* Black Warrior Review. *She has earned fellowships from Yaddo, Sewanee, Squaw Valley, and the Kentucky Arts Council, and has led fiction workshops at the University of Kentucky, the University of Alabama and North Carolina State University. She currently teaches fiction writing at the University of Kentucky in Lexington. She is also on the faculty at Murray State University's Creative Writing Limited Residency Program. Kentucky writer Silas House has said of Lynn Pruett's fiction: "Lynn Pruett's writing can break your heart and make you laugh within the same carefully structured sentence. This novel pulls off that nearly impossible feat of being both wonderfully poetic and wildly entertaining. Most of all,* Ruby River *is brimming with real life—all of its joys and sorrows and the moments of revelation in between, told with a graceful clarity that will leave readers desperate for more."*

The
Seventh
Day

Glomawr House

In Hazard, or rather up on the hill
across from Glomawr,
about three miles from Hazard,
we had our first house.
Not even all built, a spec
with a nervous, accommodating builder
who put an X on the wall when I said a window might be nice
in the lower room looking out to the back woods,
and a window appeared before I signed anything.
A big picture window with a view that early September
as green and verdant as any Monet water lily.
The woods didn't go deep but I thought they did,
they looked like they did,
and I envisioned sitting and staring at those woods.

In December after the leaves shed, we'd gaze at a
vision of the river, a dark swirl, blocked here and
there by a few stunted pines.
The pines did not make good Christmas trees
though the thought of chopping my own made me drag them in each
Noel, hiding their naked sides, the ones almost bereft of branches,
in the corner.

Our North side, stingy with sunlight,
slanted rationed doses.
Our tomatoes stretched spindly and pale green in July;
our thin sycamores turned yellow in October;
our oaks burned to rust.

Only the snow in mid-December thickened the stick arms
of the second growth trees; piled on white muscles.
A blizzard, though, burdened limbs too much.
We heard snaps and cracks in the night.
They were the only sounds.
Cars couldn't find the road when the snow piled up.
We'd be cocooned in a silence as private as any rich resort.
Just us in our first house with our poor tree hugging the wall,
in Hazard, or rather up on the hill
across from Glomawr,
about three miles from Hazard.

JOSEPH ANTHONY

"A Certain Small Shepherd"

This is a story of a strange and a marvelous thing. It happened on a Christmas morning at Hurricane Gap, and not so long ago at that.

But before you hear about Christmas morning, you must hear about Christmas Eve, for that is part of the story.

And before you hear about Christmas Eve, you must hear about Jamie, for without Jamie there would be no story.

Jamie was born on a freakish night in November. The cold that night moved down from the North and rested its heavy hand suddenly on Hurricane Gap. Within an hour's time, the naked earth turned brittle. Line Fork Creek froze solid in its winding bed and lay motionless, like a string dropped at the foot of Pine Mountain.

Nothing but the dark wind was abroad in the hollow. Wild creatures huddled in their dens. Cows stood hunched in their stalls. Housewives stuffed rags in the cracks underneath their doors against the needling cold, and men heaped oak and apple wood on their fires.

At the foot of the Gap, where Jamie's house stood, the wind doubled its fury. It battered the doors of the house. It rattled the windows. It wailed like a banshee in the chimney.

"For sure, it's bad luck trying to break in," moaned Jamie's mother, and turned her face to her pillow.

"Bad luck has no business here," Jamie's father said bravely.

He laid more logs on the fire. Flames licked at them and roared up the chimney. But through the roaring, the wind wailed on, thin and high.

Father took the newborn baby from the bed beside its mother and sat holding it on his knee.

"Saro," he called, "you and Honey come see Jamie!"

Two girls came from the shadows of the room. In the firelight they stood looking at the tiny wrinkled red face inside the blanket.

"He's such a little brother!" said Saro.

"Give him time. He'll grow," said Father proudly.

"When he's three, he'll be as big as Honey. When he's six, he'll be as big as you. You want to hold him?"

Saro sat down on a stool and Father laid the bundle in her arms.

Honey stood beside Saro. She pulled back a corner of the blanket. She opened one of the tiny hands and laid one of her fingers in it. She smiled at the face in the blanket. She looked up, smiling, at Father.

But Father did not see her. He was standing beside Mother, trying to comfort her.

That night Jamie's mother died.

Jamie ate and slept and grew.

Like other babies, he cut teeth. He learned to sit alone and to crawl. When he was a year old, he toddled about like other

one-year-olds. At two, he carried around sticks and stones like other one-year-olds. He threw balls and built towers of blocks and knocked them down.

Everything that other one-year-olds could do, Jamie could do, except one thing. He could not talk.

The old women of Hurricane Gap sat in their chimney corners and shook their heads.

"His mother, poor soul, should have rubbed him with lard," said one.

"She ought to have brushed him with a rabbit's foot," said another.

"Wasn't that boy born on Wednesday?" asked another. "'Wednesday's child is full of woe,'" she quoted from an old saying.

"Jamie gets everything he wants by pointing," explained Father. "Give him time. He'll learn to talk."

At three, Jamie could zip his shirt and tie his shoes.

At four, he followed Father to the stable at milking time. He milked the kittens' pan full of milk.

But even at four, Jamie could not talk like other children. He could only make strange grunting noises.

One day Jamie found a litter of new kittens in a box under the stairs. He ran to the cornfield to tell Father. He wanted to say he had been feeling around in the box for a ball he'd lost, and suddenly his fingers had felt something warm and squirmy, and here were all these kittens.

But how could you tell somebody something if, when you opened your mouth, you could only grunt?

Jamie started running. He ran till he reached the orchard. There, he threw himself face down in the tall grass and kicked his feet against the ground.

One day Honey's friends came to play hide-and-seek. Jamie played with them.

Because Clive was the oldest, he shut his eyes first and counted to 50, while the other children scattered and hid behind trees in the yard and corners of the house. After he had counted to 50, the hollow rang with cries.

"One, two, three for Milly!"

"One, two, three for Jamie!"

"One, two, three, I'm home free."

It came Jamie's turn to shut his eyes. He sat on the porch step, covered his eyes with his hands, and began to count.

"Listen to Jamie!" Clive called to the other children.

The others listened. Then they all began to laugh.

Jamie got up. He ran after the children. He fought them with both fists and both feet. Honey helped him.

Then Jamie ran away to the orchard, and threw himself down on his face in the tall grass, and kicked the ground.

Later, when Father was walking through the orchard, he came across Jamie lying in the grass.

"Jamie," said Father, "there's a new calf

in the pasture. I need you to help me bring it to the stable."

Jamie got up from the grass. He wiped his eyes. Out of the orchard and across the pasture he trudged at Father's heels. In a far corner of the pasture they found the cow. Beside her, on wobbly legs, stood the new calf.

Together, Father and Jamie drove the cow and the calf to the stable, into an empty stall.

Together, they brought nubbins from the corncrib to feed the cow.

Together, they made a bed of clean hay for the calf.

"Jamie," said Father the next morning, "I need you to help plow the corn."

Father harnessed the horse and lifted Jamie to the horse's back. Away to the cornfield they went, Father walking in front of the horse, Jamie riding, holding tight to the hames.

While Father plowed, Jamie walked in the furrow behind him. When Father lay on his back in the shade of the persimmon tree to rest, Jamie lay beside him. Father told Jamie the names of the birds flying overhead—the turkey vulture tilting its uplifted wings against the white clouds, the carrion crow flapping lazily and sailing, flapping and sailing, and the sharp-shinned hawk gliding to rest in the woodland.

The next day Jamie helped Father set out sweet potatoes. Other days he helped Father trim fence rows and mend fences.

Whatever Father did, Jamie helped him.

One day Father drove the car out of the shed and stopped in front of the house.

"Jamie!" he called. "Jump in. We're going across Pine Mountain."

"Can I go, too?" asked Honey.

"Not today," said Father. "I'm taking Jamie to see a doctor."

The doctor looked at Jamie's throat. He listened to Jamie grunt. He shook his head.

"You might see Dr. Jones," he said.

Father and Jamie got into the car and drove across Big Black Mountain to see Dr. Jones.

"Maybe Jamie could learn to talk," Dr. Jones said. "But he would have to be sent away to a special school. He would have to stay there several months. He might have to stay two or three years. Or four."

"It is a long time," said Dr. Jones.

"And the pocket is empty," said Father.

So Father and Jamie got into the car and started home.

Usually Father talked to Jamie as they drove along. Now they drove all the way, across Big Black and across Pine, without a word.

In August every year, school opened at Hurricane Gap.

On the first morning of school the year that Jamie was six, Father handed him a book, a tablet, a pencil, and a box of crayons—all shiny and new.

"You're going to school, Jamie," he said. "I'll go with you this morning."

The neighbors watched them walking down the road together, toward the little one-room schoolhouse.

"Poor foolish father!" they said, and shook their heads.

"Trying to make somebody out of that no-account boy!"

Miss Creech, the teacher, shook her head too. With so many children, so many classes, so many grades, she hadn't time for a boy who couldn't talk, she told Father.

"What will Jamie do all day long?" she asked.

"He will listen," said Father.

So Jamie took his book and his tablet, his pencil and his box of crayons, and sat down in an empty seat in the front row.

Every day Jamie listened. He learned the words on the pages of his book. He learned how to count. He liked the reading and the counting.

But the part of school Jamie liked best was the big piece of paper Miss Creech gave him every day. On it he printed words in squares, like the other children. He wrote numbers. He drew pictures and colored them with his crayons. He could say things on paper.

One day Miss Creech said Jamie had the best paper in the first grade. She held it up for all the children to see.

On sunny days on the playground the children played ball games and three-deep and duck-on-a-rock—games a boy can play without talking. On rainy days they played indoors.

One rainy day the children played a guessing game. Jamie knew the answer that no other child could guess. But he couldn't say the answer. He didn't know how to spell the answer. He could find nothing to point to that showed he knew the answer.

That evening at home he threw his book into a corner. He slammed the door. He pulled Honey's hair. He twisted the cat's tail. The cat yowled and leaped under the bed.

"Jamie," said Father. "Cats have feelings, just like boys."

Every year the people of Hurricane Gap celebrated Christmas in the little white church that stood across the road from Jamie's house. On Christmas Eve the boys and girls gave a Christmas play. People came miles to see it—from the other side of Pine Mountain and from the head of every creek and hollow. Miss Creech directed the play.

Through the late fall, as the leaves fell from the trees and the days grew shorter and the air snapped with cold, Jamie wondered when Miss Creech would talk about the play. Finally, one afternoon in November, Miss Creech announced it was time to begin play practice.

Jamie laid his book inside his desk and

listened carefully as Miss Creech assigned the parts of the play.

Miss Creech gave the part of Mary to Joan, who lived up Pine Mountain beyond the rock quarry. She asked Honey to bring her big doll to be the Baby. She gave the part of Joseph to Henry, who lived at the head of Little Laurelpatch. She asked Saro to be an angel; Clive the innkeeper. She chose three big boys to be Wise Men, four others to be shepherds. She named the boys and girls who were to be people living in Bethlehem. The rest of the boys and girls would sing carols, she said.

Jamie for a moment listened to the sound of the word he had last heard. Yes, Miss Creech expected him to sing carols.

Every day after school the boys and girls went with Miss Creech up the road to the church and practiced the Christmas play.

Every day Jamie stood in the front row of the carolers. The first day he stood quietly. The second day he shoved Milly, who was standing next to him. The third day he pulled Honey's hair. The fourth day, when the carolers began singing, Jamie ran to the window, grabbed a ball from the sill, and bounced it across the floor.

"Wait a minute, children," Miss Creech said to the carolers.

She turned to Jamie.

"Jamie," she asked, "how would you like to be a shepherd?"

"He's too little," said one of the big shepherds.

"No, he isn't," said Saro. "If my father was a shepherd, Jamie would help him."

That afternoon Jamie became a small shepherd. He ran home after practice to tell Father.

Father couldn't understand what Jamie was telling him. But he knew that Jamie had been changed into somebody important.

One afternoon, at play practice, Miss Creech said to the boys and girls, "Forget you are Joan, and Henry, and Saro, and Clive, and Jamie. Remember that you are Mary, and Joseph, and an angel, and an innkeeper, and a shepherd, and that strange things are happening in the hollow where you live."

That night, at bedtime, Father took the big Bible off the table. Saro and Honey and Jamie gathered around the fire.

Over the room a hush fell as Father read:

And there were in the same country shepherds abiding in the field, keeping watch over their flock by night. And, lo, the angel of the Lord came upon them, and the glory of the Lord shone round about them: and they were sore afraid. And the angel said unto them, Fear not: for, behold, I bring you good tidings of great joy which shall be to all the people … and it came to pass, as the angels were gone away from them into heaven, the shepherds said one to another, Let us now go even unto Bethlehem, and see this thing which is come to pass, which the

Lord hath made know unto us. And they came with haste, and found Mary, and Joseph, and the babe lying in a manger.

•••••

Christmas drew near. At home in the evenings, when they had finished studying their lessons, the boys and girls of Hurricane Gap made decorations for the Christmas tree that would stand in the church. They glued together strips of bright-colored paper in long chains. They whittled stars and baby lambs and camels out of wild cherry wood. They strung long strings of popcorn.

Jamie strung a string of popcorn. Every night, as Father read from the Bible, Jamie added more kernels to his string.

"Jamie, are you trying to make a string long enough to reach to the top of Pine Mountain?" asked Honey one night.

Jamie did not hear her. He was far away, on a hillside, tending sheep. And even though he was a small shepherd and could only grunt when he tried to talk, an angel wrapped around with dazzling light was singling him out to tell him a wonderful thing that had happened down in the hollow in a cow stall.

He fell asleep, stringing his popcorn, and listening.

In a corner of the room where the fire burned, Father pulled from under his bed the trundle bed in which Jamie slept. He turned back the covers, picked Jamie up from the floor, and laid him gently in the bed.

The next day Father went across Pine Mountain to the store. When he came home, he handed Saro a package. In it was cloth of four colors—green, gold, white, and red.

"Make Jamie a shepherd's coat, like the picture in the Bible," Father said to Saro.

Father went into the woods and found a crooked limb of a tree. He made it into a shepherd's crook for Jamie.

Jamie went to school the next morning carrying his shepherd's crook and his shepherd's coat on his arm. He would wear his coat and carry his crook when the boys and girls practiced the play.

All day Jamie waited patiently to practice the play. All day he sat listening.

But who could tell whose voice he heard? It might have been Miss Creech's. It might have been an angel's.

Two days before Christmas, Jamie's father and Clive's father drove in a pick-up truck along the Trace Branch road looking for a Christmas tree. On the mountainside they spotted a juniper growing broad and tall and free. With axes they cut it down. They snaked it down the mountainside and loaded it into the truck.

Father had to open the doors of the church wide to get the tree inside. It reached to the ceiling. Frost-blue berries shone on its feathery green branches. The air around it smelled of spice.

That afternoon the mothers of

Hurricane Gap, and Miss Creech, and all the boys and girls gathered at the church to decorate the tree.

In the tiptop of the tree they fastened the biggest star. Among the branches they hung the other stars and the baby lambs and camels whittled out of wild cherry wood. They hung polished red apples on twigs of the tree. They looped paper chains from branch to branch. Last of all, they festooned the tree with strings of snowy popcorn.

"Ah!" they said, as they looked at the tree. "Ah!"

Beside the tree the boys and girls practiced the Christmas play for the last time. When they had finished, they started home. Midway down the aisle they turned and looked again at the tree.

"Ah!" they said.

Saro opened the door. "Look!" she called. "Look, everybody! It's snowing!"

Jamie, the next morning, looked out on a world such as he had never seen. Hidden were the roads and the fences, the woodpile, and the swing under the oak tree—all buried deep under a lumpy quilt of snow. And before a stinging wind, snowflakes still madly whirled and danced.

Saro and Honey joined Jamie at the window.

"You can't see across Line Fork Creek in this storm," said Saro. "And where is Pine Mountain?"

"Where is the church?" asked Honey. "That's what I'd like to know."

Jamie turned to them with questions in his eyes.

"If it had been snowing hard that night in Bethlehem, Jamie," Honey told him, "the shepherds wouldn't have had their sheep out in the pasture. They would have had them in the stable keeping them warm. Wouldn't they, Father? Then they wouldn't have heard what the angel said, all shut indoors like that."

"When angels have something to tell a shepherd," said Father, "they can find him in any place, in any sort of weather. If the shepherd is listening, he will hear."

At 11 o'clock the telephone rang.

"Hello!" said Father.

Saro and Honey and Jamie heard Miss Creech's voice. "I've just got the latest weather report. This storm is going on all day, and into the night. Do you think ..."

The telephone, once it started ringing, wouldn't stop. No matter if it rang a long and a short, two longs and a short, a short and two longs, or whatever, everyone on the Hurricane Gap line listened. The news they heard was always bad. Drifts 10 feet high were piled up along the Trace Branch road ... The boys and girls on Little Laurelpatch couldn't get out. Joseph lived on Little Laurelpatch ... The road up Pine Mountain through Hurricane Gap was closed, all the way to the rock quarry. Mary couldn't get down the mountain ...

And then the telephone went silent, dead in the storm.

Meanwhile, the snow kept up its crazy dance before the wind. It drifted in great white mounds across the roads and in the fence rows.

"Nobody but a foolish man would take to the road on a day like this," said Father.

At dinner Jamie sat at the table staring at his plate.

"Shepherds must eat, Jamie," said Father.

"Honey and I don't feel like eating either, Jamie," said Saro. "But see how Honey is eating!"

Still Jamie stared at his plate.

"Know what?" asked Saro. "Because we're all disappointed, we won't save the Christmas stack cake for tomorrow. We'll have a slice today. As soon as you eat your dinner, Jamie."

Still Jamie stared at his plate. He did not touch his food.

"You think that play was real, don't you, Jamie?" said Honey. "It wasn't real. It was just a play we were giving, like some story we'd made up."

Jamie could hold his sobs no longer. His body heaved as he ran to Father.

Father laid an arm about Jamie's shoulders.

"Sometimes, Jamie," he said, "angels say to shepherds, 'Be of good courage.'"

On through the short afternoon the storm raged.

Father heaped more wood on the fire. Saro sat in front of the fire reading a book. Honey cracked hickory nuts on the stone hearth. Jamie sat.

"Bring the popper, Jamie, and I'll pop some corn for you," said Father.

Jamie shook his head.

"Want me to read to you?" asked Saro.

Jamie shook his head.

"Why don't you help Honey crack hickory nuts?" asked Father.

Jamie shook his head.

"Jamie still thinks he's a shepherd," said Honey.

After a while Jamie left the fire and stood at the window, watching the wild storm. He squinted his eyes and stared. He motioned to Father to come and look. Saro and Honey, too, hurried to the window and looked.

Through the snowdrifts trudged a man, followed by a woman. They were bundled and buttoned from head to foot, and their faces were lowered against the wind and the flying snowflakes.

"Lord have mercy!" said Father, as he watched them turn in at the gate.

Around the house the man and the woman made their way to the back door. As Father opened the door to them, a gust of snow-laden wind whisked into the kitchen.

"Come in out of the cold," said Father.

The man and the woman stepped inside. They stamped their feet on the

kitchen floor and brushed the snow from their clothes. They followed Father into the front room and sat down before the fire in the chairs Father told Saro to bring for them. Father, too, sat down.

Jamie stood beside Father. Saro and Honey stood behind his chair. The three of them stared at the man and the woman silently.

"Where did you come from?" asked Father.

"The other side of Pine Mountain," said the man.

"Why didn't you stop sooner?" asked Father.

"We did stop." the man said. "At three houses. Nobody had room," he said.

Father was silent for a minute. He looked at his own bed and at Jamie's trundle bed underneath it. The man and the woman looked numbly into the fire.

"How far were you going?" asked Father.

"Down Straight Creek," said the man. He jerked his head toward the woman. "To her sister's."

"You'll never get there tonight," Father said.

"Maybe," said the man, "maybe there'd be a place in your stable."

"We could lay pallets on the kitchen floor," said Father.

The woman looked at the children. She shook her head. "The stable is better," she said.

"The stable is cold," said Father.

"It will do," said the woman.

When the man and the woman had dried their clothes and warmed themselves, Father led the way to the stable. He carried an armload of quilts and on top of them an old buffalo skin. From his right arm swung a lantern and a milk bucket. "I'll milk while I'm there," he said to Saro. "Get supper ready."

Jamie and Saro and Honey watched from the kitchen window, as the three trudged through the snowdrifts to the stable.

It was dark when Father came back to the house.

"How long are the man and the woman going to stay?" asked Honey.

Father hung a tea kettle of water on the crane over the fire and went upstairs to find another lantern.

"All night tonight," he said, as he came down the stairs. "Maybe longer."

Father hurriedly ate the supper Saro put on the table. Then he took in one hand the lighted lantern and a tin bucket filled with supper for the man and the woman.

"I put some Christmas stack cake in the bucket," said Saro.

In his other hand Father took the tea kettle.

"It's cold in that stable," he said, as he started out the kitchen door. "Bitter cold."

On the doorstep he turned. "Don't wait up for me," he called back. "I may be gone

a good while."

Over the earth darkness thickened. Still the wind blew and the snow whirled.

The clock on the mantel struck seven.

"I wish Father would come!" said Honey.

The clock struck eight. It ticked solemnly in the quiet house, where Saro and Honey and Jamie waited.

"Why doesn't Father come?" complained Honey.

"Why don't you hang up your stocking and go to bed?" asked Saro. "Jamie, it's time to hang up your stocking, too, and go to bed."

Jamie did not answer. He sat staring into the fire.

"That Jamie! He still thinks he's a shepherd!" said Honey, as she hung her stocking under the mantel.

"Jamie," said Saro, "aren't you going to hang up your stocking and go to bed?" She pulled the trundle bed from beneath Father's bed, and turned back the covers. She turned back the covers on Father's bed. She hung up her stocking and followed Honey upstairs.

"Jamie!" she called back.

Still Jamie stared into the fire. A strange feeling was growing inside him. This night was not like any other nights, he knew. Something mysterious was going on. He felt afraid.

What was that he heard? The wind? Only the wind?

He lay down on his bed with his clothes on. He dropped off to sleep. A rattling at the door waked him.

He sat upright quickly. He looked around. His heart beat fast. But nothing in the room had changed. Everything was as it had been when he lay down—the fire was burning; two stockings, Saro's and Honey's, hung under the mantel; the clock was ticking solemnly.

He looked at Father's bed. The sheets were just as Saro had turned them back.

There! There it was! He heard it again! It sounded like singing. "Glory to God! On earth peace!"

Jamie breathed hard. Had he heard that? Or had he only said it to himself?

He lay down again and pulled the quilts over his head.

"Get up, Jamie," he heard Father saying. "Put your clothes on, quick."

Jamie opened his eyes. He saw daylight seeping into the room. He saw Father standing over him, bundled in warm clothes.

Wondering, Jamie flung the quilts back and rolled out of bed.

"Why, Jamie," said Father, "you're already dressed!"

Father went to the stairs. "Saro! Honey!" he called. "Come quick!"

"What's happened, Father?" asked Saro.

"What are we going to do?" asked Honey, as she fumbled sleepily with her

shoe laces.

"Come with me," said Father.

"Where are we going?" asked Honey.

"To the stable?" asked Saro.

"The stable was no fit place," said Father. "Not on this bitter night. Not when the church was close by, and it with a stove in it and coal for burning."

Out into the cold, silent, white morning they went. The wind had laid. Snow no longer fell. The clouds were lifting. One star in the vast sky, its brilliance fading in the growing light, shone down on Hurricane Gap.

Father led the way through the drifted snow. The others followed, stepping in his tracks.

As Father pushed open the church door, the fragrance of the Christmas tree rushed out at them. The potbellied stove glowed red with the fire within.

Muffling his footsteps, Father walked quietly up the aisle. Wonderingly, the others followed. There, beside the star-crowned Christmas tree, where the Christmas play was to have been given, they saw the woman. She lay on the old buffalo skin, covered in quilts. Beside her pallet sat the man.

The woman smiled at them. "You came to see?" she asked, and lifted the cover.

Saro went first and peeped under the cover.

"You look too, Jamie," said Saro.

For a second Jamie hesitated. He leaned forward and took one quick look. Then he turned, shot down the aisle and out of the church, slamming the door behind him.

Saro ran down the church aisle, calling after him.

"Wait, Saro," said Father, watching Jamie through the window.

To the house Jamie made his way, half running along the path Father's big boots had cut through the snowdrifts.

Inside the house he hurriedly pulled his shepherd's robe over his coat. He snatched up his crook from the chimney corner.

With his hand on the doorknob, he glanced toward the fireplace. There, under the mantel, hung Saro's and Honey's stockings. And there, beside them, hung his stocking! Now who had hung it there? It had in it the same bulge his stocking had had every Christmas morning since he could remember—a bulge made by an orange.

Jamie ran to the fireplace and felt the toe of his stocking. Yes, there was the dime, just as on other Christmas mornings.

Hurriedly he emptied his stocking. With the orange and the dime in one hand and the crook in the other, he made his way toward the church. Father and Saro, still watching, saw his shepherd's robe a spot of glowing color in a great white world.

Father opened the church door.

Without looking to left or right, Jamie hurried up the aisle. Father and Saro

followed him. Beside the pallet he dropped to his knees.

"Here's a Christmas gift for the Child," he said, clear and strong.

"Father!" gasped Saro. "Father, listen to Jamie!"

The woman turned back the covers from the baby's face. Jamie gently laid the orange beside the baby's tiny hand.

"And here's a Christmas gift for the Mother," Jamie said to the woman.

He put the dime in her hand.

Father, trembling with wonder and with joy, fell to his knees beside Jamie. Saro, too, knelt; and Honey, and the man.

"Surely," the woman spoke softly, "the Lord lives this day."

"Surely," said Father, "the Lord does live this day, and all days. And he is loving and merciful and good."

•••••

In the hush that followed, Christmas in all its joy and majesty came to Hurricane Gap. And it wasn't so long ago at that.

Rebecca Caudill

REBECCA CAUDILL

Snow Lines

The snow had drifted into the crevices so that it all looked like a level surface. Frank hadn't remembered this much flat land. He thought his three acres was all up and down, except for the shelf made for his house and a few yards stretched out from his front door. His back door opened onto a deck that spiraled over a small canyon. But they'd only been in the house since October and hadn't explored all the land and here was a flat field not more than a couple hundred yards from the house.

But he should have known better. Nothing was level in eastern Kentucky. His boot kept on plunging through the white powder, looking for solid ground. When he found it, he was up to his waist.

Rockefeller Center. That was the first thought he had as he pulled himself up out of the ditch. Which was odd. Frank had never liked Rockefeller Center. Even in 1980, it still had that 1930s, Ayn-Rand-neo-fascist look. But if anything said New York Christmas, it did. He looked over the white wilderness in front of him. He should have brought a long stick to poke the drifts. It'd be hard to keep his footing.

A fallen beech blocked his way. Beech? Sycamore, maybe. He tried to remember if that's what the surveyor had said was the border edge of his three acres. He had never owned a foot of land in Manhattan. He grabbed a branch of the Beech or whatever it was and pulled himself up and over. Put his small axe down first.

"Going to chop us some wood, honey?" They did have a wood stove, but mostly for decoration. The heat pump worked just fine.

"Going to chop our own Christmas tree," he told her, trying not to sound too ridiculous. Elaine nodded vaguely. Christmas was all part of the baggage that came with marrying a boy. But even Elaine had liked Rockefeller Center with its giant Norway Spruce brought down from Vermont, the skaters, the whole Fifth Avenue crush of shoppers. Even if you could only afford to window shop or look at the skaters. When you got too cold, you could always duck into St. Patrick's across the street. None of it was particularly Christian. They decked the altar with green boughs and spread pine trees out to the entry ways. Mixed with the candles burning, the smell was pure New York. You forgave a lot of New York sins during Christmas week.

He stepped carefully over the fallen tree, but slipped on some hidden iced rock and tumbled forward over the hill. He spread his arms out trying to catch his balance, as if he was going to take flight, and did a snow angel face down. His words, not very angel-like, were muffled by the snow. The land was full of pitfalls. He could hear some dogs starting to bark in the distance.

"You going where?"

"Kentucky. Hazard, Kentucky."

His friend Stan had roped him into going out to Belmont in June a week before the big race.

"Hazard? That near Churchill?"

"I don't think so. It's in the mountains."

"Mountains?" Stan's eyes were momentarily torn from *The Racing Form*. "Man, you're going to get shot. Kentucky feuds."

Frank didn't remind Stan of his own shooting: some junkie thinking Stan wasn't moving fast enough emptying his pockets. Or Frank's own gun-to-the-head experience when the place he managed had been robbed the year before. He didn't think Kentucky's mountains could be more dangerous. But that had been the general reaction of his friends. Either an old stereotype about moonshine and feuds or a blank stare. Mostly blank stares. His friends knew Jersey was across the river and Los Angeles across the country. But they were vague about the stuff in-between.

He picked himself up again and brushed the snow from his face. He looked around for his axe.

"Well, bring a big tree back, Honey. And maybe some bagels and lox?"

Elaine had been a blank stare, too, when he told her he had gotten a job at the community college. But Elaine never stayed blank for long. She jumped right in. Knew enough to answer all their friends who just scratched their heads in befuddlement, even her mother who cried, actually cried, about her daughter and grandbaby being brought to the wilderness.

"Mother, Daniel Boone's been gone a long time."

But she still missed her bagel and lox. And he guessed he still missed Fifth Avenue. But he'd just been a window shopper there. He owned this place.

At 17 months, their baby, Emily, wouldn't care how big the tree was. Anything sparkly would do. And Elaine sure didn't care as long as it wasn't too big. But this was his first Kentucky Christmas. He wanted something impressive, something that said woods and outdoors, not like the corner lot trees he'd dragged home in New York. They had said Long Island tree farm.

Only his hill was on the north side. The real estate agent had mentioned that and he had nodded, as if she were explaining the difference between West Side and East Side. But now he understood. Every promising candidate tree he approached ... full, lush, green ... turned bare, brown, spare when turned around. Like a Potemkin village façade: all front, no rear. Elaine would laugh him out of town if he brought one of these sorry specimens back.

The snow was deeper than he had thought ... three snowfalls adding up. The road that led down from his house had disappeared. They'd been parking on

Route 15 by the mailboxes since the first snowfall, been trudging their way up since.

"We could call the city for their snow plows," Elaine had teased one trip. She was carrying groceries; he had put on the baby backpack which Emily always treated like a trampoline. Each jump doubled her weight of 25 pounds and he was sweating. Their house was a half-mile straight up from the road.

"Don't think they have snowplows. Besides, we're in the county. Not their jurisdiction."

But they liked those hikes. They'd have to pause for breath every hundred yards or so and it gave them time to look over the mountains. The trees crowded in close to the path they were making. In the summer, they couldn't see the river for all the leaves. But the river was there now, a black line cutting through the white of the banks. The south hills on the other side just had patches of snow left. They wondered if they'd have to wait to March for a thaw on the north side.

He spotted a likely tree candidate, halfway up the next incline. It was separated from the other trees, in a little clearing of its own. Maybe it had had sun enough to fill out all the way around. He picked his way carefully down the hill and started to climb back up towards the tree. It was probably eight feet tall. Elaine wouldn't laugh, at least. He wondered if his axe was big enough.

Six feet from the tree, he heard a click. He had heard that click the year before when he was robbed. He froze, and then slowly turned his head towards it. An old woman held a rifle half as big as she was. It was pointed off to the side and looked heavy. It was all she could do to hold it steady. Two large dogs stood by her side, glued by some unspoken command. Unlike the gun, they pointed directly at him.

"You lost, Mister?"

"No," he managed to say. "I'm looking for a Christmas tree."

"They sell Christmas trees in town."

"I wanted to chop my own. On my own land." The rifle had swayed closer to the ground. The old woman pulled it back up. She was wearing a man's coat that reached past her waist though it was just a jacket. Her galoshes looked like men's, too. They reached her knees. She had pulled a knit cap over her white hair. She looked like she had dressed quick.

"This ain't your land."

"It's not?" Frank thought of the fallen beech. Oh. "I'm sorry. It's hard to tell in all this snow."

"It ain't hard to tell if you know where you're at." She looked at the axe he still held in his hand. "That what you aiming to use to do your chopping?"

He looked at the axe again himself. It looked like a toy—the blade could have been made of rubber. He shrugged.

The old woman lowered the gun. He

heard another click. Something like a smile passed over her face. "You're that professor who bought the Richie house. Got that pretty baby. Shouldn't be wandering around folks' property carrying axes. Even axes like that. Makes the dogs nervous."

"I'm sorry. I ..."

"Oh, no harm done. Except maybe to you. Look like you took a few tumbles. Why don't you come down to the house, get you something warm to drink. And I might have something better to chop that tree with than that baby axe you're carrying." She nodded to the tree he'd been stalking.

"But that's your tree. It's on your land."

"Oh, Mister. I got more trees than I know what to do with. Besides, it's a sorry-looking thing on the other side. Good Christmas trees don't grow in these mountains, Mister. You need flat land for that. Still, you're welcome to it if you want it. But come on down and get you something to drink first."

She turned with the rifle slung over her shoulders. The dogs trailed back to him, wagging-tail friendly now—some invisible sign having been made to them that he was okay.

The old woman plied him with two mugs of hot cider before he got away. Her man was gone, but her sons checked in on her regularly. And the grandbabies would be over Christmas. She gave him an axe as big as her rifle. He could bring it back when the snow thawed. Did he think it would ever? She pulled out a rag doll she had made out of old socks. Didn't know why since her sons just had boys.

"You think your little girl would like that?" she asked, shyly.

He thanked her but she waved it away.

"I hope I didn't scare you none with that old gun. Can't hardly lift it anymore with the arthritis, but my boys make me keep it, living out here, alone, by myself."

"You look like you knew what you were doing."

She looked at him steady. "Oh, I know how to shoot it if that's what you mean."

The dogs had fallen asleep in front of the coal stove, but pricked their ears up at her tone. But the old woman was smiling again and they lay back down.

Elaine laughed when he dragged the eight-foot tree in. One whole side was missing.

"Frank, that's the ugliest Christmas tree I've ever seen."

"It's a mountain tree."

Emily reached for a branch. Bringing trees indoors was a new treat for her. She didn't care about Rockefeller Center.

He picked Emily up and they both nuzzled the green pine. It smelt as good as any Norway Spruce. He grinned back at his wife. "It's made right here in Kentucky. And we think it's beautiful."

Joseph G. Anthony

Joseph Anthony

About The Authors

Joseph G. Anthony *is a Kentucky writer, born and reared in southern New Jersey. His first novel,* Peril, Kentucky *(Wind Publishing) was set in eastern Kentucky. His second book,* Camden Blues, *(Wind Publishing) a collection of novellas and short stories was a description of "the evolution and death or deterioration of the very center of what made this country great," according to James Goode, writing in the literary journal* New Madrid. *Anthony has been a community college English professor for 32 years and has published numerous essays, stories, and poems in various publications. His latest novel,* Pickering's Mountain, *a novel about the devastation wrought by mountaintop removal, was released in 2012 by Old Seventy Creek Press. A collection of stories and novellas,* Bluegrass Funeral, *centered in the Bluegrass and stretching from the Civil War to current times, was released by Wind Publications in August 2012.*

Rebecca Caudill Ayars *is perhaps one of Kentucky's best-known children's writers, having published more than 20 books between 1934 and 1985. Rebecca was born Feb. 2, 1899 and grew up as the middle child in a family of 10 who lived at Poor Fork, Ky., (now the city of Cumberland) in Harlan County. After her family moved to Tennessee, she worked her way through Wesleyan College in Macon, Ga., where she received a bacehlor's degree in 1920. She taught English and history at Summer County High School in Portland, Tenn., from 1920-21. In 1922, she earned a master's degree in international relations from Vanderbilt University. She taught English as a Second Language at Collegio Bennett in Rio de Janeiro for a short time. She also worked as an editor for the Methodist Publishing House in Nashville, Tenn. After she moved to Chicago for a job with a publishing house, she met and married James Sterling Ayars. After their two children, John and Rebecca, were born, they moved to Urbana, Ill., in 1937, where James was editor of the* Illinois Natural History Survey *at the University of Illinois campus. Her first book was the novel of juvenile fiction* Barrie and Daughter *(Viking, 1943), a partly biographical work of her experiences at growing up in rural Kentucky and Tennessee.* Tree of Freedom *(Viking, 1949) was a Newbery Honor Book in 1950, and* A Pocketful of Cricket *(Holt, 1964) was a Caldecott Honor Book in 1965. She was also the recipient of the Hans Christian Andersen Award. Rebecca Caudill Ayars died Oct. 2, 1985 at the age of 86.*

The Eighth Day

New Year

Wide tracks yawn beneath
the holly tree
here at the old hotel
where street cars sleep
dreaming linen litanies
of motion.

Like carolers, we wander
up and down
the golden street,
brave Christians
with our cheeks turned
to the night,
following
the shadow of
the orphan's candles;
listening
to the tremble of
another year
we have betrayed;
Reminiscing
in the warmth of closed shop windows,
sorting out the merchandise
receiving or rejecting or refusing
to believe,
blaming
our each defection
on the loneliness
that we cannot

clock or computerize,
the constant jingle of a memory
that no heart has
the heart to silence,
the bubble of
a dream just born,
the fantasy
of satin bootsteps
falling along
a peaceful path,
beside the silver street car rails,
up and down the golden street
following
the shadow of
our children's candles.

Jane Stuart

JANE STUART

A Christmas Memory

Instead of the wide-eyed, apple-cheeked doll I dreamed of, Susie Walker was actually a mini Brunhilde, a clunky kinder with stiff blond braids and stocky legs that resembled tree stumps. Her arms were pudgy, and her greedy little hands were open as the moon, with ray-like, spatulate fingers. Nevertheless, when I was six, I thought Susie was the most beautiful doll in the world, and that I would perish if she were not under my tree Christmas morning.

In the television commercials, Susie did not have the most graceful gait, but I thought she was darling. Now when I close my eyes and picture her perambulating, she is rigid with goose-step precision, her head cranking from side to side, as if reviewing two lines of paratroopers. The corresponding swish of her braids created a step-whoosh-step-whoosh rhythm that made me want to tap dance.

As the youngest of five children, product of a menopausal mother and 50ish father, I had no chance of having a real little sister, but Susie would bring me consolation. I did all the things little girls still do when campaigning for a special Christmas wish. I wrote to Santa, did my daily chores without complaint, and even dried the dishes without complaint so my teenage sister could sneak upstairs and talk on the phone. Just in case, I took every opportunity to mention Susie's merits to my mother, the "real" Santa, whose identity had been revealed to me by my older siblings when I was in kindergarten.

My record of perfect performance was immaculate until the day in early December when I came home for lunch and my mother gave me a house key because she would not be there after school. One of my older sisters would be less than 10 minutes behind me, so Mother trusted me to let myself in the house and stay out of trouble for that short span. I clenched the key until the ridges and teeth bit into my palm. I was proud; I felt grown up.

After lunch, Mother sent me up to the third floor on an errand, and that's when I got cocky. The third floor was my big brother's lair, off limits to little sisters unless summoned by special invitation. I had learned from the same loose-lipped siblings who had told me that there was no Santa, that the Christmas presents were hidden in a cedar closet up there.

As soon as I peeked in and saw the coffin-like box, I knew it was Susie. I crouched down to inspect. There she was in all her stiffened splendor, a plastic bag over her head. I only looked at her for a minute. Honest. And then I shut the box, closed the closet, and went downstairs with whatever I'd been sent to fetch.

By then, it was time to get back to school. As I zipped myself into my snowsuit Mother asked if I had the key. I didn't, of course, but I knew exactly where I lost it: Upstairs in Susie's cardboard

casket. To say my heart sank is usually an exaggeration, but not in this case. And since I wasn't quick enough to make up a lie, I tearfully blurted my confession.

"Good little girls aren't supposed to snoop around trying to find their Christmas presents," Mother said. "Santa Claus will have to come and take your baby back."

It was an idle threat, for I did get my doll that Christmas, but the story of my spying was repeated as part of family lore. Everyone laughed at my expense, and I blamed Susie. A few years later, when my little nieces scalped her in a game of cowgirls and Indians, I didn't really care and sometime when I was in high school, the clunky *mädchen* disappeared altogether.

By now, I suppose Susie's in doll heaven—plaid dress, silky socks and blond braids restored. I can see her now, an unblinking Aryan android, beating up Barbie and moving into her mansion so she can lie in wait for Ken.

Constance Alexander

CONSTANCE ALEXANDER

Ascension

While morning slices under
the green edge of the moon,
while leaves shake with birds
breaking glass stillness
with weighty dark,
I slip beside the rooster crow
walking a fence row of sound
down behind the Big O.

My hands become the surf
greeting piper dawn—
no, more a crucifix of a man,
one hand the dying moon
the other the birthing sun,
shadows around my head
constant thorns.

Three days now in the tomb,
the rock rolled back,
rolled back.
I ascend here beyond the bone—
my spirit, now shadow, my clone.

Lee Pennington

LEE PENNINGTON

The Christmas Chair

Annie will always be one of my favorite Christmas gifts. She did not come in December when presents are traditionally given and received. She appeared six months early on a hot day in July.

A Queen Anne chair is not the type of gift I request, since I am not a furniture aficionado. I have several family heirlooms that I treasure, but only for their sentimental history. Valuable antiques or expensive pieces have never particularly attracted me. But this chair was different, and I instinctively gave her a name as if she were a real person. She became a source of genuine comfort, a confidant who now represents the miracle of Christmas.

For many years, Annie lived with us out in the country, in a large house filled with four energetic children. Even though I have now moved to a smaller house in town, and my family is grown and gone, Annie will always stay with me. I have reupholstered her in a nubby olive green fabric with tiny flecks of bittersweet red. She sits all by her herself in my living room, which elicits decorating comments from well-meaning friends.

"Nice chair, but it needs something like a lamp or a table." Does a shrine need something like a lamp or a table? Annie deserves the sainthood I have bestowed upon her. In fact, I would give up every piece of furniture I own to keep Annie.

I first saw Her Majesty Queen Anne sitting at the curb in a very, very nice area of town, the kind of area where people manicure, not mow, their yards. When I spotted the chair from several blocks away, I felt sure that when I drove closer I would see a *For Sale* sign or an irreparable blemish in the fabric. As I stopped the van, I leaned outside the window for a closer look and to my surprise found no such sign or fabric scar.

"What's a good-looking chair like you doing in a place like this?" I asked. The chair did not seem bothered in the least sitting beside a trash can. She modeled her wing back, carved knees, and cabriole legs with style.

"You look great!" I declared, as I turned off the engine. I often carry on detailed conversations out loud with myself, inanimate objects, and God. I blame this on being a writer who never stops brainstorming. Finding an abandoned treasure opened the floodgates.

"Thank you, Lord, that something possessed me to drive the van today, even though I left the kids at home. This chair would have never fit in our smaller car. And it's not like I could have left a sign that read *Do Not Remove Chair. New Owner Will Return In One Hour.* Someone must have discarded this chair only minutes ago. Something like this does not stay around long waiting for the garbage men. I can't believe I found you, just sitting here for me on your own four feet."

I finally stopped talking and began

walking around the chair, carefully examining my unexpected find. I poked and prodded her arms and her back and her seat. When satisfied that my initial "You look great!" was right, I heaved her sideways into the van. I continued to marvel that I had come across this chair before anyone else. I could hardly wait to tell my mom, even though I knew she would not feel as surprised. She probably would ask me one of her thought-provoking questions. *Did you ever think that the chair had been waiting there for hours, just for you, carefully guarded by an angel?*

Mom was probably right. Only last week I had told my husband that I specifically wanted a Queen Anne chair for Christmas. Furniture had never before been on my wish list, nor did I give out hints for gifts so early. But I knew we needed time to save and shop for that kind of chair. I had the perfect corner, the perfect lamp and the perfect small table to accompany a Queen Anne. And now, unexpectedly, while driving past a low-end store called *The Curb*, I found the exact high-end chair I wanted, in the exact color I needed, a solid sage green. No down payment, no finance charges. Perhaps this was a Christmas miracle and not an amazing coincidence.

I looked around to see who I could thank for this gift. And I had to admit, I was also curious. How could such a fine lady have been abandoned? What dire circumstances surrounded her being unceremoniously dumped into the street? On the other hand, her history really did not matter because I was ready to adopt the chair. I could envision her nestled in the corner of our family room. I could see myself sitting there reading books to the children.

"I hope you like poetry and Shakespeare and animal stories, Annie," I said, patting her on the side as I slid the van door shut. I had named the chair so naturally: Annie for the orphaned Queen Anne chair. We had just met, and I was already turning her into a member of the family.

With Annie in the van, I forgot about my original purpose of grocery shopping, and headed straight home. Annie would be the hot topic at the dinner table that night. Before her debut, I wanted to give her a thorough shampoo and pedicure. To properly show off those curved legs, the most distinctive feature of a Queen Anne chair, I needed to touch up some minor scratches.

"You'll look good as new," I told her on the way home. I could not stop feeling giddy about this free Christmas gift. Singing parodies of well-known songs was one of my favorite forms of zaniness. I immediately knew the ideal material. Before long, songs from the Broadway musical *Annie* filled the van. "Not a hard-knock life for me, when I find a chair you

see ... Tomorrow, tomorrow, I love ya tomorrow, you're only a chair away ..."

•••••

I found the chair in July, and a month later, the doctors found cancer in my mom's bladder. Mom had awakened one night and discovered she was bleeding. She was admitted to Mercy Medical Center, the Catholic hospital in my hometown of Springfield, Ohio, for exploratory surgery that night. Several days later my world began to crumble when the laboratory results verified Mom's tumor was cancerous. I decided the doctor who told us the news must practice medicine during the day and write suspense novels at night. He painted an intense picture of the tumor with tentacles intertwining inside her bladder wall.

How could I stand a second loss? My dad had died from a massive heart attack only the previous year. In the split second I heard the word cancer, I felt paralyzed, unable to deal with the thought of losing another parent, this time to cancer. I tried to explain to my sister Rebecca why Mom, of all people, should not have this diagnosis.

"She exercises regularly, keeps a chart to make sure she drinks eight glasses of water a day, eats more fruits and veggies than anyone I know, has taken loads of vitamins her whole life, lives an active life of faith and prayer, has never smoked nor drank, does crossword puzzles religiously to keep her mind active, has never taken a prescription on a regular basis, does volunteer work with people who need her, and belly laughs all the time." But no matter how many times I replayed the list in my mind, the result never changed— cancer.

Before Mom left the hospital, we had to have the conversation every elderly person dreads— the transition from independence to dependence. I wanted her to come live with me. Yet, I knew she did not want to leave the house that Dad had built for them as newlyweds almost 53 years ago. I could not look at her, so I focused on the Crucifix above her hospital bed. I needed this tangible reminder that God was listening to our painful plans.

I waited for her response to my proposal, but there was only silence. When I eventually mustered the courage to look at her, I saw that she had closed her eyes. How did Mom know that saying nothing spoke volumes? I knew she was talking to God, asking for help to deal with the new lifestyle that her cancer would inevitably bring. She had thrived on spilling sunshine into the lives of both friends and strangers as she fed them, cleaned for them, taught classes to them, and chauffeured them. She had only recently navigated the rugged terrain of Dad's death and her adjustment to widowhood. Could she handle another drastic change so soon? Could she climb another steep mountain, a mountain whose

trail markers read: *Major Relocation, Brand New Routine*, and for her, the most arduous, embarrassing trail of all, *Loss of Control of Bodily Functions*?

Finally, Mom let out a contented sigh. "I don't want to leave Springfield, and all my friends, but I think 'My Old Kentucky Home' is calling."

I squeezed her hand. "You'll finally get to meet that chair I found. You know, the one you're convinced was guarded by an angel. That chair is in the perfect place for you to sit and enjoy the grandkids. You'll be able to observe all their violin and piano practices." She smiled, and I knew the combination of grandchildren and music sealed the deal.

Annie immediately became a bigger blessing than I had originally imagined. What else would it take to convince me Annie was a miracle? I found the chair before anyone else. The price was right. The style and color matched the family room. And now, I watched in amazement as the high back and winged sides cradled Mom's severely curved spine. She had lived with scoliosis for years without complaint, even though she had trouble sitting in a chair for longer than an hour without aggravating her back. Annie came to the rescue. Mom had never sat in a Queen Anne chair before, but they fit each other perfectly. She now had a place of rest for hours without pain. And little did I know that the corner where Mom and

Annie sat proved ideal, since the bathroom was nearby.

Bladder cancer inevitably comes with mishaps, even with the use of adult diapers. The first time Mom had an accident, she had a hard time forgiving herself. "Don't worry, Mom," I said. "Think of all the dirty diapers you cleaned up for me." I knew better than to say, "Don't worry, Mom. It's just a chair." She believed Annie was a miracle who deserved the best. I reassured her that Annie's fabric was durable, and the right cleaning products would make her look good as new. However, the night after Mom's first accident, while she was asleep, I applied some topical insurance to Annie. She received the royal treatment—Scotch Guard.

Despite Annie's prominent place in the house, her name remained private. The day I brought the chair home, I wanted to tell my family how I had proudly christened her Annie, but I knew they would all laugh like I was crazy. Their imagined reaction made me ask, *Who would name a chair?*

I would, and so would mom. At my first opportunity to be alone, I had called Mom and told her about finding the chair and naming her Annie. She agreed that the children were too young to understand our intuition about this chair. From that day forward, we decided to keep the name a secret between the two of us.

Doctor visits and daily living made

the remaining months until Christmas fly. The joy of Mom's presence tempered any stress from our new hectic pace. To say that we loved having Grandma live with us was an understatement. If she was not at the kitchen table or in bed, she sat in the green chair, orchestrating love and laughter. That chair even seemed to refresh her memory. She began to tell tales of my antics as a child that I had forgotten. For instance, while my children decorated our tree, my mom recounted the story of how I, at the tender age of seven, tried to make hot chocolate.

Fixing hot chocolate should be a simple affair—whole milk, cocoa, sugar, and vanilla. I misread the recipe, however, and instead of adding 1/4 teaspoon of vanilla, I poured in 1/4 cup. My dad, always one to take hearty first bites or gulps, spit out the hot chocolate with such force that Mom remarked, "Well, we have a choice. Touch up the walls with paint, or tell friends we're now decorating with brown Rorschach ink blots." I needed to hear that story again. Her sense of humor about my childhood mishaps illustrated how I should mother my own children. Whenever a problem arose, I must first ask, did the mess come from a child's clumsy hand or from a rebellious heart?

Once Mom moved in, I never sat in the green throne until after she went to bed. Mom looked so regal in the chair. From time to time I thought about renaming the chair. Rather than Annie, the Queen Anne chair, she might become Dottie, the Queen Dorothy chair. Although I never did change her name, I did change her location for the week before Christmas. Mom had won several recipe contests throughout the years, and loved cooking. When I scooted the chair in the kitchen, Mom could participate in our holiday baking marathon. Annie was now a director's chair, as Mom told us how to prepare her legendary cranberry salad with miniature marshmallows, our favorite on the Christmas Day dinner menu. She also directed making her recipe for real peanut brittle, so named "real" because she used a stove, a Paul Revere saucepan, and a candy thermometer instead of the microwave. *Queen Anne chair? Queen Dorothy chair? Director chair?* The name did not matter as long as Mom daily shared with us her recipe for living.

Sometimes, I turned the chair to face toward the French doors. From that view Mom enjoyed the four pine trees planted in celebration of the birth of each grandchild. My parents had passed down this holiday tradition. For my first Christmas they had bought and decorated a balled pine tree, a decision that required an unwieldy galvanized wash tub for a tree stand. Daddy had pre-dug the hole earlier in the season, anticipating that the ground would be frozen come December. After the holidays, he planted the tree in

the backyard, right outside my bedroom window. By the time I was a teenager, the pine stood at least 12 feet tall. The tree was not the only fast grower in the family. The height I had inherited from my father found me entering the eighth grade at almost six feet tall. I often cried myself to sleep because I was too uncoordinated to be the basketball player everyone expected me to be. Then one summer night, looking out my open bedroom window, I was struck by the pine tree's majesty and fragrance. She had survived harsh winters and blistering summers. She whispered a message: *Don't give up*.

•••••

When Mom moved to our home in late August, she brought an internal Advent calendar that never ran out of days. Every morning, she woke up with expectancy. Through the glories of autumn and into the cold, rainy days of early winter, she radiated the joy that others reserved only for the celebration of the Christ Child and the anticipation of Saint Nicholas. She did not change after Christmas, either. Though I had put away the decorations, nibbled the last piece of real peanut brittle, and finished my time at the return counters, Mom continued the festivities. She sang her favorite carols, swinging from the boisterous "Come On, Ring Those Bells" to the sacred and solemn "O Holy Night." The calendar and weather said January in Kentucky, but Mom's singing made us

feel like November at Macy's. Sometimes, while sitting at her feet listening, I knew she would conquer her battle with cancer. She would be a survivor.

Of course, in order for her to be a survivor, I needed to be a researcher, keeping on top of any new cancer protocol. I regularly checked websites for the latest information, determined to do anything and everything to keep Mom alive. My research led me toward nutrition, diet, and alternative medicine. Since Mom believed that seeing her grandchildren grow up and marry was sweeter than any dessert, she never complained when I adjusted her diet. My strategy included vitamin-packed vegetable juices. Spinach leaves usually were a main ingredient, so the concoctions resembled pond scum. We joked about how the drinks were in Annie's color palette.

These natural remedies helped Mom, but not as much as we had hoped. The bleeding incidents continued, unnerving us more each time. Our family doctor thought the staff at the Markey Cancer Center at the University of Kentucky might have more options. In February, we drove to Lexington for our first visit. The day of the appointment began with Mom's customary ritual of heading to her chair, where she read her well-worn Bible and prayed. Afterwards, as usual, she wrote notes of encouragement to friends. I had witnessed these habits my whole

life. Often as I child I would run into her bedroom and stop abruptly when I realized she was kneeling beside her bed, head bowed and hands clasped. Likewise, I saw the stacks of Hallmark cards that contained her personalized verses of cheer.

On this particular morning, with the oncologist appointment looming before us, I wished one of those cards had been addressed to me. I felt unusually nervous about this visit but did not let Mom know my concern. When we arrived at the Markey Cancer Center, I settled Mom in a chair and approached the desk to sign in and complete the inevitable paperwork. While scribbling her name on the arrival list, my hand suddenly stopped, as if an invisible force had reached down and firmly grasped the pen. I looked at what I had written. *This writing looks like chicken scratch*, I thought. *Of course the words look like chicken scratch. I feel like a chicken. I can't deal with Mom's cancer*. Instinctively, I knew Mom's reaction to my thoughts. *Of course you can't deal with my cancer. I can't deal with it, either. We can only do the next thing.*

Mom had allowed me to see her consistent life of faith and hope so well that I could usually read her mind about any circumstance. Her idea that we can only do the next thing was the invisible card of cheer she had sent me that day. I knew the next thing to do. Mom had always prided herself on her flowing penmanship, her word for handwriting.

Her elegant signature represented her ladylike manner. I crossed out the words I had hastily scrawled and carefully penned Dorothy Kohl Ulsh. Taking the time to write her name in a dignified way reminded me to not only do the next thing, but to make sure the next thing was well done.

The receptionist turned the clipboard around and looked at me for a moment. "First time here?" she asked.

I nodded.

She handed me the urine collection cup. "Do you know what to do?"

I nodded again. I needed no instructions for urinary target practice.

Mom hated *The Cup*. Keeping it well out of view, I suggested we go to the bathroom. She readily agreed. The handicap stall was the only one that fit the three of us— Mom, me and *The Cup*. I helped her pull down her slacks before revealing the dreaded container. She sighed.

"Can we super-size that?" she asked quietly. Less than an hour ago, we had enjoyed lunch at Wendy's, ordering our typical bowl of chili and a Frosty. I immediately burst into laughter at her word play, picturing the size of the new and improved cup.

"Think some guy named Peewee invented these?" I offered. Now it was her turn to cackle. I smiled at her reaction, but my heart was heavy. I sensed our moments

of give-and-take banter were fragile and fleeting. Less than six months previously Mom had pedaled her stationery bike a minimum of five miles a day. Now she needed my help to go to the bathroom.

Back in the waiting room, Mom's eyes did not miss the fact that we sat in a lobby filled with people wearing scarves and knit hats. Two women with a fine crop of fuzz came in and sat across from us. As I admired their confident beauty, I felt Mom stiffen. I knew she worried about being bald. "So, what do you think about a Zsa Zsa wig?" I asked in a conspiratorial whisper. She laughed and started to relax.

The wait might have been more tolerable if we could have brought Annie with us. After another half hour of reading endless articles from *Good Housekeeping*, the nurse called Mom. She ushered us into an exam room and I pulled out a pen and my list of questions. Within minutes, two men walked in and introduced themselves as the doctor and a medical student. Mom sat with her head bowed, while the doctor directed his comments to me. I sensed he thought Mom was resigned to her fate like a criminal waiting to hear the verdict, or perhaps he questioned her mental competency. I knew better. I knew exactly what habit she was practicing.

"Surgery is not an option, considering your mother's age and the type of cancer," he said, scribbling notes on her chart.

"What about chemo?" I asked, sitting on the edge of the hard chair.

"Contraindicated."

"What about radiation?"

He shook his head and closed Mom's file.

"So our options are ..." my voice trailed off, as I squeezed my mom's hand.

"Are you familiar with the services of Hospice?" He scrawled some phone numbers on the back of his business card, while I nodded numbly.

I watched them leave, closing the door behind them. Mom spoke first. "I want to go home where the grandkids and Annie are waiting for me."

The drive home was quiet. Mom dozed off, and I tried to untangle my thoughts. I began making a mental list: *Call close relatives, beginning with my sister Rebecca. Think positive. Talk with children. Ask friends at church to pray. Buy Mom a new book of poetry. Frame favorite picture of Mom and the kids.* Little quips and sayings from Mom darted in and out of my mind. I pondered one of her very favorite quotes: "In acceptance lieth peace." *I hope lots of courage comes with acceptance*, I thought.

Inside the house, I immediately settled Mom in her chair. Next, I threw away the oncologist's business card murmuring to myself, "Poor penmanship." We never spoke again about that visit to Markey. Six weeks later, Mom developed a serious cold that was leading straight into bronchitis. The family doctor suggested we call Hospice in order to qualify for a hospital

bed at the house.

"She'll sleep better in an elevated position," he explained. "And Hospice can be there to help in case she needs more." I hated the sense of foreboding that his words carried. Even though I had to look up the Hospice number in the phone book, I was glad I had tossed away the oncologist's card as a courageous act of faith. Now, my hands trembled while I dialed the number. I tried rehearsing what I should say, but my mind was numb. This path was unfamiliar and I was frightened.

"I really don't know why I'm calling you," I began. "My mom has been diagnosed with cancer, but we really don't need you since she only has a cold." The Hospice nurse did not seem offended in the least at my distorted logic and arranged for a home visit later that day. Within 24 hours, the bed was delivered. I said nothing to Mom, but I immediately disliked the rubbery smell of the mattress and the heavy-duty side rails that shouted *Invalid*. I did not need to worry about naming this piece of furniture. What could I name an object that looked like a monstrosity? And what was my mom's first reaction? "I'm so grateful for a nice place to rest."

Having the hospital bed in a downstairs room meant Mom no longer had to maneuver stairs. Our library was the perfect room. The four windows provided her with sunbeams and bird songs. Boxes of Depends, Kleenex, rubber gloves, baby wipes, and turquoise-backed bed pads now crowded the volumes of books. I hated that Hospice required me to prominently display the *Do Not Resuscitate* paper I had signed. "This is in case you call the emergency squad in a panic," the nurse explained. Did I look like the kind of woman who would change my mind and decide in the midst of a crisis to do everything possible to prolong my mom's life? Yes, guilty as charged.

Of course, the primary benefit of the downstairs bedroom was Mom's ability to reach Annie more easily every morning. Mom's cold disappeared, and normal life resumed, except the bed stayed. I began saying, "Grandma's in her chair, all's right with the world." She smiled every time I twisted that classic line from poet Robert Browning.

But one day all was not right with the world. I noticed Mom had trouble walking to the chair, so I moved Annie slightly forward, perhaps four inches. Next week five inches. Six inches. Eight inches. The chair, a green caterpillar, kept moving forward, and I could no longer ignore the stark reality— her cancer was advancing. A month later, the chair was out of the living room. In the hall. Down the hall. Outside the library. Finally, the chair was beside her bed. Then came the day when she did not leave her bed.

•••••

I walked into Mom's bedroom with a fig milk shake, singing my cheerful little refrain of "Here's a swig of fig!" I had read that fig was the most alkaline fruit available. Since cancer did not live in an alkaline environment, I had been pushing figs in the form of a morning protein shake. One look at mom, and the words stuck in my throat. She put her lips together in a small smile and shook her head.

"Just one spoonful?" I coaxed.

"I love you, baby doll," she said, still refusing her breakfast. I wanted to beg her. I wanted to shout "No!" I wanted to cry. Instead, I did the next thing and sat down in the chair and massaged her hands.

Of course, I called the Hospice nurse, panicked at her refusal to eat. The nurse came within half an hour and, noticing Mom's slightly labored breathing, started an IV with pain medication. Outside her room, the nurse reminded me that a person preparing to die did not need food. I choked out the question, "How long ...?"

"Most likely no more than 72 hours."

"Tube feedings ..."

The nurse shook her head no and patted me on the shoulder. I knew Mom did not want tube feedings, but I had to ask.

Mom whispered loving thoughts to her family throughout the day. She reminded the grandchildren how she adored them, using the special names of endearment she had bestowed during their childhood: *Virtuoso*, *Princess*, *Darling*, and *Sweetheart*. I did not realize at the time, but those names were the last words I would hear her speak.

I now had a complete picture of my mom's goodness, kindness and faithfulness. The genuineness I had glimpsed as a child was now in full view, undimmed by the trials of life. Now that I finally knew my mom, she was leaving me.

That night, I wearily sent my family to bed, and stayed beside Mom. I dozed off and on, accepting the comfort Annie gave. Mom's heavy breathing lulled me to sleep. Then, when her breathing became soft, I was startled awake, fearful the end was close. By morning, Mom seemed rested and peaceful. She smiled faintly at my one-sided conversation with her but kept her eyes closed.

I had been reading the Bible to Mom for several weeks, and this morning all the family surrounded her as we read Psalm 23, "The Lord is my shepherd ..." I looked at the frightened faces of my children and knew we formed a broken unbroken circle. As we sang Mom's favorite hymns, I watched her mouth the words to "Count Your Many Blessings." She was dying like she had lived. I planned to sit beside her all day, soaking up her peaceful spirit while reading her favorite poetry. Those plans were interrupted by a knock at the front door. My friend Karen stood on the porch with a basket of food. She refused to

come in, saying she only wanted to deliver a meal and a hug. I thanked her and took the food to the kitchen. When I returned to Mom's side, I gave her a kiss and said, "I love you, Mom." She gave a long contented sigh.

I sat down in Annie and waited to hear the sounds of her breathing, but there was only silence. I looked at Mom's face and realized she had gently gone Home. Mom often told me of our first moments together, when she took me into her arms and placed us heart to heart. Instinctively, I had chosen to mirror that moment. I took a deep breath, called out for my family, and sat down again.

•••••

Annie became my therapist. After Mom's death, I sat daily in the chair, crying and praying and crying some more. I could not bear to move Annie back to the family room corner without Mom. Nor could I bear to sit in the chair and read to the children. I felt Annie needed to stay in the place where Mom had taken her last breath. And thus, the library became my sanctuary.

Gradually, the days brightened as I focused on the wonderful memories. Two months later, on what would have been Mom's 83rd birthday, I returned Annie to the family room. It seemed a fitting gift to Mom and Annie. I survived the Thanksgiving holidays, fixing Mom's favorite recipes. However, the closer Christmas came, the more depressed I became. The Hospice staff had warned how difficult December could be, as we remembered Mom's last Christmas with us. I suggested my husband take the children to his parents' house for the holidays. I needed to be alone.

On Christmas morning, I woke up and walked downstairs to Annie with a new box of tissues. I lit the small candle on the table beside her. I prayed for my family and friends, and read the Christmas story from the Bible. I had never noticed before how many journeys were part of the birth of Christ: the journey of Joseph and the expectant Mary to Bethlehem, the journey of shepherds to see the King in a stable, the journey of the Magi based on directions from a gigantic star. I thought of the journey Mom and Annie had made, and I cried.

After I calmed down, I decided, in memory and honor of Mom, to use my best handwriting and write a few notes of encouragement to friends. The act of putting words on paper lifted my spirits so much that I soon found myself making a list of words or phrases that represented Mom's legacy— dictionary, puns, classical music, gratitude, poetry. One word overshadowed all the others as my favorite Mom word: Boobam. I smiled, recalling how she had created that word on Christmas day years ago during a friendly game of Password.

I remembered as if it it were yesterday, the two of us sitting at the dining room table, each sliding a piece of cardboard filled with blue-encoded words up and down a red plastic folder. "This should be an easy word for you to guess, Mom. Almost too easy."

As the sand trickled down the tiny plastic hourglass, I tried every synonym I knew to entice Mom into calling out the word. Every clue I gave seemed to confuse her more.

"Tropical," I began.

"Palm."

"No, grass."

"Lawn mower."

"No, woody."

"I don't know," she said.

I decided to change tactics. Maybe Mom would be able to supply the word as an adjective. "Mmmm ... furniture."

"Furniture?"

"Mmmmm ... poles," I countered.

"Fishing?"

None of my tricks of vocal inflection and hand gestures worked. As the last grains of sand passed through the narrow tunnel, she suddenly stood up and yelled, "I know it! I know it! Boobam!"

She stopped. We looked at each other and said in unison, "Boobam?"

"Mom!" I could hardly talk for laughing. "The word is bamboo." She joined me in uncontrollable laughter for several minutes.

"Remember how we watched *The Andy Griffith Show*?" Mom asked.

I had not thought about that program for a long time and wondered where Mom was headed. "Do you remember Gomer Pyle, the gentle auto mechanic who was awestruck by the simplest of things? He had all those catchphrases like 'g-o-l-l-y' and 'shazam!'"

She paused for dramatic effect. "And we have ..."

"Boobam!" we shouted together, and began laughing even harder.

Finally, Mom held up her hand, and we sputtered to a stop. "You know, baby doll, Boobam is a great word. It's the word that describes the kind of day I want. Full of 'sur-prise, sur-prise.' That's what Boobam is — a word powerful enough to get you through the day with a song in your heart and a smile on your face."

•••••

On July 23, 2003, the one-year anniversary of my mom's death, my family celebrated her life as I prepared a meal of her best recipes. We finished dinner with angel food cake. Mom had considered that dessert the perfect birthday cake for Jesus. My children loved her serving that cake for Christmas breakfast.

Later that night, I stood and looked out the family room window, watching the fireflies blink their fluorescent lights. Suddenly, I felt tired from the emotions of the day and knew where to find the best

seat in the house. Sitting down in Annie made me remember seeing her for the first time on that hot summer day. I had looked utterly amazed, while Annie had looked regal and inviting. What July day was that exactly? I wondered. Without warning, I felt goose bumps run up my arms. My heart knew the answer. *The day that Annie went home with me and the day that my mom went Home were one and the same, one year apart.*

"Annie," I whispered gratefully. "You will always be one of my favorite Christmas gifts. Mom was right. You were the miracle that came during an ordinary day. I did not find you. You found me."

Jacqueline J. Kohl

JACQUELINE KOHL

About The Authors

Jessica Jane Stuart *is the daughter of famed Kentucky writer Jesse Stuart and Naomi Deane. She was born Aug. 20, 1942 at Ashland, Ky. After graduation from Stuart Hall in Staunton, Va., she received her undergraduate degree at Case Western Reserve, earned an master's degree in classical languages from Indiana University, and a doctorate in Latin from Indiana University. She has published 19 books of poetry, three novels, and a collection of short stories. She started publishing when she was only 14. Some of her poetry titles include:* A Year's Harvest *(1957),* Eyes of the Mole *(1967),* White Barn *(1973) and* Journeys: Outward/Inward/Home. Eyes of the Mole *is considered by critics her best book of poetry to date. While under contract with McGraw-Hill, she published three novels:* Yellowhawk *(1973) and* Land of the Fox *(1975), and* Passerman's Hollow *(1974) which was also translated into Italian, and a collection of short stories* Gideon's Children *(1976). After her father's death in 1984, she published* Transparencies: Remembrances of My Father, Jesse Stuart *(1986). Today, she lives in the Jesse Stuart homestead, adjacent to the Jesse Stuart State Nature Preserve on land her father donated to the Kentucky State Parks system in W-Hollow near Greenup, Ky.*

Constance Alexander *is an award-winning columnist, poet, playwright, public radio commentator, and civic journalist. She has received grants and awards for her writing from the Kaiser Foundation, Kentucky Foundation for Women, Kentucky Arts Council, Kentucky Press Association, Pew Center for Civic Journalism, Robert Wood Johnson and Benton Foundations, the Ragdale Foundation, the eKaiser Foundation, and the Poets & Writers Exchange. Her poetry chapbooks,* dreamfish *and* Letters From Down Under *were published by Finishingline Press.* Kilroy Was Here, *a book of poems, and* Who Needs June Cleaver?, *a collection of newspaper columns and public radio commentaries, were published by Motes Books. Her plays have been performed in the U.S., South America, and at Edinburgh's Fringe Festival. Alexander completed her undergraduate work at University of Copenhagen and The College of New Jersey. She has an master's in Humanities, an master's of Business Administration from Pace University in New York, and is a candidate for a MFA degree candidate in fiction at Murray State University. A New Jersey native, she has lived in Murray since 1988. She is married to Roy Davis, artist and custom coffin maker. She has been faculty scholar in Arts & Humanities at Murray's Teacher Quality Institute since 2004.*

Lee Pennington *is the author of 19 books including* I Knew a Woman *(Love Street Books, 1977) and* Thigmotropism *(Green River Writers/Grex Press, 1993)—both nominated for the Pulitzer Prize. He is a retired Professor of English, having taught with the Kentucky Community College System for 34 years, 32 of those at The University of Kentucky Jefferson Community College in Louisville, Ky. He holds a bachelor's in English from Berea College and a master's in English from the University of Iowa. He has an Honorary Doctorate of Literature from World University and an honorary doctorate of philosophy in Arts from The Academy of Southern Arts and Letters. His publishing credits also include numerous poems, short stories, essays, and articles in national and international magazines and newspapers, nine plays that have been produced, and a movie script for the film* Moonshine Wars *produced by MGM in 1970. His writing has appeared in* Alaska Review, South and West, Southern Poetry Review, Red Clay Reader, *and* Playgirl. *Between 1990 and 2008, his film production company JoLe Productions produced 21 documentaries related to the study of ancient cultures. He has served as editor for several publishing companies and magazines.*

Jacqueline Kohl *and Annie live in Winchester, Ky. She loves teaching students of all ages and she works as an adjunct professor of English at Eastern Kentucky University and Bluegrass Community and Technical College. She also owns Cardinal Music Conservatory, where she trains some 30 piano and violin students ranging in age from 4 to 40. She considers herself a life coach who uses the discipline of music and writing to encourage students to achieve their potential. She graduated from Miami University with a degree in English and journalism and earned a MFA from Murray State University, where she received the Jesse Stuart Fellowship. A recipient of a Rotary International Journalism Fellowship, she also studied in England. In her spare time, she loves spending holidays, especially Christmas, with her grown children, writing, remodeling her house, laughing with her best friend Jenny in South Carolina, walking with her Maltese dog named Webster, and, of course, reading in her favorite chair.*

The Ninth Day

Lipstick Like Lindsay's

In the fourth century, when the tales and memory of Christ were still young, there lived a man named Nicholas who was bishop of the city of Myra in Lycia, Asia Minor. History has it that he was persecuted and martyred by Emperor Diocletian. Thereafter he became the patron saint of children, remembered for the gifts he left in secret in memory of Christ's birth. While much about his life is legend, his custom of giving gifts is a fact, and it is a custom that has without fail been entrusted to willing disciples throughout the centuries.

Under such a discipleship, and acting under St. Nicholas's guidance, I hoisted my daughter to my knee and inquired as to her secret list for Christmas. I take this assignment from St. Nicholas seriously. I always have.

Jennie spoke directly and to the point.

"I want crayon lipstick like Lindsay Schell's."

"What else would you like!"

Jennie thought long and hard. She was only four years old and had not learned the words "BMW/J" or "mink." In fact, it became very clear that she had thought long and hard in anticipation of this moment of list making, and the "crayon lipstick like Lindsay Schell's" was not only paramount, it was exclusive. I suggested a few odds and ends and we sealed the letter to St. Nicholas with love and kisses.

Jennie's discovery of the crayon lipstick in question had been fortuitous. She knew about real lipstick, of course, and about play lipstick that was barely visible to the naked eye and totally innocuous to the keeper of a child's clothes. But this was a look-like-a-crayon deep-colored-apparently-harmless-and-supposedly-hypo-allergenic stick of chemicals that spread like real lipstick. Lindsay, age six and more worldly wise, had come to the house one night for pizza with her mother and father and shared her lipstick with Jennie. From that point on it became a fixed object on Jennie's wish list.

I was, at first, amused and delighted. God's miracles come, on occasion, in small packages, and I knew that one day Jennie might develop a similar fervor for more expensive gifts. Thus, for this year, Jennie's wishes and Santa Claus's orders to me were commensurate with my budgetary constraints. The crayon lipstick could not possibly cost more than $2.50. In short, an easy task had been laid out for St. Nicholas and therefore myself as his agent.

My wife urged me not to delay. She was wise, and I was not. A few weeks passed. The memory of Thanksgiving faded into December and Christmas preparations. Work at the office took on a double-time cadence as every attorney in town tried to pack the month of December into its first two weeks, knowing that the only thing that would be packed in the last two weeks would be the bags of every attorney

in town. It was the 15th of the month before I began to catch up with the joy of the season.

We bought our tree, and Jennie spoke about "crayon lipstick like Lindsay Schell's." We finished our Christmas cards and began reading our favorite Christmas stories, and Jennie giggled in anxious anticipation of a "crayon lipstick like Lindsay Schell's." We lit our Advent candles, and I could tell that she was dreaming not of sugar plums but of crayon lipstick. I smiled, knowing that St. Nicholas would allow me to fulfill that desire at any of a dozen drugstores, department stores, and even supermarkets within two miles of our home.

And then one early evening, after a medical deposition in the vicinity of numerous shopping centers, I decided to make a quick trip to the local Children's Palace and swiftly accomplish my assignment. Through most of the year, the roads which lead through the chaos of shopping center land are merely an endless array of erratic lights and signs. At Christmas time, they become a snarling mass of harried Christmas shoppers. Inching my way through the traffic to the correct curb cut for Children's Palace, I turned in just as a steady downpour erased all possible visibility through my windshield.

It will rain from here on in. All the way to Christmas. That is not literary license.

It just happened that way. It rained and didn't seem to stop. If it did stop it was while I was asleep or in the office. If I made the slightest move for the door or got into my car to drive anywhere, it would start raining.

I found the only parking place available, having hovered about the lot for what seemed a modest eternity. Typical fortune found me about 10 yards from the expressway and 60 yards from the front door of the store without an umbrella. I sighed, "Such are the wages of virtue," rolled up my pants a turn or two, thrust open the door, and puddle jumped to the entrance of the toy store.

Inside the store, a light steam rising off of my suit, I began wandering up and down the aisles in search of either the play makeup or an employee. Since all employees in discount stores are either on break or disguised as customers, I found the play makeup first. They had Tinkerbell, Bo-Po, Barbie, and numerous other concoctions, but no crayon lipstick.

After a modicum of stealth, I trapped an unsuspecting employee and asked her for the crayon lipstick. I carefully described the object of my search and slowly, as "through a glass, darkly," she showed a glimmer of recognition.

"Yeah. We had that."

"Great," I replied, trying to ignore her use of the past tense, "where is it?"

No one in this position ever gives a

completely straight answer.

She responded, "It was on aisle 13."

"I looked on aisle 13, and it's not there," I began, "but maybe if you'll come with me, we'll find it. I probably just didn't see it." I have learned that a plea of stupidity will often work wonders in such instances. She smiled and nodded and we walked together to aisle 13.

"It used to be there," she said. "But we must have sold out."

"Could you check for me?" I asked.

"Hey, Margie," she called out. An older woman emerged from a wall of boxed Big Wheels where she had been hiding. "This man wants to know if we got any play lipsticks."

Before I could interrupt, Margie had educated me as to the various other lipsticks that could be found on aisle 13. I then noted politely that I was searching for a specific crayon lipstick like Santa Claus had brought Lindsay the year before. She noted that Jennie would not know the difference. I assured her that Jennie would.

"Well, we had them. But they sold out. I don't know if we'll be getting any more in before Christmas or not."

There was really nothing more to say. I thanked them, and thinking to myself that I had just dried out, I went back into the rain. "This might be a little harder than I thought," I told myself as I hugged the wall of the building in a futile attempt to avoid the downpour, and went around the corner to Service Merchandise.

I was no more fortunate in the home of catalogue sales. "I remember those. They looked liked crayons. Real popular a while back."

"Right," I said eagerly.

"We don't have 'em."

"Gonna get 'em back?"

"I couldn't say. You never can tell."

I went on to the Walgreen's drug store next door.

"Crayon lipstick?" I believe the woman thought I was a little odd.

"It's for Christmas ... my little girl," I said.

"Try aisle five."

I tried aisle five and found only real lipstick. Evidently she hadn't believed my story about Christmas and my little girl. I checked aisle seven for toys and found only the usual collection of non-crayon, and therefore inferior, children's play makeup.

I made my way back to the car, got in, and turned on the radio, only to have the newscaster remind me that it was December 17, "just seven shopping days left before Christmas." I pulled the car back into what is euphemistically referred to as the "flow of traffic," but which was at the moment actually more like a trickle or a drip, and worked my way down the strip.

An inconsequential errand, casually made on the heels of a deposition, had not gone at all as expected. Rather than

leave well enough alone for the time being, I stopped at Thornbury's, the oldest toy store on the strip, knowing that I would pay a lot more, but confident that I would find what I wanted. While the young girl was far more interested in my request, she had even less help to offer. She knew what I wanted, but they hadn't stocked the item for weeks—maybe months.

The word "months" sent a sudden chill through me. What if I had not just run into a streak of bad luck, but an outright famine? I walked away from Thornbury's Toys with growing concern. They hadn't even suggested a place I might purchase a stick of crayon lipstick.

I glanced at my watch and noticed it was almost seven. Already late for dinner, I headed down the road for home, determined that the next day would bring better luck. Then, like a gambler drawn to that one last slot machine prime for the plucking, I noticed the Woolworth's sign over to my right. "Well, why not?" I asked myself, signaling quickly and pulling into a space.

The store was everything a dime store should be. Musty, dusty, and old, it was the type of place that still sold rubber spoolies for women's hair. It was perfect for my purposes. I went straight to the manager.

"Do you have … or have you carried … a type of play lipstick that looks like a crayon?"

"Sure," he said. Here was a man's man. A giant among men. A hero from his clip-on tie down to the pointed ends of his shoes. "They're right back here." And he personally led me to a pegboard at the back of the store.

Our eyes searched the pegboard together. There was an ominous metal hook that was empty. He didn't have to tell me, but he did anyway.

"They *were* right there."

"But you sold out the last one a week or so ago," I offered.

"That's right." He smiled. "But the other stores might have some left."

"Could you check?"

"I'll be glad to," he said. And with that, he initiated a series of phone calls, during which I found that Woolworth's was closing its stores in the area. All of their stock had, in fact, been moved to Lexington. But they did remember the crayon lipstick.

"I'm awful sorry I couldn't help," he said. I knew that he was sincere and thanked him for his help and his sincerity. My way home was filled with a grim determination shadowed by slowly increasing panic.

I laid the situation out to my wife and she stated that which I already knew.

"You started too late, sweetheart."

"You are right," I said with a certain amount of hurt pride. "But do you have any ideas?"

"Keep trying drug stores and dime stores."

"I will," I said. "I will," I mumbled to myself. And the next day I began the phone calls.

I started with the remaining toy and discount stores. An entire morning of otherwise billable hours was spent in large part "on hold" while the search for the elusive lipstick was made. I have no idea whether they all searched their counters and shelves or stood around waiting for the light on the phone to go out so they could go back on break. But I never hung up. And finally a pleasant enough woman at a Target Department Store acknowledged my request, telling me she was familiar with the product and that she had it in the store. My excitement knew no bounds.

I made my excuses at the office and slipped away during lunch. The store was a good 15 minutes away by car and under normal circumstances I would never have made the trip. By now, of course, these were not normal circumstances. And I was glad to give up lunch if I met with success.

I didn't. I searched the Target Store and found neither lipstick nor helpful employee. My informant had been ill-informed and I had been led astray. I ate a Hershey bar for lunch as I drove back to the office.

On Thursday night Jennie and I were in the kitchen making cookies when the phone rang. I answered. I could tell it was long distance. "May I speak with a little girl named Jennie?" I knew immediately it was the Boss himself, the man in charge, in two words: Santa Claus. I gave the phone to Jennie.

"Hello. Yes, this is Jennie." There was a pause, then a giggle of delight. She cupped her little hand over the receiver. "It's Santa Claus, Daddy," she whispered.

"I know," I whispered back. For the past two years, my special contacts with St. Nicholas had prompted this annual phone call. It was made from a friend's house in Cincinnati, 100 miles away.

I kept stirring the oats into the batter as I listened to her conversation.

"Yes, I've been a good girl ... another pause while I held my breath, "I want a crayon lipstick just like Lindsay Schell's." My heart sank. The conversation had quickly taken on the tenor of a conspiracy. If ever I have wished that the cup would be passed on to a more worthy agent of St. Nicholas, it was at that moment. Jennie ended her conversation, aglow with the magic of Christmas.

The next morning, I took desperate measures. First, I called Carol Schell, Lindsay's mother. I explained my dilemma.

"Carol, could you look at Lindsay's lipstick and give me the name of the manufacturer?"

"Of course," she said, immediately responding to the shrill edge of abject fear

in my voice. "But I'll have to find it first."

"I'll wait," I replied. And I waited, until Carol returned to the phone several minutes later.

"Are you still there?"

"Where else?" I laughed, ignoring the mounting stack of return phone slips which my secretary was dutifully placing before me.

"I've got it. Have you got a pencil and paper?"

"You bet," I responded, and meticulously repeated and copied the information.

When I had thanked Carol and hung up, my secretary came in and stood at the end of my desk. She looked at me and smiled warmly.

"I overheard what you were doing. You are a very special daddy."

"If I were really a special daddy," I said, "I wouldn't be in this fix now."

"Hmmm," she said, and handed me a piece of paper with the Manhattan area code written on it.

I got the number and tried to remain calm as the receptionist answered.

"Hi, my name is ... well you don't care about that, but you see, I'm a lawyer ... and ..."

"You want the legal department?" she interrupted.

"No, no ... I want ... uh ... your consumer ombudsman."

"Just a moment," she responded. I was momentarily impressed with my ability to move right to the source of all knowledge. That apparent skill, however, was soon outdistanced by my persistence. Three more departments and 10 minutes later, I finally stumbled onto the appropriate party.

"Yes," the woman said with a heavy north Jersey accent, "I am familiar with that product. Did you say you are a lawyer?" I noted caution in her voice.

"Yes, I am ... but please, this isn't business. I just want a stick for my little girl. I'll pay for you to Federal Express it ..."

"Oh ..." she laughed. "Four years ago we sold millions of those lipsticks. You know how fads go, though. Two years ago the market dwindled to nothing. We dropped the stuff. Listen, you don't want last year's news. This year it's glitter stickers. You can get 'em everywhere!"

Her words hit like the proverbial ton of bricks.

"But Jennie doesn't want what every kid wants this year. You don't have maybe a few sticks left ... you know ... for old times' sake?"

"Take my word," she replied, "they're out ... o-u-t out!"

"Right, well, thanks for the information." I hung up. The big "NO" had come from the "Big Apple," and I realized that I was in considerable trouble.

That night, my wife and I regrouped.

She was the first to deal with the problem head on.

"I'd say you are up the well-known creek," she said.

"I'd say you are right," I said.

"Well," she began after a pause, "maybe we should just let Jennie know in a note that Santa Claus tried as hard as possible, but that we can't always get everything we want."

"That's fine for Jennie," I chuckled weakly, though I knew it wouldn't be fine for Jennie, "but what about me?"

She looked at me solemnly, realizing for the first time how deeply this test of my traditional principal-agent relationship with St. Nicholas had cut to my core. The conversation drifted, and I began to compose in my mind the note explaining why there would be no crayon lipstick like Lindsay Schell's.

Officially, the search ended that night. I am, after all, an adult of sorts. To anyone who asked at the office, I adhered to the party line: You can't have what isn't available.

Secretly, I continued to pursue every possible avenue as the days moved all too quickly toward Christmas. I called my sister in Cincinnati and my mother-in-law in Birmingham. After a few pleasantries I got to the point, mercilessly shaming myself and offering eternal gratitude if they could find the lipstick in Ohio or Alabama. They tried, but my operatives met with no success.

On my way to see a client in Frankfort, I purposely took the long way through Shelbyville, hoping to myself that one of the old, small-town drug stores ignorant of the outdated nature of the stuff might have some of the crayon makeup left on a dusty shelf.

"We had some, dear," said the jolly little lady with the purple rinse in her hair, "but we sold out."

"I know," I said with resignation. "I didn't really think you'd have any." She showed me another, very nice lipstick, but I knew it would never do. I was 20 minutes late for my meeting, and I said I had been delayed by "business." As Marley said to Scrooge, "mankind was my business."

My efforts became calmer, more fatalistic. On December 23, when I went into the old Woolworth's that still remained in downtown Lexington, I was almost as amused as they when I revealed that I knew some of their stock had been shipped over from Louisville.

"How did you know?"

"Oh, I get around," I said, feeling a little like a Fuller Brush man. "Now, about the crayon lipstick ..."

Like the kind man in Louisville, the lady walked me to the aisle where it had been and was no more. I thanked her and walked back into the rain. For it was still raining.

I finished my business and headed north out of town. I mentally reviewed my efforts and realized that I had covered more square miles in my search for the perfect present than during any other Christmas. I also realized that I had failed. The drizzle, which continued in a light but steady stream, fit my mood perfectly.

It was not the nature of the gift that prompted my frustration, nor my failure to attain its purchase that fed my melancholia. In years past, and I was sure in years to come, I had reminded and would remind myself and my family-Jennie and, later, my son John foremost-that the greatest gift which St. Nicholas would have us give or receive in Christ's name would be our love. Certainly baseball gloves, dollhouses, fur coats, gold jewelry, or even automobiles are merely second-class attempts at showing that love. The wise men knew that even as they came forth with their frankincense, gold and myrrh.

It was more a sense of a failed entrustment that overcame me. St. Nicholas had made me the trustee for his simple little gift to Jennie, and I felt like I had somehow breached my fiduciary duty to both of them. I knew in my head that my wife's recommendation of a note explaining the lipstick's absence would be a helpful passage to maturity, but in my heart there was no solace for failure.

These were my thoughts as I shifted into fifth gear and began to pass the Northland Shopping Center on my way out of Lexington. Out of the corner of my left eye I noticed the sign of another Begley's Drug Store, just like the one I had investigated in Shelbyville. I felt it was as good a time as any to buy the substitute lipstick, so I switched on my left-hand signal and pulled into the lot.

Wet as usual (had I ever been dry), I dripped into the store and began the now well-practiced craning of my neck to determine on which aisle I might find their stock of Bo-Po, Tinkerbell, and so on.

A heavyset woman in her late 40s came over to ask if I could be helped. By now a certain similarity of features had begun to emerge in the ladies who worked at the Begley's, Walgreen's, Taylor's and other drug stores. Modified cat-eye glasses dangling from a gold elastic band, heavily rouged cheeks moving rhythmically with the cadence of her chewing gum, her hair coiffed in frozen perfection—this was the lady who stood before me asking, "May I help you?"

"I was looking for play makeup," I said. "Specifically, lipstick."

"We have some in toys," she began, pointing off to a spot at the back of the center aisle. I began ambling back to toys.

"We also used to have some on the hang-up displays over on the specialty racks."

I slowly turned, careful to contain my

curiosity. "Did it ... uh ... have a little girl on the front ... and look like a crayon?" I asked, my mouth turning to play-dough.

"Sure did, honey. Let's see, follow me."

Nearly stumbling twice, I followed her to the far side of the store, beginning to babble incoherently about how I had been looking for this certain type of lipstick, but couldn't find it, and if they had any, well, I would be very happy, but I would understand if they didn't, and so on. I'm sure I was saved from being heard, since she had gotten several steps ahead of me and was already thumbing through the pegboard displays when I caught up with her.

"Here we go," she said. I stared in dumbfounded amazement as she went on. "I'm sorry, I don't see the lipstick. I guess we sold out ... but here's the nail polish ... in cherry ... strawberry ... and here's cologne ..."

I had never gotten this close before. Like a squirrelly, bearded bookworm who has found a first edition of *Oliver Twist* on the dollar book shelf, I savored the mere sight of this now-antiquated line of children's makeup. There was no lipstick, but perhaps this might be my substitute.

"I'm sorry the lipsticks are gone," she continued, "but we have all of these ... " she didn't even change her tone of voice, "well, I'll be darned, look what somebody has stuck back here on the wrong hook."

At that moment, the blessing of St. Nicholas descended upon Begley's Drug Store in the Northland Shopping Center and caused to appear before my very eyes the only unpurchased, fresh, and unopened package of crayon lipstick like Lindsay Schell's in the Commonwealth of Kentucky. My MasterCard would have been hers for the asking, but it was reduced for clearance to $1.37, and she held it toward me.

"Is this okay?" she asked nonchalantly. I restrained the urge to embrace her on the spot and kiss away the rouge on her cheeks.

"You do not know." I said slowly, trying to keep the lump down in my throat, "how you have helped to make my little girl's Christmas and my own. I'll take it." She smiled passively, not revealing if she knew just what I meant, or was perhaps slightly embarrassed at the *event* she had stumbled upon.

I gathered up a modest collection of the remaining makeup and followed her in stunned joy to the check-out counter. I went on to ask her if there were any more lipsticks in the stock room or at another store, and while she was kind enough to check for me, I needn't tell you that I had uncovered the last stick known to mankind.

The rain continued on my way back to Louisville and neither cleared nor miraculously turned to snow by the time I got back home. I am but a crass human,

agent for a greater principal for whom
we joyfully toil at this time of year. Yet
even I realized on the trip home alone, as
I was reminded on Christmas morning
when Jennie found her lipstick and held it
gleefully upward for all to see, and again
whenever I have thought about it since,
that a Christmas trust had been fulfilled on
aisle one of Begley's Drug Store that rainy
December day. It had little to do with play
lipstick and everything to do with love,
and beyond that, no more need be said.

GERALD TONER

The Birds' Tree

Everything's forgotten. This remains: patted
peanut-butter ball we pressed seeds into for
the birds' Christmas—a cold winter—, and
they were around us everywhere, in the shabby
cedars. Stick your fingers in the jar, don't be
afraid—this is not every day, this is the day
before Christmas—pat that ball of brown stuff
round, press in a handful of these nameless
flat black seeds! My brother had to run to wash
his gummy fingers, the baby put the stuff in her
little greedy mouth, and they are gone now, too,
and not remembered. But the birds' tree, that
small unshapely cedar, still stands in the dry
grass of the fenced-in yard, and the little black-
and-white birds, the greedy, the starved,
still gather there.

SALLIE BINGHAM

A Hawk at Christmas

Cold board fences
Divide the pasture,
Running parallel lines
Along the snow this Christmas day.
I am with the lone hawk,
Gliding into the trees across the gully—
Our wings skimming thin branches
As we land on a muscled oak limb.
Our curved claws
Grip icy bark—
Our feathers
Wind fluffed
To keep us warm.
We wait
For the Great I Am,
Turning our sculptured heads
And watching
All this miracle
With eyes
Sharpened
By His words.

James B. Goode

A Wet Christmas

My father was a man of regular habits. He was up with the birds, off to the office by 7:15 a.m., home by 5:30 p.m. unless, on rare occasions, he was held up in court or at the office. Seldom did he break his routines. A defense lawyer, he was accustomed to schedules and deadlines set by judges and the *Kentucky Rules of Civil Procedure*. As might be expected of someone whose working life centered on gauging cause and effect and legal consequences, he preferred the predictable to surprises. Attuned to these patterns, my mother, who managed the household and much of the messy randomness of rearing three children, miraculously had dinner on the table at six o'clock each evening, feeding her husband, "Buzz," her bachelor brother (my Uncle Louis), my older sister, younger brother, and me substantial meals that did not spare either butter or calories—a meat loaf, roast, pork chops (Welsh rarebit on Fridays for my uncle who was a reformed but residual Catholic). Born and bred a city girl, my mother served the hearty fare of the country—plough food that for some reason did not turn us all into blimps. Though the locus of dinner might be changed to the back porch during the summer months, especially before air conditioning, the routine always remained the same as though the schedule was cut in cuneiform on a clay tablet unearthed among the Sumerians. The pattern was ritualistically set, except for once a year as offices and courts slowed down or closed in the days before Christmas.

•••••

Unlike more than one of his partners, my father was a moderate drinker. I can say this with authority because, for a time, I clerked in his office while I was in school at the Brandeis School of Law at the University of Louisville (and before I quit the law profession, my gift to the Commonwealth).

One of my jobs was to drive Henry V.B. Denzer home at the end of the day. A lumpy, scholarly-looking man who wore bland suits and unenviable ties, he won few cases through his personal charisma. Capable as he was as a trial lawyer whose bread and butter was automobile liability cases, he did not drive, never had. Blind in one eye from a childhood BB gun accident, he was a certified expert on insurance law as it affected negligence in accident cases and knew, my father acknowledged, as much on the subject as any man in Kentucky. He had a very dry humor. When the receptionist and secretaries at work would gossip, and guffaws could be heard in the outer office, Mr. Denzer would stick his head in the doorway, roll his glass eye, and bellow, "What's all this frivolity?" No one was the least bit intimidated, nor did he mean them to be. Not marrying until late middle age, Mr. Denzer would have me accompany him to the Delta, a bar and restaurant at 434 Market Street a block and

a half from the law office, the third floor of a three-storey building overlooking several magnolias and the east elevation of Gideon Shryock's classically-designed Jefferson County Courthouse.

The proprietor of this watering hole for the courthouse crowd, Buddy, who then tended bar himself (though aided by two waitresses, Joanie and a redhead known as "Shively Red") knew the tastes of his patrons, and almost as soon as Mr. Denzer stepped off the street and entered this dim-lighted refuge, there were not one but three or four double-double bourbons queued along the polished surface of the long bar where he was wont to stand or sometimes perch on one of the high-backed stools placed there for weary barristers. Eyeing those about him, some through what he could see reflected in the beveled mirror with its tiers of bottles behind the bar, Mr. Denzer would tilt back his head, his wall eye fixed on the ceiling, and suck down his bourbon with just a whisper of water in one long draught as he commented on a case or shared a howler: "Why wasn't Jesus born in Letcher County? Because they couldn't find a virgin or a wise man in the whole county." Most of the regulars were lawyers—Johnny Knopf, Henry Sadlo, Henry A. Triplett, Walter Redmon, Thruston "Redbird" Crady, and Chester Allen Vittitow, who always carried breath mints and once went home from the Delta

and tried, unsuccessfully, to give his dog a haircut. Toping one night at the old Pine Room on River Road—a favorite suburban watering hole—he sang song after song at the piano bar with Mabel, the bar's longtime performer. When he excused himself to visit the loo, Mabel leaned over to Chester's wife and commented, "He knows all of the words and none of the tunes." All of these men savored a taste at the end of the day.

Often as he held forth reporting how some witness let slip a word that won or lost a case or quoting the judge's ruling on some motion for summary judgment, the phone would ring, and Buddy would pick up.

"Yes, Mrs. Denzer," he would say. "Yes, m'am. I'll see if he's still here."

Of course, he was. Buddy, a man who honored his customers' right to privacy and a nip or two after working hours, would cup his palm over the receiver and catch Mr. Denzer's attention, asking if he were still there.

"Tell her I left 10 minutes ago and am heading straight home," he would perjure himself saying, downing whatever remained of his unemptied glasses before finishing whatever it was he was holding forth about and settling up. "Better go," he would mutter to those within hearing. Then I would drive him to his home in the suburbs.

•••••

My father was not a big drinker, nor did he have much time to linger at downtown bars. But what about his father, the last full-time farmer of generations of farmers? Not that came down to us in family stories—with one exception. When my father was about 10 (about 1915), he accompanied his father by horse and wagon (amazing to me) along the old Brownsboro Road and Frankfort Avenue to the hay market in downtown Louisville. What his father was transporting or selling he did not say—or I don't remember— but my brother informed me he was in fact driving cattle and that they were taken not to the old hay market but to the Bourbon Stock Yards. From the family farm at the end of Wolf Pen Branch Road on Chamberlain Lane to downtown Louisville must have been at least 15 miles, taking most of the day to reach. What I do remember his saying is that it was the dead of winter and very cold, and that on the way home his father stopped at Bauer's, the well-known restaurant-bar that had been a stopping place for travelers since the third quarter of the previous century. His father led him into the bar, and the barkeep asked what he would have.

"A shot of straight whiskey," my grandfather said, "and something less strong for the boy!" This meant some predecessor of the Coke or something like sarsaparilla. And that was all I knew about family drinking history.

• • • • •

Whatever the case, my father was not a regular at the Delta. When Mr. Denzer would try to cajole him to come for a drink or two, he would make excuses except for what became a yearly exception. "What's training for," we would say today, "if not to break it occasionally?" His excuses were that he had something more he had to do at the office or something he had to accomplish at home—gentle perjuries. Neither priggish nor intolerant, he acknowledged the need, and the right, of others to take the edge off the day. Fact was, he was even-tempered and showed little of the tension that beset his partners. Alcohol was not for him the elixir of life. My own brief experience was that most of the fraternity of lawyers I encountered, especially trial lawyers, were either neurotic or alcoholic, or both, by age 40. There was a great deal of pressure on them that could only be released with a drink or two.

• • • • •

But once a year, and just once, almost always in the days before Christmas, at six o'clock my father's seat at the set table sat empty, the rest of us seated, potatoes steaming in their bowl, gravy cooling in its cradle, spinach marinating in its liquor, my mother at first looking concerned and then a little exasperated as the truth dawned on her.

"Where's Buzz?" my uncle would ask

abstractly. And no one had an answer though my mother and sister Treva had a good idea.

As the minutes clicked toward the 6:30 news with Walter Cronkite, my mother would roll her eyes and do what she could to hold the meatloaf or roast or whatever it was on the kitchen stove, eyeing the kitchen clock as the minute hand descended toward its nadir at 6:30, then slowly rose toward its zenith at seven o'clock. She would wait as many tolerant minutes as she could, then tell us to eat before the food got cold. When we'd scraped the last green bean from our plates (which we had to clean), she would clear the table and begin washing dishes without my father, his dish towel in hand.

Then, at seven o'clock or a little after, we would hear a fumbling at the front door. In would step my father, a little flushed, vaguely apologetic, grinning. My mother, never a nag, acted as though everything was normal and helped him hang up his overcoat.

"Oh, Buzz!" she would finally say, not really scolding, more resigned and relieved than angry. He offered no explanation, no excuses, as though this breach of implied promise was not really an infraction so much as a slight deviation from the norm, one to which he was entitled. His red face told the story. Keeping his natural dignity (despite the tie misaligned in the inverted V of his collar), he would seat himself at the empty table, his children off doing homework or watching Milton Berle, Jack Benny, or *The Lone Ranger* on our first TV, a Motorola in a bulky wood cabinet at whose center was a smallish screen, its surface almost perpetually a blizzard of snow, the rabbit ears of its crude aerial requiring subtle adjustments. Now it was his own screen that was snowy, a little blurry. My mother, in the kitchen, continued washing the dishes.

•••••

Never a boisterous drunk like some of his friends and members of the legal brotherhood (he could name the women who practiced law in Louisville on one hand), he had no time for prattle and courthouse gossip. Alcohol didn't loosen his tongue. Yes, during the winter evenings of early dark he liked a glass of red wine before dinner, often a carefully prepared gin and tonic (with an antique lime squeezer I use to this day) during the sweltering months of summer. Occasionally, if there was a social event—a game of poker or Buck Pitch on the back porch, he might indulge himself with a Miller High Life or a Manhattan, the latter maybe a carryover from the time during his college years when he bussed tables at a New York night club, once serving and proudly meeting the celebrated band leader, Paul Whiteman. Predictably, each Christmas he edged my mother from the kitchen so that he might concoct his

famous eggnog, real eggnog, with fresh ingredients: egg whites, heavy cream, sugar, Myers dark rum and brandy, topped off by sprinklings of nutmeg in each poured mug that specked its milkshake-thick liquid a stippled brown—an eggnog that bore no resemblance to the pale surrogates sold now at Kroger.

For him, alcohol, seldom and sparingly consumed, served as a seal of contentment. The year was winding down and things looked pretty good. There were challenges and obstacles ahead, certainly, but he could worry about them another time. Mint-flavored gumdrops clustered in a bowl on his desk at work, a large tin of peanut brittle at home. In the Frigidaire there was the eggnog he made ritualistically each year, the tree (a scraggly cedar with prickly needles usually cut on some farm he'd known from his Worthington days) decorated and lit (presents decorously withheld until Christmas morning), a fire in the grate—black locust he'd sawed on some desolate hillside with whomever he could conscript to lift and load, an involuntary but grudging servitude, starting with my brother and me. All was well. His daughter was a model student; his sons did not embarrass him often and showed occasional signs of gradual reformation from the world of lackadaisical studies and active nightlife. His wife, my mother, was even-tempered and undemanding,

tolerant to a fault. After his own warmed-over dinner, he would modestly ensconce himself in his accustomed armchair or stretch out on the sofa pretending to watch *Gunsmoke* or Groucho Marx, adrift in a state of mute euphoria. He wore a sheepish grin that assured us things were as they ought to be, even if he wasn't. If there was a UK basketball game, he would climb the stairs to bed, listening as long as he could to the tense announcements of free throws over the hullabaloo of Wildcat fans. If there wasn't, he would read himself to sleep over *American Horticulture*, *American Muzzleloader*, or *American Field Trials*, magazines that were his recess from the sterile prose of legal opinions, pleadings, and depositions. Never since childhood a churchgoer (though Christmas Eve would find his children in vestments choiring or acolyting in St. Mark's Episcopal Church where even the C and E Boys [Christmas and Easter] would make a showing), he would doze off and finally rise to climb the steps to bed.

•••••

According to my brother Doug, a day or two before our school break the weatherman forecast snow. Never one to be impeded by the elements, my father retrieved the set of cumbersome tire chains from the basement and worked hours connecting them to the tires of his Chevy Bellaire, opting, for some reason, not to take his Willys Jeep which had four-wheel drive. Next morning when he discovered

that no snow had fallen and there was not time enough to remove the chains, he dropped us off by school, the clanking chains creating a racket that embarrassed everyone but him.

He would be up early the next morning to peruse the morning edition of *The Courier-Journal* as though nothing had happened. "Up and at 'em," he would call through our bedroom door an hour later, as if the day were an enemy which we must prepare to attack. That weekend, snowfall or freezing, he would make his annual pilgrimage to Worthington, the small farming community out U.S. 22 toward Brownsboro (where he, his parents, and siblings now lie) about 10 miles northeast of Louisville, the farming neighborhood whose fields are now backyards of an East End subdivision that were then countryside with farms he'd known as a boy with neighbors (some clients for whom he wrote a will or contract) he'd known all his life—whose precincts would always be home to him. He prided himself on his ready self-reliance, always too glad to escape the desk chair and circumspect town life to which he was resignedly tethered. Dressed in khakis and olive Navy-surplus shirt (though a K.M.I. graduate, too young for one war, too old for the second, he never served) on that weekend before Christmas, he would steer his old mud-colored Jeep with the orange hubs through Crescent Hill and east of the city, finding refuge no amount of alcohol could rival in the unbroken fabric of farms whose landmarks were familiar from boyhood, barren fields and shorn trees contracted into winter stasis. Parking, he would carry his clippers and a hank of clothesline straight to the tree he'd scouted that summer, shinny up to a mistletoe-ladened crown ("He can scramble up that tree like a damn squirrel," a friend would say), and surgically clip bunches of the berried pagan magic and lower it to J.B. Myers or Mr. Mercke, his neighbor who came along because he couldn't bear to contemplate his friend falling. They would load enough in his old Willys Jeep, his balance steady (and sober enough) into his late 60s to stock the neighborhood, a healthy clump hanging from the lintel that separated the living and dining rooms.

Eggnog, peanut brittle, car chains, jumbo clumps of mistletoes, stalled dinners—these were landmarks on my map of Christmas memories.

The Delta caters to another generation now, maybe wiser if not more temperate. MADD (Mothers Against Drunk Driving) has curbed most of the excesses of Delta-goers. And those who go off the deep end—if they have no law clerk to drive them home—have a designated driver or have someone summon a reliable taxi to ferry them through the Yuletide season unscathing and unscathed.

Richard Taylor
RICHARD TAYLOR

About The Authors

Gerald R. Toner *is a practicing defense attorney specializing in medical malpractice, product liability, and first-party insurance liability. His practice has law offices in Louisville, Ky., and New Albany, Ind. He is a graduate of Harvard where he was awarded a bachelor of arts in government, cum laude, and Vanderbilt School of Law where he was awarded a juris doctor. In addition to publishing widely in prominent law journals, his short fiction has appeared in* The Saturday Evening Post, Redbook, Ladies Home Journal, *and the* Louisville Courier-Journal. *He has authored and published four books of Christmas stories:* Lipstick Like Lindsay's and Other Christmas Stories *(Pelican, 1990),* Whittlesworth Comes to Christmas *(Pelican, 1991),* Holly Day's Café and Other Christmas Stories *(Pelican, 1996), and* The Christmas Turkeys and Other Misadventures of the Season *(Butler Books, 2010).*

Sallie Bingham *has been widely described as a teacher, writer, feminist activist and philanthropist. Bingham was born in Louisville, Ky. Sallie's family is the former owners of the* Louisville Courier-Journal. *She has worked as a book editor for* The Courier-Journal *in Louisville and has been a director of the National Book Critics Circle. She is founder of the Kentucky Foundation for Women, which published* The American Voice. *Her books include:* After Such Knowledge *(novel) Houghton Mifflin, 1960,* The Touching Hand *(short stories) Houghton Mifflin, 1967,* The Way It Is Now *(short stories) Viking Press, 1972,* Passion and Prejudice *(memoir) Alfred A. Knopf, 1989,* Small Victories *(novel) Zoland Books, 1992,* Upstate *(novel), Permanent Press, 1990,* Matron of Honor *(novel) Zoland Books, 1994,* The High Cost of Denying Rivers Their Floodplain *(poetry) privately published, 1995,* Straight Man *(novel) Zoland Books, 1996,* Transgressions *(short stories) Sarabande Books, 2002; French edition published by Gallimard, 2007,* Cory's Feast *(novel) Sunstone Press, 2005,* The Hub of the Miracle *(poetry) Sunstone Press, 2006,* Nick of Time *(novel) Sunstone Press, 2007,* Red Car *(short stories) Sarabande Books, 2008, and* If in Darkness *(poetry) Tebot Bach, 2010. Her short stories have appeared in* Atlantic Monthly, New Letters, Plainswoman, Plainsong, Greensboro Review, Negative Capability, The Connecticut Review, *and* Southwest Review, *among others, and have been anthologized in* Best American Short Stories, Forty Best Stories from Mademoiselle, Prize Stories: The O. Henry Awards, *and* The Harvard Advocate Centennial Anthology.

Richard Taylor *is a widely published poet, novelist, and historian who served as Poet Laureate of Kentucky from 1999-2001. He holds a bachelor's degree in English from the University of Kentucky (1963), a master's degree in English from the University of Louisville (1964), a juris doctor in Law from the Brandeis School of Law at the University Of Louisville (1967), and a doctorate in English from the University of Kentucky (1974). He served for many years on the faculty at Kentucky State University, where he was selected as Distinguished Professor in 1992. He served as director of Poetry in the Schools for the Kentucky Arts Commission and dean of the Kentucky Governor's Scholars Program. He has won two creative writing fellowships from the National Endowment for the Arts and an Al Smith Creative Writing Award from the Kentucky Arts Council. His publications include eight collections of poetry, two historical novels, and several books of non-fiction and history. Most notable novels are* Sue Mundy: A Novel of the Civil War *(UP of Kentucky, 2002) and* Girty *(Wind Publications, 2006), a history* Three Kentucky Tragedies *(UP of Kentucky, 1991), and poetry collections:* Earth Bones *(Gnomon Press, 2002),* Rail Splitter: Sonnets on the Life of Abraham Lincoln *(Larkspur Press, 2009), and* Rare Bird: Sonnets on the Life of John James Audubon *(Larkspur Press, 2011). Taylor is the current Kenan Visiting Writer at Transylvania University in Lexington, Ky.*

James B. Goode *biography can be seen on page 69.*

The Tenth Day

One Hundred and One Christmases

Mamaw was mean: to begin with. There is no doubt whatever about that.

Mamaw didn't like most people, and most people, if they were honest, didn't like her. Topping the list of people she didn't care for were those to whom she was related—her siblings and her parents, closely followed by her neighbors, the members of her church, her deceased husband, and, well, to be honest, most "other" people.

Mamaw was in agony and not prone to suffer in silence. Everyone knew exactly what she thought of them and in 19 of 20 cases it wasn't nice.

One of the many people Mamaw liked least was her younger sister, Mabel, if for no other reason than Mabel lived a better life. Mabel left home early, married for love, traveled the world, and by Mamaw's 50th Christmas, Mabel was a rich widow living on a massive estate in central Florida. Jealousy carved a gorge between them. And despite my mother's claim that the falling out centered on a team of white ceramic reindeer pulling Santa's sleigh, Mamaw's distain was not limited to one holy day or one festive season.

I cannot claim witness to Mamaw's first 50 Christmases, but I've heard the stories repeated enough that I believe I was actually there. Dozens of times I heard about how she'd *never* gotten what she wanted or how she *always* did without. I heard about how awful her brothers treated her. I heard about how her mother forced her to raise her brothers and sisters, and how she knew that's why they all resented, despised or hated her. "Not a one of them ever appreciated me," she said. "It's simply not fair. They all got anything and everything they ever wanted, and all I got was ... nothing."

Maybe Mamaw was compensating for her childhood. Whatever the reason, while some denominations celebrate the 12 days of Christmas, we celebrated the four days of Mamaw. The homage to Mamaw began on her birthday, December 22, and continued through a required Christmas Day visit or agonizing phone call.

•••••

It was sometime during my childhood, sometime after Mamaw's 55th Christmas, that Aunt Mabel made a set of ceramic reindeer for each of her sisters—Mamaw, Alice and Naomi. In the version of the story Mom tells, Mamaw politely told Mabel she had nowhere to put it. Mamaw changed her mind several weeks later and drove across the swamps of northern Florida to retrieve it. When she arrived at Mabel's house, on the banks of the Ocklawaha River, just across from the Ocala National Forest, Mabel told her she'd already given it away. "Well," Mamaw said indignantly. "How could you give *my* reindeer away?"

"You said you didn't want them."

"That has nothing to do with it," Mamaw said. "You were never going to give them to me in the first place. You, little missy, have disrespected me for the last time." Mamaw then turned, stormed down the driveway to her car, and drove back home, vowing never to speak to Mabel again.

"See if she gets a Christmas card from me again," I can hear Mamaw huffing at my mother. "She'll be sorry."

•••••

My first Mamaw memory, which would have been her 61st Christmas, centers on "a picture pendant tree" I have in a place of honor in my office. It once stood on the nightstand next to Mamaw's bed—first in Latonia, Kentucky, and later in New Port Richey and Clearwater, Florida, where she moved after my grandfather died, after celebrating 42 Christmases with her, leaving her to celebrate 41 more Christmases alone.

When I visited Mamaw as a child, I would sit for hours staring at that small, golden tree. There was a doctor holding a stethoscope, a couple of friendly-looking ladies whom I assumed to be my aunts, and a couple of kids. I was less than six when I first asked her to tell me about the people pictured in the little round frames.

"Mamaw," I said, "one of these days you have to tell me about the people."

"What people?" she said.

"The people in the little tree in your bedroom. My family. My great-grandfather, the doctor, my aunts, my cousins."

"Are you daft?" she said. "Boy, those are the people who came with the blasted tree."

"Huh?" I thought.

"Yep," she said. Then, after a long pause, she added, "I like the looks of them better."

•••••

Every year while watching *A Christmas Carol* on television or on stage, I would envision Mamaw as Scrooge. I would fantasize about the spirits coming to visit her. They'd reveal her past, present and future, and she'd undergo some amazing transformation, and she'd surprise us for Christmas dinner with smiles and genuine good feeling, and across town, Tiny Tim would bless us, every one.

Mamaw's permanent move to Florida came before her 64th Christmas, and for the next 20 years her visits were rare. However, even with her 800 miles away, Christmas revolved around Mamaw. We would gather in the kitchen, call her at an appointed time, and take turns bellowing into the phone so that we could be heard over the roar of her television.

"Merry Christmas, Mamaw."

"What?"

"Merry Christmas."

"What?"

"MER-EE CHRIST-MAS!"

"Oh ... all right. Merry Christmas to you, too."

Every so often someone would ask, "Don't you think Mamaw is lonely all alone down there in Florida?"

My dad would say, "Naw, I think she likes her independence."

That was the polite way of saying she didn't want the noise and confusion and clutter that was our Christmas. To her, the thought of paper and ribbons and boxes scattered across the living room was a nightmare. She liked order. Everything had its place and needed to be in it.

When she would send a gift, she had a place in your house where she knew it should go, and she would check from time to time to see if you were following her instructions.

Case in point: the brass eagle she ordered from the Home Shopping Network that she sent me for my desk. Its five-foot wingspan would look majestic on my four-foot-wide desk. "Not many people have an eagle like that one," she said. She was right.

In Mamaw's mind, she was a giving, loving person, which she sometimes was, but she could also be brutally honest. As Pastor Dave said at her graveside service, "Her initials were B-A-M, and from what I gather, she was a firecracker."

⁘⁘⁘⁘⁘

First, you have to understand that it was required that two presents from each member of the family arrive in Florida prior to her birthday. One present needed to be clearly marked "Birthday," and the other was to be marked "Christmas."

During the phone call, each of us would ask her if she liked what we had sent. "Oh, yes, it was nice," she would say. If, however, she didn't like it: "What in the world were you thinking? Are you afflicted? Are you retarded?"

That was one of the great things about Mamaw, really. You always knew exactly where you stood, and there was no—absolutely no—chance you might be left guessing.

"When did you start gaining all that weight?"

"Did you think that haircut looked good when you got it?"

⁘⁘⁘⁘⁘

But I'm not sure Mamaw actually said I was daft. It was a word she used, but I'm not sure she flung that one at me. What she did say was that I was afflicted, troubled, a mistake anyone with half a brain should have known better than to make, and flat-out retarded. Or when she spoke of me in the third-person, looking me square in the eye: "He just ain't right, Margie."

In response, we were taught that if you didn't have something nice to say, don't say anything. That meant, in practice, that when Mamaw was around, there was a large vacuum left for her to fill, and she

was more than up to the task. Dad could hold his breath under water longer than anyone else in our family. It shouldn't come as a great surprise that, when Mamaw was around, Dad could spend three weeks without saying more than a half-dozen words. In time, I learned to do the same.

One of the best slices of Mamaw lore came in 1974, Mamaw's 68th Christmas, at Standiford Field (now the Louisville International Airport). It was Christmas Eve, and Mamaw was coming to town. By chance, WAVE-3 had a camera crew wandering through the airport and magically captured my adorable, blonde, five-year-old niece, Tammie, running up to the gate to greet Mamaw. The two hugged and Mamaw, with her freshly permed, pure white hair, hoisted Tammie off her feet. Then, looking directly into the camera, Mamaw smiled the biggest smile I ever saw from her.

It was one of those great television moments. So great that it was re-aired on live broadcasts until the tape wore out. I'm not kidding: the last time we saw it air during WAVE's Christmas Eve news, Tammie had graduated from high school.

When I said that Mamaw's television smile was the biggest I'd ever seen, that was because I seldom saw Mamaw smile other than in the yearly Olan Mills photo she had taken of herself to give each of us for Christmas. In the portraits, framed in

gold, that still line the spare bedroom at Mom's luxury, adult-living community apartment, Mamaw wears an assortment of starched white pantsuits.

That's the lasting memory I have tried to keep of Mamaw, but it's hard. When I think of Mamaw, I see anger, pain and humiliation. I get a knot in my stomach and want to curl up and cry.

About once every 10 years, Mamaw would visit during Christmas. She thought her return should be celebrated, appreciated as a rare holiday treat. Phone calls were made and we, the extended family, would gather in some northern Kentucky restaurant—usually a jumbo buffet near the interstate—to exchange gifts appropriate for near strangers. We could catch up on the scantest details of the lives of our cousins and the cousins of cousins.

Listening around the table, it's easy to pick up the shouted answers. For the answers, it's simple to guess at the questions.

"No, this is my eldest son, and he's the quarterback at the University of Akron."

"No, Mamaw, we haven't lived in Indiana in years. We live in Ohio now."

"No, he's my oldest by my first husband. You remember my first husband, right?"

Relatives would come from three states and hundreds of miles away. Even

Aunt Mabel attended at least one of these gatherings as she was visiting her baby sister, my Aunt Naomi, for the holidays more than two and a half decades later, but in my memory Mamaw and Mabel sat on opposite ends of the small room at Ryan's Steakhouse.

"Mother," I can hear 75-year-old Mom pleading with her 95-year-old Mamaw. "Don't you want to wish Aunt Mabel a Merry Christmas?"

"Why in damnation would I want to do that? That's utterly ridiculous. She still hasn't apologized for giving away my blasted reindeer."

"But you said you didn't want them."

"That's of no concern to you, little missy. That's between me and her."

"But ..."

"But nothing," Mamaw barked. "I'll not hear another word."

It was easy to imagine the hand or the switch being drawn back and Mom being placed across Mamaw's knee—yes, right there in the Ryan's Steakhouse. Mom stopped talking.

Not hearing another word was one of Mamaw's skills. You could argue with her all day, and if she disagreed with what you had to say, she simply wouldn't hear it.

Why anyone showed up at the Christmas restaurant gatherings still amazes me more than a decade after the last one was held. "Why would anyone allow someone to talk to them that way?" I can remember asking Mom.

"Because they're family," Mom said. "They all know that's just the way she is."

"Right," I said. "That's why I'm surprised they'd bother."

"Stephen Matthew, she's my mother," Mom would say, using my first and middle name as a cue for me to watch my words. "I know she can be difficult, but she's my mother."

•••••

In the winter of Mamaw's 100th Christmas, I auditioned for a community theatre production of *A Christmas Carol*. The dozens of television and stage productions I had seen over the years always made me tear up when Scrooge begins to change.

While the transformation I dreamed of never came, Mamaw's memory wasn't always what it once was. Most days, every single wrong, each and every grudge was top of mind, but some days, she was actually daft-fully happy.

That same winter, Naomi visited Mamaw in the nursing home. They hadn't spoken in two decades. Naomi never really understood why Mamaw was mad at her, and that day, at least, Mamaw couldn't remember.

On Mamaw's 100th birthday, 100 free onion-fried White Castle hamburgers were delivered to the nursing home for the extended family and assorted guests. She didn't say a single nasty thing to anyone,

but we all, thanks to the sliders, had the same uneasy stomach feeling anyway.

●●●●●

Each and every time we were together as a family, I remember Mamaw giving the same speech about how we should treasure our time together because it might be the last time. "I'm not going to live forever," she'd say. The first time I heard the speech was her 55th Christmas. My brother had heard it a dozen times before that. Months shy of Mamaw's 101st Christmas, she died, catching us all off guard.

●●●●●

Today, Mamaw's little family tree still resides in my office. Atop the tree remains the thoughtful-looking doctor, holding a stethoscope. I have since learned it's cropped from an iconic Norman Rockwell print "Doctor and the Doll." Featured on the cover of *The Saturday Evening Post* on March 9, 1929, it depicts a concerned little girl holding up her doll for a white-haired doctor to examine. His expression is so thoughtful and caring that you might think he was examining the girl herself. In the second row is a young girl in a straw bonnet next to a woman wearing a flowered hat. On the left of the bottom row is a fresh-faced boy with short, well-groomed red hair. The other pendant is missing.

Like Mamaw, I have never replaced the Rockwellian images with actual family members as was intended. When I'm

honest with myself, which is a dangerous thing, I guess I like the looks of them better, too.

STEPHEN VEST

When Christmas Was Just An Orange in a Red-Wool Sock

Puh-Leezee ... !
Take me back to a time
long before
Commodore 64,
Pong,
Casio,
Xbox 360,
PlayStation3,
Nintendo DS,
Sega,
Atari,
Game Boy,
Intellivision,
Wii,
Gizmondo,
And Amiga CD32,
Before Gamepads,
Mice,
Keyboards,
Joysticks
And Haptic peripherals
Take me back to a time
Before "Rayman Origins"
And places where the Glade of Dreams
Is overrun by nefurrious Darktoons,
Where the Fairy Councils hastily invoke Rayman
To save the day...
before "Assassin's Creed: Revelations"
Touting itself as the acclaimed

Online multiplayer experience
Refined and expanded,
With more modes,
More maps,
And more characters
That allow players to test their assassin skills
Against others from around the world.
Before "Grand Theft Auto"
Posed the seminal question:
Want to be bad to the bone
Without suffering any pesky legal and moral consequences?
Where the unfriendly neighborhood crime lord
Orders you to
Steal cars,
Kidnap citizens,
Run drugs,
So you could be rewarded with more "Hos,"
And generally become a menace to society.
Where each unsavory mission completed
Is a rung in the ladder to criminal status and success.
Puh-Leeze!
Take me back to when Christmas was an orange in a red-wool sock
Topped with dark crystal horehound sticks,
Peppermint candy canes,
And sticky chocolate cream-filled candies
When the Christmas tree was free—
One of the Cedars
That had spread like green fire
Across the rocky fields

Dragged feet first into the house,
Leaving its tiny needles
In a path across the flowered linoleum floor
The aromatic tree then strung with popcorn
And hollow, colored eggs
Missing the yellow and white liquid
That had been red-faced blown
Into a chipped drinking glass
gotten as a prize from a round Crystal Oats box
When it was big multi-colored bulbs
The size of my daddy's thumb
That had been mashed in a rock fall in the mines
When it was
Raggedy shimmering silver tensile
And itchy angel hair
And strings of dull red cranberries
And a foil-covered cardboard star ...
When it was magic newspaper angels holding hands
As they fell
from the black handled pinking shears
And then followed each other in circles
Around the tree.

James B. Goode

JAMES B. GOODE

Little Bird

(a novel excerpt from The Birds of Opulence*)* December 1962

The pin oaks and the birch, the elms and the maples droop like weeping willows and the winter birds are out of sight. Each branch glistens thick with the weight of ice and talk of the weather has begun to replace the resounding thud of the baby being dropped to the floor at the Goode place. At the edge of town, just past the Jude place, a small line of bushes shroud the Clark house.

Inside, Francine Clark presses her ear to the wall and listens to the muted scratch of mice. She has spent 10 years training herself to enjoy the occasional rustlings of some creature or a twig scratching the window, a little bit of music low, even the company of the tomcat she feeds on the back porch but no people. People come plagued with disappointment. Her husband Sonny died leaving her with the overwhelming company of her own thoughts and she has nearly made the adjustment.

This town is his. So it was only love when Sonny got homesick, that had convinced her to move here. When gray-eyed Sonny Clark, who had been considered a prize among women, arrived in Opulence with Francine, citified, dark and big boned, all eyes were already peeled toward the house before they moved in. And the gaze has held steadfast.

In town they say she is an odd one—hincty and soft—all that weight, those small, useless hands and feet on such a big woman. Even the skinniest women in town, though thin as runner beans, would make two of big ole Francine Clark on any given work day.

Francine runs her hand down the wall and crosses the living room to the kitchen. The swish of her fleshy thighs and the occasional skittering inside the wall are all the sound in her world on this night.

She is making fudge, stirring black walnuts into cocoa, confectionary sugar and butter with a wooden spoon. Gospel twangs through her radio and though she doesn't particularly enjoy the country sound of the music, the words soothe her.

Pass me not oh gentle savior
Hear my humble cry
While on others Thou art calling
Do not pass me by

Her mind only on Sonny and the Lord.
Savior Savior
Hear my humble cry
While on others Thou art calling
Do not pass me by

The chocolate bubbles up and splatters against the sides of the pan. She stirs and takes in a breath deep enough to make her large breasts lift a little. She hums along with the song, her voice lifting out every time the woman singer emphasizes *Savior*.

She puts the teapot on.

At night sometimes she thinks she can feel her own heart thumping against

her chest. She rubs the coldness of the sheets where Sonny used to lay. These are the moments she believes that dying was something Sonny could have prevented if he had loved her enough.

It was just Sonny's time—her rational mind knows it, her God-fearing heart knows it, but that part of her that remains empty, the part Sonny used to fill up, still nudges her into questioning, even now, so many years later.

A spring storm. Power lines down. Her husband up before daylight. Even when day came the sky was still dark and the clouds full. She shoved a paper sack filled with a piece of chocolate cake, a fried chicken breast and two slices of light bread into his hands.

Or did I just give him one slice that morning?

She has always imagined him with one of those black metal lunch boxes like other working men but they never got around to buying it.

"And where's my sugar?" he asks before he goes.

The memory of that kiss makes her cheek warm, but she lets the burning flame underneath her skin blister.

Needs more walnuts.

She pours the remains of the kernels into the mixture.

Saw the white lightning strike.

A beautiful thing, lightning, zigging and zagging like …

Pictures of heaven in her King James Bible, her Sonny, surrounded by light like a halo.

"Struck by lightning, what were the chances of that?" one of the men who dragged Sonny into the living room had said.

"And living?" another added.

… lit up like fireworks on The Fourth.

… like Jesus.

Francine adds more confectionary sugar to the mixture.

They came in, two of them, wet and dirty, and placed Sonny on the sofa. He was groaning out like a wounded animal, his face twisted to one side like he'd had a stroke.

The smell of burnt flesh, like meat cooking. The toes of his shoes blown out by the force of the current, his clothes shambled down to his underclothes.

Those men taking little glances around like they were let in on a secret.

"I still feel it go clean through me," Sonny tells her. He holds his hands out to her, "My fingers and toes, my arms …" He had hollered out in the night in pain. Doctor came, said he'd be alright. Sonny coiled up like a baby, laid up on her breast, like she was his mother.

"I can't go back out there," he said just like a scared little boy and she had held him like that, comforted him like that, like some child. "I can't go," he said.

But he did.

He went back to working on the power

lines, came back to himself. And then just when Francine had gotten some Sonny back, not the one she had married, but some Sonny that was enough to satisfy her, all was lost again.

He died, just lay down and died, took something as simple as a headache one night and died. Aneurysm they'd said.

Fought off a lightning bolt for no reason.

She stirs the fudge again, feels a funny yank in her belly and mistakes it for grief.

Francine still looks all around this house like it doesn't quite belong to her. It seems small, somebody's fairy tale house, bright yellow with brocade high back chairs that barely hold her and an enormous sofa on swirling gold claw-shaped feet. Everything is clean. When she's not reading the Bible she's scrubbing the sink, the baseboards, the floors. The walls are covered in blooms: Gold roses in the back bedroom, lilac on the other, daisies in the living room and morning glories in the kitchen. The lilac room will become Mona's, but for all these years there has been no Mona. How could there be?

Though Francine Clark's mind has just returned from a ten year journey, she now stands in her own kitchen and is 46 years and 112 miles away. She is seven years old, in the house she grew up in on Oak Street in Louisville. A large house, enviable by any standards, that could swallow the small house she lives in now, at least

twice, even three times she suspects. It had a winding staircase that connected the two floors and shiny hardwood floors that made *clickety* sounds when someone walked on them.

Her parents descending the stairs all dressed for the Black Masons' Ball, a cocktail party or a church outing, looking like some magazine couple. Her honey-coated father, hair slicked back, shiny as rain, his navy suit fresh from the cleaners, and her mother, deep, deep, brown just enough Europe dancing in her face—the elongated nose, the pointy chin and thin lips—to give her a flair of Lena Horne. Her hair swooped up in a massive bunch of curls, and pearls dangling from her ears and the sleek line of her neck.

Francine, at the bottom of the stairs, in her nightgown, looking up at her parents, her thoughts swimming in the possibilities of her own future. But those memories are like lightning bugs—they flit, glow with hope, and then disappear.

Nervous breakdown: What a funny way to describe someone's malady. Breakdown as though she was an appliance or a car. Breakdown as if her mother could be fixed if they found the right mechanic.

Francine hums it all back to where it came from.

She is spooning the chocolate out onto the wax paper, has just licked her fingers clean, when a sharp pain hits. She paces a few steps bent over, holds onto the

counter, hoping this kink in middle of her will work itself out. The pain subsides a little and though she's startled and still feeling a little bit of pain, Francine straightens her dress and returns to the stove. She wipes the brown splatters from the stove with her dishcloth, then another pain strikes and this one takes her to her knees.

Even as she lies down to rest on the linoleum (the azure linoleum ... azure, one of her mother's favorite words), she notices a spot of dirt that she has somehow missed, a tiny spot, the size of a half dollar, shadowed by the table leg. She tries to get at it with her finger.

The teapot whistles.

Help me, Lord.

She cooks for the church members when there's occasion, a funeral, a baptismal, a baby born, but refuses to talk to them outside what is necessary. She is merely Sonny's wife. That woman. Still a stranger after all these years. She cherishes this. Folks don't bother strangers much, they just let them be.

People clamoring around isn't the kind of thing she wants. And even if she had taken full notice of the tiny twitches in her belly before this pain now, she would have never thought them to be a sign of a child. But she did think about calling on somebody before she remembered the people pouring out of the Minnie Mae Goode's house into the July heat like bugs and carrying the story with them. She wanted no part of that even if her gallbladder was bursting.

When the pain lessens again, Francine pulls herself up on all fours. *Francine Lynette Clark, get yourself in order.* She stands, though she keeps her back humped to ease this agony, and places a tea bag inside one of her china cups. She pours a bit of hot water and dowses the bag several times. *Maybe this will settle my stomach.* She leaves the fudge cooling on the counter, part of the mixture remains in the pan and is scorching. The cabinet door still hangs open on its hinges. That spot on the floor. These things haunt her from the sofa chair where she manages to ease herself, but she is glued to the chair by uneasiness. She tries to relax her muscles, rubs at the small of her back, her side. The black tea scalds her throat as it goes down. The silver wedding ring still gleams on her finger and sometimes just looking at it calms her mind.

Must be 10 people standing on top of me.
Something I ate?
Sonny Clark, your wife is vexed.

A band of pain wraps around her waist again and suddenly just like a bolt of lightning on a rainy night there is clarity. The reason comes to her.

There are women who do this all the time, women who don't know where their babies come from, ones who have menstrual cycles all through

their pregnancies, women who refuse to remember tragedy, women who were raped. Then there are women who live one life by day and another by night. It is not known which category Francine Clark is in so each resident in town puts her where they want her to go. Some will shift her to the double-life category, others will place her neatly in the box labeled, "rape," but nobody knows for sure. Some of the women will later say they noticed that she had gained more weight, but nobody had expected she was pregnant. Pregnant was the last thing they thought she could ever be. All except Minnie Mae Goode who had rightly said no more than six months ago, even during her own family's chaos "Something funny 'bout that woman, there." But even she had dismissed it as a sign of something else.

On this night, Francine misses Bible study because she isn't feeling well. Some will say she knew. Some will say she couldn't have known. That if she had, she would have called in some of Sonny's people, even though she doesn't speak to them. No woman in her right mind would willingly do this, a scared teenager maybe, but not some old widow woman. Not in these modern times. The word will make its way: Francine Clark, church-going widow woman, calls the life squad for a bellyache and pops up with a black-headed baby girl. And brought the baby home swaddled in a green blanket donated from some white church in town without a diaper or a bottle to her name. "Old as she is? Ought to know better," the women will add.

And this is how Minnie Mae Goode's tribe will reclaim a little bit of their dignity. All that other talk from six months back, about Lucy Goode Brown having a baby amid the squashes, then losing her natural mind and whooping and hollering and dropping the baby right in the middle of the floor for all to see, will be put to rest for a while. This new story fills up every dusty corner, every sly grin, every single drop of spit from every working tongue.

Mona's entrance into the world will make men's heads tilt in confusion and cause old women to gossip with their hands on their hips. Over sweet hot tea in each other's kitchens for the rest of the winter they will speculate that a woman like Francine Clark will be apt to run off or give the baby up. "She don't know nothing," they'll say. "Ain't seen an honest day's work in her life."

Three days later, when Francine brings her baby home, curtains and shades open and close all up and down the road until the strange car headed down the road toward the Clark place is out of sight. Francine steps from the car and thanks the woman, her back straight but her eyes cast slightly downward. The plump, short white woman, a social worker from the hospital, watches as Francine walks

gingerly across the icy sidewalk balancing the baby and the bag of starter items that the hospital provided—bottles and powder and such. A gust of cold wind picks up the edge of Francine's brown skirt tail and she grimaces. The hospital woman focuses in on the house. She has expected something different, something low-class and run down, especially with no father to be seen. What kind of nigger-woman is this?

"Yoo-hoo, Miss Clark," she yells from the window her breath puffs out smoke from the cold, "You need some help in?"

Snow is beginning to fall again.

"No, thank you kindly." Francine trundles as quickly as her frame will let her, up the porch step and around the tomcat weaving in and out between her legs. She fumbles for her keys with one hand, and has the door open before the hospital woman is out of the car. A flock of sparrows takes off up at the edge of the house and dusts the fresh snow to the ground.

"Mrs. Clark." The woman runs behind Francine like she's forgotten something, "Wait ... just wanted to wish ..."

Francine Clark steps across her own threshold, steadies her senses against the stench of burnt chocolate that remains in her air, and quickly closes her door. She shrugs her arms out of her coat and lays it across one of the kitchen chairs. She uncovers Mona's face, traces the roundness of her cheeks and lips with her finger. A

little bird, she is, a little bird. Francine can hear the white woman's boots crunch in the snow outside the door, the sound going away and away out into the night.

And then it hits her: Christmas.

"Oh Sweet Sonny it's Christmas," she says. "And look what I've done."

CRYSTAL WILKINSON

The Christmas Ornament

1. The Mouse and the Moon

In a grinning quarter moon's curve
a mouse sleeps under a patchwork quilt:
one of Susan's handmade scenes.

The moon's single eye, blue and wide
somehow watches both mouse
(who never wakes) and me.

The time now is Christmas
but next week and next month
the moon will remain in my window,
its pale yellow brighter in the sun,
the big-eared mouse almost blinking.

2. For Susan
The mouse never blinks
and the moon may be blind
but tonight we saw each other
for the first time in years.

You pressed the ornament into my palm,
a present between cousins
who are nearly strangers—
a decoration for all our seasons, love
suspended by a string.

Don Boes

Don Boes

Elves

For Helen Ewing

Santa couldn't come
until my fingers and arms ached
from cutting up raisins and walnuts
after carrying blackberry jam
flour, sugar, and eggs
wax paper, vanilla
and boxes of Duncan Hines
all the way home
from the A&P uptown

until Rudolph, Frosty
the Grinch, the little Drummer Boy
and the Nutcracker
danced across the screen
and the smell of tangerines
and the last jam cake
overpowered
the fresh-cut pine in the air
until Aunt Helen put on her lipstick
Avon perfume
her good wig
and stood in the screen door, waiting
for the shadowy figures
to drop off toys
and stay awhile

he couldn't come
until Mamma teased me
out of my slumber
and sent me tipping through the snow
door to door
armed with screwdrivers and extra batteries
in case somebody else's daddy
forgot

FRANK X WALKER

About The Authors

Stephen M. Vest *is the editor and founding publisher of* Kentucky Monthly, *which was the 2005 winner of the Governor's Award in the Arts. He is a graduate of the University of Louisville (1986) and holds a MFA degree in creative nonfiction from Murray State University (2011). He is the author of two collections of columns:* Briar Bits *(Vested Interest Publications, 1993) and* THAT Kind of Journalist *(McClanahan Publishing, 2008). His work has been anthologized in* OF WOODS AND WATERS: A Kentucky Outdoors Reader *(UP of Kentucky, 2005). He and his wife Kay reside in Frankfort with their children. Prior to the launch of* Kentucky Monthly, *Vest wrote and edited newspapers in Kentucky, Indiana and the Carolinas and served as news editor of* The Blood-Horse, *an international Thoroughbred racing magazine.*

Don Boes *was born in Louisville, Ky. He received his bachelor's from Centre College and his MFA in creative writing from Indiana University. Boes has been awarded three Al Smith Fellowships from the Kentucky Arts Council. He has also been a resident at the MacDowell Colony in New Hampshire and the Ragdale Foundation in Illinois. His books of poetry include:* The Eighth Continent *(Northeastern University Press, 1993), which was the winner of the Samuel French Morse Poetry Prize, and* Railroad Crossing *(Finishing Line Press, 2005). His poetry appears in two recent anthologies:* What Comes Down To Us: 25 Contemporary Kentucky Poets *(UP of Kentucky, 2009) and* Bigger Than They Appear: Very Short Poems *(Accents Publishing, 2011). He is an Associate Professor of English at Bluegrass Community and Technical College.*

James B. Goode's *biography can be seen on page 69.*

Crystal Wilkinson *has published two collections of short stories:* Blackberries, Blackberries *(Toby Press, 2009) and* Water Street *(Toby Press, 2002). She was reared by her grandparents in Indian Creek, Ky. She graduated from Eastern Kentucky University with a bachelor's and from Spalding University with a MFA in creative writing. Crystal is the 2002 recipient of the Chaffin Award for Appalachian Literature and is a member of a Lexington-based writing collective, The Affrilachian Poets. Her latest work is* Water Street. *Her work appears in numerous anthologies including:* Confronting Appalachian Stereotypes: Back Talk from an American Region *(UP of Kentucky, 1999),* Gifts From Our Grandmothers *(Crown Publishers, a Division of Random House, May 2000),* Eclipsing A Nappy New Millennium *(Purdue University, 1998),* Home and Beyond: A Half-Century of Short Stories by Kentucky Writers *(UP of Kentucky, 2001),* A Kentucky Christmas *(UP of Kentucky, 2003) and* Gumbo: Stories by Black Writers *(Doubleday, Harlem Moon Press, Fall 2002). Her work has appeared in various literary journals including:* Obsidian II: Black Literature in Review, Southern Exposure, The Briar Cliff Review, *and the* Indiana Review. *She has taught at Indiana University and Spalding University. Wilkinson is former assistant director of the Carnegie Center for Literacy and Learning. Wilkinson is visiting professor and writer-in-residence at Morehead State University.*

Frank X Walker *is best known for co-founding the group "Affrilachian Poets." Born in Danville, Ky., Walker is a graduate of the University of Kentucky, and earned a MFA in writing at Spalding University in May 2003. He is the author of four poetry collections:* When Winter Come: The Ascension of York *(UP of Kentucky, 2008);* Black Box *(Old Cove Press, 2005);* Buffalo Dance: The Journey of York *(UP of Kentucky, 2003), winner of the 35th Annual Lillian Smith Book Award; and* Affrilachia *(Old Cove Press, 2000), a Kentucky Public Librarians' Choice Award nominee. He has been widely published in magazines and anthologized in numerous collections including:* The Appalachian Journal, Limestone, Roundtable, Spirit and Flame: An Anthology of Contemporary African American Poetry, Role Call: A Generational Anthology of Social and Political Black Literature and Art, *and* A Kentucky Christmas *(UP of Kentucky, 2003). Walker is an Associate Professor in the Department of English at the University of Kentucky; and is the proud editor and publisher of* PLUCK!, the new Journal of Affrilachian Art & Culture.

The Eleventh Day

The Tides

On Christmas Day, Tom and Elly sat in the living room next to the four-foot Scotch pine Tom had bought. He insisted on a real tree, though Elly had lobbied for years now for the convenience of an artificial one. Maybe she had something, he admitted to himself, as he stared from the plane tickets in his hand over to the small tree. This one had sat in a tub on the deck for two weeks waiting for them both to be home at the same time to put it up, which had turned out to be last night— Christmas Eve, after he'd returned from working at Estelle's.

Though he had brought all the boxes of decorations down from the attic, they'd decided to just put lights and a new set of crystal stars and icicles on the tree. Both of them were too tired to get into the musty boxes of ornaments, some of which dated back to their childhoods. To Tom those boxes represented a merging of their lives, and it was hard for him to give up at least taking them out to look at them. In her excitement at the trip she'd planned, Elly vowed that this year she'd repack all the decorations in plastic boxes as soon as they returned from Florida, but Tom was fairly certain he'd end up quietly putting these same containers away again after the new year. Besides, some of them were still wrapped in softened strips of old newspaper that dated to the fifties — pages his mother had torn from the local paper to protect the ragtag assortment of glass figures and homemade paper chains. The smell of the worn paper, the old ads brought back a lost world. Something his wife seemed unable to appreciate.

Elly lounged now on the creme-colored rug. She wore the red satin pajamas he'd given her last year at Christmas. Her skin glowed in the light from the tree and the fire in the fireplace. She looked nearly as young as when they'd met. Leaner, though. Elly had had a young girl's fragile softness about her back then. Now muscles defined her neck, and her face had an angular, hungry look. *When had this happened? After she'd lost the third baby in '85*, he thought. When she'd thrown herself into aerobics and weight-lifting.

"What are you thinking?" she said, grinning up at him.

"Nothing. I just wondered how you liked your gifts. Did I get the right kind?"

She'd opened hers first—a new watch that counted calories and heart rate as well as time. Its black bulk incongruous on the slim wrist that peeked from the deep red silk of her sleeve. The pedometer she'd also requested lay in its opened box on the floor.

"Yes," she said, "exactly right. But I already told you I liked them." She flexed her right foot back and forth, back and forth. "You're the one who hasn't said anything about your gift." She reached out with her foot and gave a soft poke to his calf.

Tom sat in the side chair in front of the fire he'd laid and lit in the hearth. At Elly's words, he gave his attention to the packet of tickets, reservations, and brochures for The Tides, a golf resort in Florida. He didn't play golf, though Elly had taken it up a couple of years ago. She'd bought the tickets, made all the plans. A New Year's trip for the two of them. Except it wasn't really a getaway, more like a command appearance.

Brent Hardin, owner of the chain of gyms where she worked, wanted to reward some of his highest producing trainers, and Elly had brought in more clients than anyone. This was a real chance for her to consolidate her position there; she'd beamed when he'd opened the package, going through a sequence of nested boxes to finally discover the envelope at their heart. Elly looked as if she'd burst as he'd worked through the layers. The gym was her future, she said. This trip meant she was on her way.

All her aerobics friends would be there. He'd really like them, she'd added, if he'd only give them a chance. Brent owned a winter home in Destin Beach. She and Tom and the other guests would stay in condos, built around three golf courses.

A piece of red oak gave a loud pop, sending a shower of sparks against the fire screen. Tom startled and leaned toward the fire to make sure the log had not dislodged itself.

"Tommy." Elly stood next to him now. She pushed herself onto his lap and put her arms around his neck, looking into his face. "Maybe I shouldn't have surprised you," she said, running her index finger across his forehead. He realized he was frowning. "You can go, can't you? I mean, you will?"

Tom's frown tightened under her touch. Then he sighed and pulled her to him, partly so he didn't have to look into her eyes.

"Of course, Elly," he said. A half-dozen feelings pressed through him. "Sure, we'll go," he said. "It's important to you, and that makes it important to me," he added, hoping his voice held an enthusiasm he didn't feel.

"Ummmm ..." She snuggled deeper into his lap. He felt the point of her elbow, then the hard round of her hip as she scooted herself into him. She twisted her head into the crook of his neck, nibbling at the skin there in an old gesture of desire. "You'll see," she murmured into his skin. "You'll have a good rest ... and we'll have time together."

He gathered her in more closely and kissed the top of her head, then her eyebrows and lashes, finally her mouth, waiting for his body to respond.

In a little while he sat her up away from him. "I guess I've just been working too hard lately. I'm sorry, Elly. Maybe later."

She got up and looked down at him.

"It's okay, Tommy." She gathered their coffee cups. "I'll start some brunch. You sure you're all right?"

"Just getting old, I guess," he said and turned to look into the fire. "I'll be in to cut up the fruit for the salad," he added.

The room opened out with her absence and settled into a stillness punctuated by the hiss and snap of burning wood. The patterns in the flames held him. He had no desire to go to Florida. He didn't even like Florida. But if Brent had invited them then, hey, who was he to object?

He remembered meeting Brent at a party once. The guy was okay. A little too perfectly built, maybe. "Body proud," Tom's grandmother would have called it, the way the guy carried himself around like a prize. But Elly liked Brent, there was no doubt about that— "admired him," she said. It was "Brent says this" and "Brent says that" half the time when they talked anymore. How impressed she was with the success of Brent's gym, how Brent "had seen the fitness wave coming and caught it as it crested"— that was the way Elly had put it.

Sometimes Tom wondered why Elly never mentioned his own— their own— success. Wasn't Reed's Restoration their success? Sure, there were no "bricks and mortar" to it, no fancy building with a shiny reception area. There were drawings rolled and set in the cubbies he'd built in his study. Landscape designs and sketches of remodeling work he'd been hired to do. There was a Rolodex beginning to bulge with client's numbers. There was the separate phone line for his business and the separate business checking account. More money in the bank and a growing array of tools neatly stored in the workshop out back and on his truck. All invisible to her, he thought.

Separate checking accounts. That was part of the reason Elly didn't notice their changed income. They'd had separate accounts for years now— since that big fight five years ago. Elly's habit of overdrawing their account and their trouble sharing a checkbook had caused him to blow up at her. One of their few really terrible fights, and from it, he remembered now, a sweet time of making up and their last all-out try at getting pregnant.

Elly had turned 30 during that time, and they'd gone to enough doctors to finally convince them that they wouldn't be having any children together, even if the tests weren't all that conclusive. Their relationship hadn't seemed to change that much at the time, but it had, and the change was lasting. And the separate accounts— they'd lasted, too.

"Tommy, are you going to cut up the fruit?"

"Yeah. Sure. Be right there."

Their tickets were for tomorrow. Elly had already started packing a bag for him.

Guess he'd have to find some books to take along. He couldn't get interested in golf, though Elly had tried to get him to. He just hadn't had the time for it. He picked up the torn wrapping paper and ribbon from their gifts and threw them on the fire, watching the colors released as the dyes burned. As he stared at the flames lapping the paper, he wondered if he'd be able to reach Estelle before they left.

•••••

On their last night in Florida, Tom and Elly were late to Brent's New Year's party. Elly had slept in that morning since there wasn't a golf outing that day. Tom got up early to walk along the ocean one last time, to feel the sun and salt mist on his arms.

He got back to the condo just before lunch. Elly paced in the living room.

"Where've you been?"

"I took a walk, Sweetie. What's up?" Relaxed from his morning, Tom kept his voice light.

"Why didn't you wake me up?" she asked.

"I didn't know you wanted to go," he said. He ran himself a glass of water from the tap.

"I don't know how you drink the tap water here," she said. "It tastes salty to me. Besides, it's full of all kinds of junk. There's bottled water in the fridge." She got herself a bottle. "And it's cold, too."

"Sink water is fine for me," Tom said.

"We haven't spent any time together during the day," she went on. "You could have stayed in this morning to be with me."

Tom refrained from pointing out that she'd been the one playing golf all day every day, that he'd been the one left to his own devices. Instead, he pulled her into a hug and asked where she wanted to go.

"I want to see what they have in the shops here," she said, snuggling her head into his chest. He was surprised at how tiny she felt. His body responded to the fit of her against him.

"Why, sure. Let's shop, then."

"You really don't mind?" she said, pulling away. She looked into his eyes and his body stirred again.

"Nope," he said.

A half hour later, they walked through shops filled with resort wear. Elly took her time looking through things. He idly followed her or looked at racks of shirts with parrots and palm trees printed on green or yellow backgrounds. By the third shop, his attention wandered, and he tried to imagine what Estelle was doing. The whole trip he'd felt guilty that he hadn't been able to reach her before they'd left— or since they'd arrived. He'd tried a couple of times at the pay phone at the service station down the way, straining through the roar of traffic for her voice on the line. But the phone had rung on and on. He hadn't talked with her since the last time he'd stopped by. God! She must think the

worst of him.

"Tommy! I said what do you think of this one?" Elly held up a filmy white night gown, looking at him provocatively.

"Great," he said, automatically.

"Well, thanks for your enthusiasm." Elly's face tightened. She shoved the gown back onto the rack.

"I'm just sleepy," Tom said. He'd better pay attention. He moved close to her and put his hand on her waist, leaning his head in to brush a kiss across her hair. "Guess I got up too early."

She jerked away from his touch. He straightened and stuffed his hand into his pocket, his jaw tense. Their love-making this trip had been this same kind of out-of-synch approach and retreat. They'd laughed it off, blamed it on aging, even talked a bit about how much their individual lives had diverged lately. They'd promised each other to try harder. The whole thing exhausted him.

"I think I'll go on back to the condo," he said in a minute. "I need a nap before tonight. I'll leave you the car."

"Fine," she said.

He walked the half mile along the road, sweating in the heat that rose from the asphalt. The wash of hot air from cars speeding down the strip kept him off balance. They were on vacation, for God's sake. Couldn't they slow down a little? At the service station near the turnoff to the resort, he went into the phone booth.

He checked to be sure Elly wasn't driving by before he closed the door and put his quarter in the slot.

His stomach did a small flip. His face and hands tingled with anticipation and pleasurable fear as the phone rang on Estelle's end. He must be crazy. He nearly hung up, but his heart lifted in anticipation at the mechanical buzz of each ring. He stayed on long enough to be sure that Estelle was out again. Had something happened to her? How would he even be able to find out?

• • • • •

That evening, late, tense from the rush to get there, they walked across the lawn toward Brent's place. Elly tugged at his hand, all smiles now that they'd arrived. She fairly skipped toward the knot of people clustered on the patio.

"Hey, Rachel! How's it going, Hans?" Elly had called out. "You okay, Lesley?" Tom recognized most of them by now. He nodded and smiled behind her. She made a bee-line for Brent, cool and composed as a magazine ad in his circle of guests. Tom felt how his tropical shirt stuck to his sweating back. Wet patches surely darkened the parrot heads under each of his arms. He must look like a clown.

"Hello, Brent," he said. His voice sounded stern, almost fatherly. Shit. Next to Brent he felt huge, his arms too long, his barrel chest just that — a barrel.

"Tom." Brent's firm handshake

matched the level look he gave Tom. He was "personable, but restrained," Elly's praise echoed in Tom's head. "Nice of you to make it down for the trip. Hope you've found enough to keep you busy."

"Thanks. I did a couple of fishing charters ...," Tom began.

"Elly!" Brent had turned away, his voice rising like a cheer as he pulled her into a quick, hard hug. "What can I get for you guys? Wheat grass? Sparkling water?"

"Wheat grass," Elly sang back.

"Tom?"

"Got any beer around here?"

Brent hesitated just a fraction. "Sure. I'll go get you one."

"Oh, I'm sure I can find it. In the kitchen?" Tom said. He thought of the cool silence inside the house, away from Brent and all the people whose eyes he imagined were glued to him right now.

"Yeah. Middle shelf in the fridge."

Tom walked off without a glance around. The French doors closed behind him with a click, and the dim air inside cocooned him. He looked around the expansive room. Decorator done, everything black, white, or tan. The whole place, inside and out, could have come straight from the pages of a slick magazine.

The kitchen opened off the large, airy great room. The refrigerator one of those room-sized Sub-Zero models some of Tom's clients asked for.

Imported beer in hand, Tom took a look around. The kitchen was huge— sleek stone countertops. Elly would love it. He wondered if she'd already seen it. He ran his hand along the face of the minimalist cabinetry and pictured their kitchen at home—raised panel oak cabinets, 15-year-old appliances, ceramic tile countertops he'd been so proud of when he installed them.

He went back into the great room and sat down on the couch, afraid to lean back in case his shirt was still wet. The beer was cold and better than he could afford. He downed it quickly and went for another one. No sense staying in here—the place made him tense. His presence there felt like a spill on the upholstery or a spot on the rug. He left by way of the mud room.

Outside, he found Elly and draped his free arm over her shoulder. "Hey," he said, nodding to the group clustered around her. Elly shot a pained look at his beer and turned back to her conversation.

"Interval is the real thing. It's the future," an incredibly fit blonde was saying, punching her pita hors d'oeuvre in the air for emphasis.

"Well, yes," Elly agreed, her forehead wrinkling, "but aerobics—now that's essential or all the rest is wasted."

"No. No," a beefy, russet-haired man cut in, "you can't say that. It isn't that simple."

Tom lifted his head to stare above the

group. He half-listened as they went on. At the foot of the yard, he saw a line of small trees, the telltale meander of a creek, he thought. The sky was cottony, filling up with humidity. Hot for New Year's Eve.

"Excuse me, folks," he said overtop of the talk that went on non-stop around him. He disengaged from Elly and walked off toward the trees.

He found the creek that was, indeed, there and picked one of the larger trees to sit against. Looked like this was a man-made waterway, he thought, for all its meander. Basically a dry creek, meant to catch run-off from the yards and golf course, though it might also carry the flow of an old waterway displaced by construction. The trees were neatly positioned. Someone had taken pains to make the whole thing look natural. He breathed in the smell of hot grass and tree bark, a pleasant mix of sharp scents. He lowered himself to the grass and leaned back.

He sipped his beer and wondered what Estelle was doing. He imagined her at work, moving through the grocery aisles with that sway that felt languid to the eye, even as she darted from crisis to crisis on the floor. He imagined her coming home, worn out, taking off her uniform, rubbing her feet, fixing a cup of tea. He let himself sink into the pleasant tension of his thoughts.

When he'd finished his beer, he simply sat for a while. It felt good to unwind. It took too much effort to placate Elly and make conversation with her new friends. He'd found nothing in common with them during this stay. And, though he and Elly had begun to find an ease together in evenings of eating out and walking the beach, their love-making had left him feeling she was not there. Or maybe he was the one absent. She seemed preoccupied, and he kept wondering what it would feel like to make love to Estelle. He looked up through the leaves into flashes of sunlight.

He must have dozed, because the next thing he noticed the light had changed, grown furred and dimmer. He stretched and got up. When he reached the patio, it was nearly empty. The two couples who stood there gave him an odd look. People must have moved indoors, he thought.

He walked around the side of the house and eased in through the mud room door, hating to make an entrance if the great room were crowded. Better to just slip back in.

Elly's voice caught his ear. "... just so absent," she was saying. "I don't know where he is, even when he's in the room."

Tom stopped in the kitchen door. Brent leaned over Elly protectively. Had she been crying?

"What's going on?" Tom said.

Brent pulled Elly closer against his chest, his hand shielding her face, touching her hair.

"What's going on?" Tom stepped into the kitchen, swinging his head back and forth. The ring of guests pulled back a little and held their glasses closer. His mouth felt like cotton, his chest burned. "Is this why you stay away all day?" he turned to his wife, his breathing harsh. "Elly. Is this what you want? This muscle-bound prick?"

"Tommy! Stop it right now," she said, stepping toward him and pushing Brent away. She shot her boss a look of concern. Brent had a slight smile on his face.

"Someone tell me what is going on," Tom said, his fists clenched at his sides. No one moved. He peered around the room, his face hot, sweat making its way down his temples.

Elly burst into tears and turned her back on him to pull Brent to her in a brief hug. She moved as if blinded, snatching her purse from the pile on the couch, feeling her way to the door.

Tom watched her leave. Brent kept his smile, as if the whole thing were a joke. Tom walked straight up to him and pulled his fist as if to throw a punch. He clamped his jaw tight against the urge to say something that would erase that look. A woman behind him whispered, "Should we call the police?"

Tom swung his rage toward her. "What do you all think I am?" he said. He dropped his fighter's stance, his shoulders slumping. He wiped the back of his hand

across his mouth, his eyes on the floor. In a moment he walked out.

Elly stood rigid by the car. He unlocked the doors.

They rode back to the condo in silence, the only noise Elly's uneven breath, her swallowed sobs. She stared out her window, her body stiff. Tom made no move to touch her or to talk.

Elly stalked into the front door of the condo and threw her purse onto the couch. She faced him then. He could feel all the force of her he'd always taken lightly. *His little Elly— the wildcat.* Only this time her anger was aimed at him.

"He's gay!" she exploded. "What can you be thinking, Tom, to talk to him like that?" She stood balanced on the balls of her feet, like a boxer. "He was not coming on to me," she said, her voice cold. "I couldn't find you. I was worried—about you. He was simply listening to me— something you never do."

"I never do?" Tom said. His head swam, he couldn't get his feet under him, as if he were trying to stay upright in heavy waves. He gathered himself and shot back, "Since when do you listen to me or care about anything I have to say?" *Gay? Brent?* He tried to process this.

"You've made a fool of me— maybe even jeopardized my position with the gym," she said. "I can't believe you. If you ever even half listened to me, you'd have realized Brent is gay."

"How?" he said. "How am I supposed to know all these people who seem to be your life now?"

The thoughts and feelings of the past weeks tumbled out. They shouted until he walked away, ending up on the back deck with yet another beer, Elly in the bedroom on the phone with her friend, Rachel—at least she was talking to Rachel when Tom crept up to their door. On the deck, alone again with a beer he didn't want, he'd replayed his entrance at Brent's. Damn. He'd looked ridiculous. Now he stood outside their room, trying to think how to apologize. The hard edge to Elly's voice turned him away. He went down the steps and picked up the car keys.

The wash of waves in the distance sounded like high tide. A surge ready to withdraw. He got into their rental car and drove toward the lights of the highway.

He couldn't bring Estelle to mind, couldn't get a clear sense of her in the muddle of his shame and anger at the events of the night. Over the weeks he'd worked on her old house, it had begun to feel like home to him. Maybe it was the house he'd fallen in love with. He'd come to dread the small empty rooms of his and Elly's place. The quiet. How their schedules kept them from seeing each other. Something had to change.

Nothing was open. No diner or coffee shop. He stopped at the service station where he'd tried to get Estelle earlier that day. The lighted phone booth glowed yellow through its dirty glass. He got his coffee and drove to a parking lot on the beach. The ocean rose and fell like breath— almost regular. Its pulse steadied him. His own breath settled.

Christmas seemed far from this warm night. At home the tree would have dried in its tub in the garage. The ornament boxes and strings of light would be where they'd left them. A new year had begun, and he'd hadn't cleaned up from the old one. Why hadn't he just told Elly he didn't want to come? Would she have come alone? He sipped the coffee as it cooled. The ocean pulled at the sand as the tide receded.

When he got back to the condo, the door to their room was closed. He sat on the deck for a while longer looking at the sky, then went in and tried the knob.

"Is that you, Tommy?"

"Yes. I'm here." He couldn't see anything clearly, but he moved toward her voice.

Leatha Kendrick

Nativity Set

Every Christmas season, my mother wrested a splintery, sepia-toned nativity scene from the bottom of a cardboard box and lovingly assembled it on the counter or the top of the TV, along with whatever wispy vestiges of hay had survived another year of holiday hustle and post-holiday hibernation.

The nativity scene was made of some extremely fragile material—certainly not ceramic, and not plastic. Something that flaked off if you touched it wrong or dropped it. Maybe it was some sort of cheap plaster. Joseph and at least one of the camels bore deep scar tissue down the sides where they had been Elmered back together. They were slightly shinier along those scars, where the glue had dried.

But Mom clung to that nativity scene with a doubting priest's desperate fanaticism, afraid that turning loose of it meant turning loose of something it represented—or more accurately, something she wanted it to represent, along with all the other flashy, sparkly Christmas trinkets and ornaments she kept in boxes stacked neatly in the back left corner of the tiny little storage shed clinging to the side of our house like benign growth. Strands of tinsel hung from the boxes like limp spaghetti, shrugging at you with off-season ennui when you went in to retrieve a box of junk in the middle of summer.

Sometime around Thanksgiving, the boxes always made a conspicuous appearance in the living room, stacked again, but this time with the casual skew that indicated progress, movement: Here we are again, a break in the routine. A change in the atmosphere around you, the one that you don't even notice most of the time because it's so goddamned boring and NORMAL. A change in the feel of everything, from the crisp, dry weather to TV and radio ads. I have always loved breaks in routine above almost all else, even when the result is pain and change. It's a strange addiction, really: I like to shoot anti-immanence straight into my veins. Never mind stability and predictability. Those are the scary things. *What if everything stays this way forever?* is the equivalent of that line at the end of the ghost story, the one that never changes, no matter how much you alter the story itself: *I want my golden aaaaarm!* or *The call was coming from inside the house!*

My nightmare scenario as a child always culminated in the same horrifying climax: *What if life is ALWAYS like this?*

●●●●●

It's not that my childhood was absolutely horrible. It was pretty damned dysfunctional in that house, yes, but I also have my share of good memories. And I was bored sometimes. No one living a nightmare finds himself bored, I would imagine.

No, for me the dreaded scenario was

for ANYTHING to last forever. I think the instability I experienced early on (which I didn't even know to label "instability") became such the norm for me that I came to relate to it as a comfort. If things don't change abruptly every once in a while, I feel as if something is amiss. I get nervous.

The Christmas of my youth was a *petit mal* encapsulation of the change I craved, a temporary but concentrated shot of upheaval. I knew that after the gaudy, groping season finally fizzled, things would change again, this time back to "normal." But I could always count on Christmas coming back next year, no matter what else was going on around me, no matter how poor we were, and this was a comfort.

It is also a contradiction, of course: To value the predictability of pre-packaged change is to not really value change at all. But I don't really care to apologize for the inconsistency. In my mind at least, those strangely derived feelings of comfort and joy explain why I love Christmas to this day, in spite of the fact that most intellectuals I know tend to smirk at it, and in spite of the fact that the Christmases of my youth ended almost without exception in chaos, frustration and tears.

•••••

Take this as Exhibit A: It's the 1983 Christmas season. I am home from boarding school on winter break (everyone still calls it Christmas Break), and the Diana Lee Christmas Express is in full chug. The crumbling nativity set is set. The too-symmetrical artificial tree is in its place where the hanging wicker pod-chair usually goes. A few packages wrapped in primary colors lie optimistically under the tree (the fire department didn't give us toys this year, so things must be a little better for Mom). I haven't believed in Santa for a long time (I don't think I ever really did, although I can't remember for sure), but the whole place reeks of him, and this makes me happy. A cardboard cutout of him hangs from the wall. It is in segments held together with metal clasps, so that one can manipulate Santa's arms and legs, make him wave or dance a jig. This has been part of the Christmas menagerie for a few years, so it is a bit frayed and faded; but I am young and still in deep love with the whole happy idea of the fat elf, so I soak up every commercial and song and cheesy Claymation special about him and his whole milieu like mothermilk. I love that segmented, aging Santa.

And then I turn from the happy Santa, and there is my brother Todd in the narrow hallway, kneeling in front of the bathroom door, straining to see under it. My mother is in the bathroom. She is showering, but the water is no longer running, which means she is out, drying off or putting on lipstick or whatever mothers do in bathrooms.

"Todd!" I stage whisper. This screws up everything, I think, ashamed immediately for thinking the f-word. But even the shame retreats to the back of my mind as I try to process what is happening. "What are you doing?"

"Shut up, Eric."

I stand at the entrance to the small hallway and

consider what to do next. My palms are damp, and I am holding my breath. If I tell Mom, what will happen? The colorful tree and the dancing Santa will be no match for the ensuing ISSUES. ISSUES always trump everything else.

Also, it is my duty to keep the house happy at any cost. I know even then that this isn't as noble as it sounds. It is the beginning of a long life of enabling and keeping the peace not just for the sake of peace (although, yes, for that reason too), but for the sake of everyone just getting along without hurting each other. Everyone must always get along.

I breathe again. I go sit across from the tree on the brown and beige couch and watch TV. Clay Rudolph is about to prove that he is worth something of American value by being functional and productive. This seems a much easier to follow logical progression than the disturbingly mythological vision of your brother dropping to his knees to gain a better vantage point from which to see your progenetrix nude, so I invest myself in the show, feeling appropriately warm as Rudolph is embraced by his jumpy, stop-motion peers, having proved his usefulness.

·····

At the heart of this essay is an attempt to better understand my love for Christmas. Any time we seek to understand our choices and tendencies, we run the risk of having a major existential breakthrough. It is a risk I am willing to take.

Plus, my love for it really makes absolutely no sense, in spite of my fancy explanations about change and stability.

By all accounts, I should hate Christmas, mainly thanks to my brother. Sure, we had no money, my parents were divorced, and my mother suffered from often-paralyzing anxiety and depression. All of those things are sad and tragic, but popular culture is full of visions of poor, sad families gathered around the hearth on Christmas Eve gifting each other oranges and handcrafted wooden trinkets, saying prayers of thanks for the birth of the Christ child. A stiff upper lip in the face of want and disease is an archetype we understand. But we tend to turn our faces away in embarrassment and shame when to tragedy is added perversion and destructiveness. We don't know what to do with it, and the discomfort is almost unbearable.

And *perversion* and *destructiveness* have been apt descriptors for my brother for as long as I can remember, especially around Christmas, which seemed to bring out some kind of Extra Special Evil in him. Things like Peeping-Tomming my mother were, as unbelievable as it may sound, typical behavior in our house on a week-to-week basis, but we never quite knew what to expect around Christmas.

It's not that his behavior that Christmas Break was typical in terms of *severity* of offense, at least not at that point. Years were still ahead that would see Todd and Mom in a hypnotic death roll of dysfunction year-round, culminating

in more and more surreal Christmases each year, my mother's yuletide dreams sustaining fracture after fracture, each one harder and harder to Elmer back together.

But not yet. In my memory, that disturbing Christmas break was the beginning of new things for Todd, new realizations of boundaries to be ignored or annihilated. I admit I was surprised to see him kneeling in front of that door, but the surprise dissipated almost immediately, replaced by cold comprehension. My heart tightened like a cold scrotum: *Here we go*, I thought beneath my shock and outrage. I did not at that time know the psychological term *escalation*, but I recognized the idea immediately when I encountered it my freshman year of college. *Todd*, I remember thinking. *Todd is escalation.*

In the wake of the hallway incident, I began to recall other recent bellwethers of just how much Todd's psychosis had advanced, and this in turn started me worrying about my mother and my sister living there with him while I was away at school (he had been expelled twice for a host of violations, including performing esoteric, allegedly Satanic rituals in a barn off campus with his roommate and sliding his hand down his girlfriend's pants during class on more than one occasion). His contempt for normalcy and convention had been apparent since he could speak, but now he was discovering the joy of acting on that contempt.

Don't get me wrong: I am no lover of the "normal." I pay no attention to fashion rules or trends; I don't brush my hair; I have patchy, oddly proportioned facial hair that any normal person would shave right off; I love to play the role of the gadfly. I have no loyalty to "normal."

But abnormal or not, I apparently somehow dodged an arrow that struck Todd somewhere in his id and lodged there quivering for the entire world to see, forming an existential stoma that would eventually manifest itself in criminal behavior.

And lest I come off as a self-aggrandizer shaking his head in pity at the *Bad Seed*, let me remind you that I have already confessed to sitting my ass on a couch and watching heartwarming Christmas specials rather than telling my mother she was being victimized. I don't even remember it being a hard decision. I just knew I wanted zero conflict going down in that house, and I knew telling Mom her son was trying to see her naked would bring Christmas to an absolute stand-still.

This was cowardly at best and downright immoral at worst. The constant avoidance of conflict, the bailiwick of my childhood, is a psychosis of its own. But whether through a blind domino chain of evolution which made my behavior acceptable in society and his not, or the unfathomable and capricious doling

out of fate and grace by some god, my strangeness has yet to land me in the social valley of death, a wilderness Todd has wandered most of his life.

•••••

One thing I can say for Todd is that he was never subtle about how he felt, and he was especially mouthy about Christmas. He had always made it clear that it was a stupid tradition, but he had begrudgingly participated because he had to. But he had of late apparently become aware of just how strong the will is of someone who simply does not want to do something, so over the last two or so Christmases, the atmosphere had become more and more poisonous, Todd inveighing against the holiday like a medical examiner explaining evidence to a jury. If these traditions were silly and not grounded in anything purely logical, he said, we should all quit being babies and just abandon them.

The best way to deal with such a person is to just dismiss him from the proceedings and forget him for a while. Why make someone participate in something they find so patently ridiculous? Everyone would be much happier with a mutual segregation of activities. Instead of insisting that he sing along (not only be present, but actually *sing*), my mother would have saved herself—all of us—a great deal of turmoil if she had just rolled her eyes and told Todd to go to his room if he didn't like it. But she seemed incapable

of this, just as she seemed incapable of not being drawn into his philosophical diatribes, which were actually quite insightful and sometimes even brilliant. There had always existed between them an animosity, a clash pulsating up from roots that could not be accounted for by his short decade-and-a-half of life, a clash that seemed as much a part of their collective chemistry as their identical chins and the blank, uncomfortable facial expressions they both put on in photographs.

Mom operated from a place of parental entitlement—she felt that as her child, Todd should be quiet when she said be quiet and do what she told him to do. Yet she was unwilling to enforce compliance the way her father did, at the bayonet-like tip of violence and humiliation. Polio had foreshortened his right leg and rendered it useless, but he had found many uses for his crutches beyond bearing his weight. We had often heard stories of crutch-jabs in the ribs, whacks across the legs and buttocks, and threats.

Mother refused to treat her children in such a way—she was, in fact, determined at the cost even of death to not treat us in such a way. This was courageous and heroic and is no small thing, as were her decisions to refuse public assistance and take a job working third shift with a bunch of aggressive men at a peanut butter factory to support three children.

But since she knew no other way

to effectively discipline, she paid for nonviolent parenting with her peace and ours. Like many single mothers, she had to invent parenting strategy on the fly, and the only thing she seemed to be able to come up with was *Put Your Foot Down And Be A Hardliner*. Perhaps she thought her father's demanding nature minus his abusiveness would tally up to a healthy sum of discipline. (She certainly couldn't look to her own mother as a parenting model: She had remained silent throughout the abuse and died at an early age.) But when one takes a hard-line approach, once must link the crossing of that hard line with some sort of believable and motivating consequence. Mom was transparently inconsistent in following up her threats. All of us knew we could get away with a lot of things, because Mom's words were louder than her actions.

The patent untruth of her threats and ultimatums embarrassed me, but they incited Todd. He responded with his own version of the same fundamentalism, as stubborn as any backwoods revivalist preacher; stubborn for the sake of stubbornness to the point of violating Mom's most crucial edicts rather than give in to demands he found unreasonable, or even to do things he didn't want to do. I remember hour-long shouting matches that need never have happened, except that neither of them was willing to let the other have the last word. In Todd it was

born of hatred; in Mom, of love. But the consequences are equally tragic.

The rare times when Mom's attempts at discipline were effective were usually when she punished us on a whim, before she had time to talk herself out of it. But these incidents usually occurred in the heat of the moment, tainted by anger, which is the primary ingredient for creating resentful children. It was certainly not a recipe for a peaceful home.

This is especially true when you have a child like Todd, who can sense when something is important to you and thus calibrate their contempt more specifically. Todd intuited that she really, really wanted Christmas to be special, a desire that proved to be a bloody *Sacré-Cœur* on her sleeve, an apt target for Todd's venomous slings and arrows.

•••••

The sing-along around the tree on Christmas Eve is an essential part of what Mom wants Christmas to be. She has made chocolate chip cookies, the tree stutter-glows with blinking lights, and she is playing her guitar. Her sweet, sentimental, untrained voice unfurls guilelessly. From the Christmas boxes she has produced a creased spiral notebook full of traditional Christmas numbers like "Silver Bells," "Away in a Manger," "It Came Upon a Midnight Clear" and "Frosty the Snowman." My little sister Angela and I love Frosty because we get to yell "Stop!" Mom plays them all in variations of the same plodding, hypnotizing strum pattern, and she demands that everyone sing along.

"Everyone" means Todd; we all know this. Angela and I love anything even slightly fun, so we always voluntarily sing as loudly as we can, as we are singing to "Frosty" right now. Maybe Mom and I will even sing in harmony on some of the songs. There are no good harmonies in "Frosty the Snowman," but "O Come! All Ye Faithful" is in that book, I know, and so is "Have Yourself a Merry Little Christmas," both of which have interesting tenor parts. I want Mom to play those songs, to sing and look into my eyes, but I am also, as usual, a little uncomfortable singing with my mother. As soon as I really get into it, really feel it, she looks right at me with such earnestness I have to look away. This seems to violate some rule I don't understand, and I know when it happens I will withdraw a little and hope she doesn't notice. I think this started a few years back when she took us to see Coal Miner's Daughter. She can't seem to shake the idea that she could be just like Loretta Lynn, if she only had a man to market her like Doolittle marketed Loretta—and if we children would just sit still and listen, like Loretta's did. This embarrasses me for reasons which are as yet mysterious to me.

But uncomfortable as I am, I sing along. For one thing, it makes Mom happy, and other than cleaning the house while she's sleeping off third shift, I don't get a lot of opportunities to do that. Her problems are just too big for a 12-year-old to fix, I know that. But I can sing along and make her smile and imitate Loretta. So I will.

But I also love it. I always have, and I know I always will, because it's part of Christmas. Angela loves Christmas too, and not only because she is almost guaranteed to find a Cabbage Patch doll under the tree tomorrow. For weeks, she and I have become more and more excited, hugging each other gleefully every time Christmas is mentioned. We even have a certain way of saying "Santa Claus" that makes us collapse into giggle fits. We sort of growl it from the back of our throats, but not in a mean way, keeping our teeth together and moving the lips only. We have been counting down the days and watching Santa Claus read kids' letters on TV on Saturday afternoons. All of this is swirling around our heads that night as we glance at each other during the carols, eyes wide at the expressive moments, hands clapping when it feels good, happy as idiots while my brother crosses his arms and withdraws further and further from all of us.

Angela notices his withdrawal too, and our looks at each other change from excitement to concern. Ever the optimist, I close my eyes and say a prayer that this year will be different. I don't want to think of anything except happy Christmas times.

But it is not meant to be. Todd huffs so loudly the music flutters off Mom's stand. I see her rounded cursive script somersault and seesaw to the carpet, along with the evening's fun.

"I don't know why we have to sing the same stupid songs every year," Todd says. He shoves a present further under the tree with his foot. "Why doesn't somebody write some new songs?"

Turns out people are always writing new songs, but we have no way of knowing this. Also, I think he is kind of right. Some of these songs are just terrible, if you just look at them as songs, apart from Christmas. "The Little Drummer Boy"? Who thinks a drum solo is a good gift for an infant? The

kid already has to put up with farting livestock and some stranger who brought him burial perfume. And "Silent Night"? What a strange, caterwauling pitch you have to climb to on the word "virgin," which of course embarrasses me.

Sure, I know the songs stink musically and lyrically, but so what? Why can't we all just put aside art and style and enjoy something different? Normally that time of night we would have been lying around bored, watching something on prime-time TV and complaining about the lack of snack food in the house. So why not enjoy the cookies and the Something Different?

But Todd seems incapable of that.

"Hush, Todd, if you're not going to sing," Mom says, trying to pretend that his lack of participation doesn't faze her. But none of us are buying it. We all know it won't work. The play has started, and Todd has the next line.

"This is stupid," he grunts, and gets up from the couch. He disappears down the hallway, past his kneeling spot as if it's just another square inch of thin carpet, and slams the door to his room. On cue, we hear the stereo come on and the volume immediately skyrocket.

The sing-along is over. Mom gathers up the spilled sheet music and places it and her guitar in the guitar case. "You all can do what you want," she says, and walks away before we can see the tears in her eyes. But we see them.

"But we want to sing, Momma," Angela says, and she, too, is on the verge of tears. At that moment it feels like the entire universe is treading delicately on that watery, narrow ledge between almost-crying and crying. I cannot bear the suspense. I know there

will be either tears or yelling, but I do not know which to hope for.

And what if there are both? Would things end as badly as they always feel like they're going to when that happens? How many more meltdowns were left in the chamber before things really started to fly apart?

We exist in this electric, awkward balance for a while, the fabled calm before the storm. Mom pretends to do things around the house, always with her back to the floor space in front of the TV where Angela and I are now camped. This means the tears have started. She also pretends not to notice Todd's music and its steadily increasing volume. He knows this will incite her further, move things to the next level. So does Mom. So do all of us. On cue, Mom balls her hands into fists and thrusts them downwards by her side, just like Angela does when she throws a tantrum. Her arms become rigid and she plods down the hallway.

"Todd!" she yells at the door. We all hear her yell sometimes—as a single mother, she is under pressure constantly—but this is the yell she reserves exclusively for her fights with Todd. I cringe.

"Todd! Turn that down!"

"Down?" Todd yells back. "It's already way down! If I turn it down any more, I won't be able to hear it!"

"Turn it down or turn it off, Todd! If you can't sing along with our music, we don't want to hear yours."

"Ours" and "yours." It is always this way now, us against him, and that makes me hurt. I blame most of our family problems on him and part of me really hates him for it, but I can't help think of

how lonely he must feel around all of us "normal" people.

"Dang!" Todd yells, somehow managing in his awkward puberty to combine both high and low pitches in a single, short word.

"Just turn it down, Todd," Mom yells, and walks away with her fists still clinched tightly except for one boney index finger, convinced she has won the battle even though we all know that the stereo volume is still louder than she wants it. We can all still hear it. This, too, is part of the play.

"Wanna watch this, Ericky?" Angela asks. Her voice quavers a little but she is trying to sound excited, trying to tap into our mutual Christmas excitement. This makes me love her a little more and Todd a little less.

"What?"

She points at the TV. "Charlie Brown!"

"Yeah," I say. "I'll be right back."

I intend to go to the bathroom and read, to tap out of things for a few minutes, but I find myself at Todd's door instead. We used to share the room, but lately I have been sleeping on the living room floor when I am home on breaks. I don't mind sleeping on the floor—I could use the couch if I wanted. And sleeping in the living room means I can watch TV until the signal goes off the air late at night. No bedroom in the house has a TV in it, so this is a big deal.

Also, I just can't bring myself to sleep in a room with Todd, for reasons I can't yet articulate. It may have something to do with the primal, animal odor his body gives off no matter how clean he is. It may have to do with his selfishness and sense of entitlement; he constantly reminds me that there is no such thing as a truly selfless act and there really shouldn't be, and he lives according to that philosophy.

I knock on the door.

"What?" The high-low voice again. He thinks Mom has come back for another round. It suddenly occurs to me that that is what I have come back here to prevent. I don't know how to do it, but it has to be done.

"It's me," I say, and walk in. The first thing I notice is that he has Becky, our dog, by the paws and is trying to dance with her to "Aqualung." I feel a stir of surprising panic, but I don't know why. The dancing actually looks funny. Becky looks over her shoulder at me and loses her balance. Her paws slip out of Todd's hands and she runs for the door.

"Stop her!" Todd yells over the music. I shut the door to keep her from leaving. I want to make peace, and this is my offering.

"Thanks, 3-Ric. Here, Becky. How about some Sabbath?" This is a calculated move. Mom hates Black Sabbath more than any of Todd's musical choices. She is convinced that Satan is not only real but inhabits most rock music. I, too, hate Sabbath; I am not convinced they worship Satan (I figure if they worship anything, it's money), but I feel a vague dread when I listen to them all the same. Styx, his second-favorite band, seems safer, even though I recently found out they are named after the river to the underworld. "Underworld" seems a lot safer than "Hell."

"Come on," I say. "Let's play chess and listen to Paradise Theatre."

"Playing chess" involves him beating me in two or three moves, but he loves to play, so that might do.

"No, 3-Ric! Go away. Me and Becky are dancing." He calls me 3-Ric because I wrote my name that way when I was learning cursive.

He has Becky by the paws again, twirling her like she's wearing a poodle skirt. I smell his peculiar smell and I suddenly want to leave. Angela is watching Charlie Brown without me, and who knows what's coming on next. Todd and Mom can work things out for themselves.

"Never mind," I say, laughing. I don't want to laugh, because I can't shake that vague feeling of unease at seeing him and Becky together. It's not like I think he will hurt her—Todd is destructive and hard to get along with, but he isn't violent. Maybe it's Becky herself who makes me uneasy. Angela loves Becky, but (while I won't admit it to anyone) she is a pathetic dog in my eyes, the kind I don't like: a needy, head-ducking, tail-drooping apologizer. Everyone loves a loyal dog, and poor Becky is certainly that. But she seems so cowed and sad. Maybe it's the breed: wispy bags of nothing who get poop stuck in their fur a little too easily. Perhaps seeing her and Todd together just reminds me a little too much of how imperfect everything in the world is. It is something I struggle with.

"You're crazy," I say. It's just something you say, of course.

"Check it out," he says, and dips Becky. Dogs aren't meant to be dipped, but Becky handles it honorably, stumbling backward but maintaining balance. I start to laugh again, but Todd places his lips over hers and pretends to kiss her.

"Eeew!" I yell. "What are you doing?"

"What?" Todd says, letting Becky drop to all fours again. "I wasn't really kissing her, stupid." He falls back on his bed and picks up a paperback novel featuring a dragon and a cowering, shapely woman in a tattered bikini on the cover.

I stand looking at him, hating him. I hate hate. I preach non-hate to my friends at boarding school until they are sick of me, but I suddenly and completely hate my own brother.

"What?" Todd says from the bed. He raises his eyebrows impatiently, waving the book at the door.

I open my mouth to speak, but I have nothing. I don't even know how to form the sentence.

Instead, I leave. I shut the door behind me and look at the open bathroom door, the kneeling space in front of it, the hallway. Mom needs to know ... what? What should I tell her? How do you form such a sentence? Doesn't the fact that I am thinking what I am thinking say more about me than anyone else?

Charlie Brown is almost over when I sit down on the floor next to Angela. She smiles and leans over on me, resting her head on my shoulder.

On the television, Linus lectures about the birth of Christ.

•••••

My daughter knows all of these stories by heart. She's only 14, but we are a strange family that way. I sometimes think I tell her too much about life, but I made a commitment early on that she was only going to hear the truth about everything from me. I was not sheltered from dysfunction in my childhood, unfortunately, but I was most definitely sheltered intellectually, and I am determined that this will not happen

to her. No one ever told me anything; I compensate by telling her everything. It's a gamble.

I have noticed that she is like her Uncle Todd in many ways, even though she has no real memory of him. (I haven't talked to him in almost 10 years. Last I heard, he was confined by his multiple felonies to Tennessee.) For instance, like her Uncle Todd, she doesn't like Christmas. But unlike him, she doesn't make the rest of us miserable about it.

It seems the similarities between them end at advanced intellect and an unwavering commitment to questioning everything. These things I love and encourage in her, while trying to teach her respect for other viewpoints. So far, it seems to be working: whereas Todd demanded everyone bend to his will or descend with him into havoc, she just shrugs her shoulders and says, "Do whatever makes you happy."

I actually took her to visit Todd once in the Larue County jail when she was a toddler. God knows why. I think I wanted to ask him to explain a few things about our childhoods to me, since I still believed such things could be explained. But as soon as we were all gathered in the same cluttered, inhospitable visiting room, I knew I had made a mistake: I never want Todd to touch or even see my daughter. It is not a good feeling to have, and I won't try to argue that it is completely justified,

even in light of his string of sex crimes, although that argument could be made. Instead, I will just confess the truth: I want my brother to stay away from my daughter. I'm afraid the young, peace-wrecking version of him will magically reappear and gobble up her childhood like he did mine.

Although he didn't gobble it up completely, I am happy to report. I still love Christmas, after all. My daughter doesn't, and she isn't really shy about telling you that if you ask her. She'll tell you she doesn't understand it and is more than a little amused by my love for it, since she knows how counter-culture I am about most things.

But she is not rude about it, and I choose not to insist that she share in my yuletide cheer. I do admit that every year, I hope that she and my wife will get into the spirit with me and help put up the tree and decorate the house, but they really have no interest. Sometimes they will be good sports and half-heartedly play along, but they lose interest about an hour into it, leaving the rest to me and our black Lab, Lucy, who sniffs around and tries to figure out what is changing while I string lights on the fake tree and think about buying a nativity set. Then the four of us watch Christmas movies together and eat cookies. Those parts we all love.

LEIF ERICKSON

Leif Erickson

Waiting for Insanity Clause

Today is Christmas Eve
And I think I will clean my
Toilet, perhaps dust my socks

And underwear and other personal
Ornaments too private to be hung
On the public mantle to be stuffed

With Holiday cheer. Later, I might
Wrap what's left of my youth and
Place it beneath the tree, a gift I

Can no longer keep nor one I am
Able to give to another—tonight I
Will wander the streets in search of

Lazarus and Diogenes to hear what
They might have to tell me—alas I
Am not optimistic: I am skeptical of all

Information received from third parties;
When I tire, I think I will come home,
Crawl under the covers and listen

For sleigh bells and tiny hooves—
A childish act, I know—but I yearn
For immortal illusion to bring the

Morning, not for fulfillment or wonder,

That would be too much here at the edge
Of dawn—but perhaps the morning could

Bring a modest gift, even if it's just
A brief, if chastened
Smile.

GARY WALTON

No Christmas in Kentucky

Christmas shoppers shopping on a neon city street
Another Christmas dollar for another Christmas treat
There's satin on the pretty dolls that make the children glow
While a boy walking ragged in the cold Kentucky snow

CHORUS: No, they don't have Christmas in Kentucky
There's no holly on a West Virginia door
For the trees don't twinkle when you're hungry
And the Jingle Bells don't jingle when you're poor

There's lots of toys for children when the Christmas time is near
But the present for the miners is a stocking full of beer
In the dark hills of Kentucky there's one gift that may be found
The coal dust of forgotten days that's lying on the ground

CHORUS: No, they don't have Christmas in Kentucky
There's no holly on a West Virginia door
For the trees don't twinkle when you're hungry
And the Jingle Bells don't jingle when you're poor

Let's drink a toast to Congress and a toast to Santa Claus
and a toast to all the speeches that bring the loud applause
There's not enough to give, no, there's not enough to share
So let's drown the sounds of sorrow with a hearty Christmas cheer!

CHORUS: No, they don't have Christmas in Kentucky
There's no holly on a West Virginia door
For the trees don't twinkle when you're hungry
And the Jingle Bells don't jingle when you're poor

Have a merry, merry Christmas and a happy new year's day
For now's a time of plenty, and plenty's here to stay
But if you knew what Christmas was, I think that you would find
That Christ is spending Christmas in the cold Kentucky mines

CHORUS: No, they don't have Christmas in Kentucky
There's no holly on a West Virginia door
For the trees don't twinkle when you're hungry
And the Jingle Bells don't jingle when you're poor

PHIL OCHS

About The Authors

Leatha Kendrick *is the author of three volumes of poetry, the most recent one* Second Opinion (2008). *Her poems and essays appear in journals and anthologies including:* The Southern Poetry Anthology, *Volume III:* Contemporary Appalachia; What Comes Down to Us—Twenty-Five Contemporary Kentucky Poets; The Kentucky Anthology—Two Hundred Years of Writing in the Bluegrass State; Listen Here: Women Writing in Appalachia, *and* I to I: Life Writing by Kentucky Feminists, *and others. She co-edited* Crossing Troublesome, Twenty-Five Years of the Appalachian Writers Workshop *and wrote the script for* A Lasting Thing for the World—The Photography of Doris Ulmann, *a documentary film. She leads workshops in poetry and non-fiction at the Carnegie Center for Literacy and Learning in Lexington, Ky., as well as at workshops and conferences in Kentucky and elsewhere. She works as a freelance editor and writing mentor.* "The Tides" *is an excerpt from her novel-in-progress.*

Leif Erickson *was born and reared in Lexington, Ky, although he spent his formative years at a Baptist boarding school in Clay County, which he says explains a lot of things about him. Leif is a graduate of the Murray State University Creative Writing Program with a MFA degree in creative nonfiction. Erickson's work has appeared in* New Madrid, Quarter After Eight, *and* Standing on the Mountain: Voices of Appalachia. *He teaches English in Lexington, where he lives with his wife and daughter, both accomplished artists. He enjoys reading, writing and otherwise being a nerd.*

Gary Walton *was born in Covington, Ky., and grew up in Fort Thomas, Ky. He received his bachelor's from Northern Kentucky University in 1981. He studied writing and publishing at the University of South Dakota then moved to Washington, D.C., receiving a Master of philosophy degree in American literature in 1985 from the George Washington University and a doctorate in international modernism in 1991. His areas of special interest are 20th-Century American Literature, the Irish literary renaissance and international modernism. His dissertation was a poststructuralist comparative study of James Joyce's Ulysses and the fiction of Donald Barthelme. He has published stories, poems, non-fiction and letters in* The Washington Post, The Baltimore Sun, California State Poetry Quarterly, *and* The Cincinnati Poetry Review. *His books of poetry include:* The Sweetest Song *(1988),* Cobwebs and Chimeras *(1995),* Effervescent Softsell *(1997),* The Millennium Reel *(2003), and* Full Moon: The Melissa Moon Poems *(2007). His new book of poetry* Eschatology Escadrille: Elegies and Other Memorabilia *is to be released in 2012 from Finishing Line Press. His books of fiction include:* The Newk Phillips Papers *(1995 collection of short stories) and his novel about Newport, Ky., in its heyday as a gambling Mecca:* Prince of Sin City *was published by Finishing Line Press in 2009. Walton has taught writing and literature at The George Washington University, The University of South Dakota, The University of Cincinnati, and Northern Kentucky University. He has also worked as an editor for the United States Coast Guard and several literary journals including* Clifton Magazine, The Vermillion Literary Project *and* The Kentucky Philological Review. *In 1994 and 1995, Walton was nominated for the Pushcart prize. He is Editor of Northern Kentucky State University's* The Journal of Kentucky Studies.

Phil Ochs, *political songwriter and performer of the 1960s and 1970s, was born in El Paso, Texas, Dec. 19, 1940. He attended Ohio State University, majoring in journalism. After three years of college, he dropped out and moved to New York City, where he flourished in the heyday of the Greenwich Village folk music movement of the 1960s. He started out singing at open mikes in the local clubs but by 1964 was well enough established to release his first album* "All the News That's Fit to Sing," *followed by his second album* "Ain't Marching Anymore" *in 1965. By 1966, he was able to sell out Carnegie Hall for his first solo concert. Most of Ochs' songs were political in nature, but often with a blend of humor and seriousness. His subjects were the hot topics of the day—Vietnam, civil rights, hungry miners, protests and tribute songs, mostly to those involved in the fight for justice. He was admired by most all his contemporaries, including Bob Dylan, who once said:* "I just can't keep up with Phil. And he's getting better and better and better." *He released eight studio albums before his death by suicide in 1976.*

The Twelfth Day

Christmas in Store

At Fitzpatrick's Grocery,
Mr. Fitz, Mrs. Fitz,
two of their daughters, and even one granddaughter
had a job in mid-November
when the bulk boxes of candy arrived –
bonbons, orange slices,
chocolate-covered peanuts and raisins,
mixed nuts and hard candies.
The girls lined up at the dining-room table
as close to a factory as the family would ever be:
donned plastic gloves, filled the bags, weighed the bags,
folded down the tops neatly
and, holding carefully,
stapled four times to seal them shut.

The day after Thanksgiving,
when customers came through the blue door
paneled with window panes and
topped off with a bell on a wound strip of copper,
there were Mrs. Fitz and the girls
putting silver-tinseled limbs into the thin metal trunk
and Mr. Fitz raising the tree up
onto the glass-sided table,
where it was set sparkling by a light's spinning filter
of red, green, yellow, and blue.

Underneath the store's tree,
the bags of candy were gifts that never dwindled,
built up as the pile under their tree

growing deep like December,
waiting for the red number on the Chenault and Hoge calendar
on the wall between Fitzpatrick's Grocery
and the Fitzpatricks' home.
Only a door and the bell on its curve of copper
separated the two.
When customers came in, jingling the bell,
Mrs. Fitz would turn down the stove and hurry to wait on them
or Mr. Fitz would get up from his La-Z-Boy
never to know how things turned out
on the TV program he'd been watching.
There was no question: The bell rang, one of them went.
And every customer had a name they knew,
most written on the spine of a charge book,
a drawer of them lined, names up,
with carbon pages filled neatly in handwritten ink:

1 lb ground chuck 35¢
2 potted meat 25¢
1 salt block 42¢
1 candy bar 5¢

No bills were ever sent
but some customers came round
religious as payday to even up.
Some never came back.
When she was there,
the granddaughter stood
in the green folding chair

behind the counter,
a front row to commerce and characters,
a behind-the-scenes view
of the graduated paper sacks
in their perfectly sized compartments.
With an expert snap,
a bag would open so certain
it would set upright to receive each item,
first written into charge book or tapped into adding machine,
the tape double-checked.
People left with what they needed
and more arrived,
knowing each other's hardships,
commenting to one another as they passed
then to whatever Fitzpatricks were there to listen.

Christmas Eve brought customers in search
of a last little something –
a yard of pretty material in a plastic bag
and a package of ric rac,
a carton of Camels,
two bandannas, one red, one blue,
a Vick's inhaler,
or smell-with, as the granddaughter called them,
the smallest paper bag filled with cinnamon balls
to tuck in a stocking,
a cap gun and play money from the spinning toy rack.
The store—which didn't close till 9—
made the family gathering late,

the moon glittering off Elkhorn Creek through the back windows,
everyone present and watching the kitchen clock,
listening hopefully for the last customer to leave.
Finally, but not a moment before nine,
Mr. Fitz would turn off the store lights,
turn the lock,
turn off the spinning light
casting its colors through the darkness
and finally he would step through the door
and take his place in his brown chair beside their tree
loaded with ornaments, lights of every color,
and
piled high with gifts into the middle of the floor.

Tammy Ramsey

TAMMY RAMSEY

Shepherds in Bathrobes

When I was a child, I thought the three wise men and the shepherds really had worn bathrobes and black socks when they came to adore the Christ child. This was the way they were always dressed in the Christmas pageant at our church, and I assumed the costuming was historically accurate. I wasn't quite sure why biblical men had wrapped terry cloth towels around their heads, but since Christmas is often cold in Kentucky, I figured they probably wanted to keep their bald heads warm.

Our tiny Methodist church thought big, and we staged an elaborate re-enactment of the Christmas story every year (although the director made an annual announcement that she would never do this again). To pull this off, everyone in the congregation was drafted into service. Even the youngest served as stable animals, and the most elderly turned the light switches on and off at critical moments. Were it not for the kindness of the Baptists across the road, we would have played to empty pews. We cast them as the audience, and they obliged by dismissing their Sunday night service to help us out.

I can still recall the angels' wings. They were shaped out of baling wire from the hayfield and then covered from span to span with multiple layers of ivory crepe paper. A creative, genial woman, who died much too young, tediously shaped the overlapping layers of fragile paper into thousands of feather-like ruffles. The wings were magnificent, and I'm pretty sure God added Margaret Carr's design to his pattern book.

Our choir of angels who sang on high was small, but their voices were fine and pure and covered every part. Mr. and Mrs. Bell could not be equaled at bass and alto; Cousin May hit the soprano notes with the skill of a trained opera singer; Bill—who later became a Baptist but got his start in the Methodist choir—sang a fine tenor; and his future wife Faye handled the keyboard with skill. There were a few other angels, too—even I—but mostly we only hummed.

Mrs. Prather was the perennial director, and in real life, she was a fifth-grade schoolteacher accustomed to being obeyed. Every year, about halfway through the month of rehearsals, she would have a mild breakdown, alternately crying and yelling, because no one was listening to her. Once she spoke sharply to a wise man who'd been hastily recruited to fill a bathrobe from the ranks of loitering boyfriends hanging around the Methodist Youth Fellowship. Admittedly, he was flirting when he should have been following yonder star, but he was so taken aback at being reprimanded that he vowed never to darken the door of a church again. I hope he didn't keep that vow—I'd hate to think our Christmas pageant sent him

straight to hell.

Years later, though, whenever I found myself standing in the midst of pandemonium trying to lead people who did not want to be led (have you ever tried to build gingerbread houses with 20 Brownie Girl Scouts in a small room?), I would think about Mrs. Prather and carry on for her sake. I wish I'd told her when I could how much the pageants meant to me. One memory, in particular, remains vivid.

Our shepherds were no-nonsense farmers, recruited from the adult men's Sunday school class. I can only imagine how their Christian faith was tested when they were asked to don ridiculous-looking bathrobes in public, wrap towels around their heads, and come to play practice every Sunday afternoon. To compound their stage misery, one year Mrs. P. surprised the shepherds at our first rehearsal by altering their perennial silent tableau. This Christmas, she had said, the shepherds would have lines to recite. Then, she instructed the shepherds to move forward one by one and read their assigned paragraphs. When shepherd No. 2 was called upon, he gamely stepped up. He read the first word "the," but then stopped. He looked at the floor. He cleared his throat. In an instant, I understood. Shepherd No. 2 could not read, a least not well. He was one of the most honorable, pleasant men I've ever met, hardworking and capable, too. I'm sure that in today's schools he would have been diagnosed with dyslexia or some other synapse glitch that made reading more difficult for him than for others. But in that awful moment, he stood mute on the altar of the church.

That's when the good thing happened. Without a look passing between them, the other shepherds began to read the lines for him; their tongues turned to silver, and then they seamlessly moved on to their own. The wise men joined in, too. I've never heard a choral reading more deftly executed. The powerful rhythm of their conjoined voices erased all embarrassment, and we went on to have the best rehearsal we ever had. By the next Sunday, Shepherd No. 2 had memorized his lines, and the incident was never mentioned again.

So it came to pass that I learned the true meaning of Christmas from farmers wearing bathrobes and towels on their heads. Whenever I find myself uncertain of my performance in life, I think about those good men—unsure of themselves, too, but unafraid to look ridiculous in the trying.

Georgia Green Stamper

GEORGIA GREEN STAMPER

There Was a Silence

When he was born
I know
There was a silence
In the Christmas snow
Within the woods
Where squirrels slept
In hollow Beeches
Filled with mast
And last year's leaves.
Glistening, humbled Maples bent
Like bows
With feet, and heads,
and hands
Upon the ground.
From half-way around the world
He leapt from the virgin's womb
And
Mountains,
Already risen
And worn,
Paused ...
Holding breaths
Like precious babes
And waited
For the world
To be transformed.

James B. Goode

James B. Goode

The Christmas Snow Angel

My people always warned each other about getting lost in the doubles of the Pine, whether they were going out to hunt or to cut Christmas trees three hollows over in Sawbranch. After all, this was the great mysterious Pine Mountain where all of the hollows and ridges jabbed their fingers into both sides of a 190-mile-long string of mountains that stretched all the way from Tennessee, through Kentucky and on to Virginia. Many of these heavily forested formations were identical and people often lost their bearings if they crossed from one to another without paying close attention—especially when snow was on the ground.

Every Christmas tree we ever had came from one of these places in the Pine, carefully selected, cut with a pruning saw and dragged home on the back of a sled fitted with curved sourwood runners. Several of the men in my family took turns pulling the sled toward the house, until it landed in the front yard, the tree taken down and fitted with a rough-board stand, then gingerly carried into the front room where it was to reign until just after New Year's Day. Our Christmas trees were always strung with popcorn, crepe-paper chains, pine cones, and hollow, brightly colored eggs. Granny took a big sewing needle and made a hole in each end of the brown eggs. When I was a child, I placed my mouth over one of the holes, puffed my cheeks out like a frog, and blew the raw egg through the opposite hole into a cereal bowl. We painted the shells with watercolor Christmas designs—primitively drawn holly, mistletoe, pine-bough wreaths, hemlock garlands, pyramids of pine Christmas trees, and red bows. Granny and I draped the tree with strung popcorn and links made of brightly colored crepe-paper fashioned into chains. We collected big pinecones from the soft-needle beds beneath the pine tree forest and tied loops of string around their bases. I circled the tree, hanging the decorations on the sweet-smelling pine branches.

•••••

In many ways, the Christmas of 1954, when I had just turned 10, was the same as all the others had been, but one event was to change all that forever and became one of the favorite stories to tell when we gathered for Christmas at Granny's in later years.

"This will be a 'skinny' Christmas," Granny said that year. "We just don't have much money this time around. Granddaddy just ain't worked much this year. Work has been awful slack for the past two years." She sighed and looked at the tree.

"I got an idea," I said. "Let's gather up some things from around the house, wrap them up and pretend-like they are presents."

"I sure like that idea," Granny said. "You go gather up some stuff, and I'll hunt

the tissue paper."

We spent the next hour wrapping everything from doorstops to stove wood and putting them under the tree. I had saved some money made from selling kindling and bought Granny a new set of knitting needles and Granddaddy a two-blade Barlow knife. I had slipped up and wrapped their presents in my little loft room when they weren't looking and placed them carefully on a low branch so they could be easily found.

Just as we finished, something moving along the back wall of the kitchen caught my eye. Traveler, Granny's old black tomcat, was making his way toward the living room, and I knew if I didn't get him, he would be in serious trouble.

My Granddaddy Larkin had made three cat holes in the back door to the old farmhouse where they lived near the Auburn Ash coal camp. He had fashioned flaps for each one out of pieces of old, worn-out, leather mining boots to help keep out the cold air. "Why do we need three cat holes when we only have one cat?" Granny asked as she screwed up her face like a dried persimmon and wiped her red, dishpan hands on her blue apron.

Granddaddy sat at the yellow Formica kitchen table with his crooked stemmed pipe clamped between his yellowed teeth. His bushy eyebrows stuck out over his steel gray eyes as he scowled at Traveler, who peeked cautiously from behind the kindling box near the coal cookstove.

"Because, when I say SKAT! Dad Gummit, I mean SKAT!" His voice was loud and gruff and the startled Traveler spun both hind paws as he tried to get traction on the slick linoleum, enough to make a dive for one of the holes in the bottom of the door. He had barely made it to the rough-sawed hole when Granddaddy clapped his big rough hands and let go with a loud whoop.

"Yaiiiii cat!" he bellowed.

Traveler slid through and into the pitch black of a cold winter night. Granny winked at me as she wadded up her wet dishrag and threw it at Granddaddy. He ducked just in time. The rag hit the stove, sizzled as it stuck to the hot metal, and then fell to the floor.

"It's beyond me why that poor cat gets in under your skin like that," she said as she scooped up the dishrag. "He ain't hurtin' nothin' by being behind the stove … and besides, he's a good mouser, as good a mouser as I ever saw."

"Yeah, and it's so cold and blowing out there tonight," I said from my perch on the sawed-off stool next to the stove. Where's he gonna sleep in a knee-deep snow?" I went to the window, rubbed the steam away, and tried to peer out into the yard.

Granny had supper almost ready. The smoked jowl had been fried and placed in the warmer above the cookstove. Kennebec potatoes sliced length-wise had been

placed in the hot bacon grease and fried to a golden brown. She had seasoned and boiled some home-canned kale in an iron pot. She waited for the iron skillet of cornbread that had been placed on the top rack of the oven to brown. She removed an eye from the stove with the lifter and selected some short pine kindling wood from the wood box. Granny had an uncanny ability to control the temperature of the oven by choosing the right sizes of split wood and setting the stovepipe draft in just the right place.

I couldn't stop thinking about Traveler during supper. I knew he was cold and hungry—maybe even lost in the deep snow. I tried to hear him meowing, but I couldn't because of the clanging of Granddaddy's fork on his old chipped plate, his loud slurping as he saucered his coffee, and the rustle of Granny's apron as she shuttled between the stove and table. Once Granddaddy sat down at the table, that was that. He asked questions like: Got anymore coffee? and Is that all the gravy we have? Or he would just lean over, look in the bowl, and grunt. These were all signals for Granny to fetch whatever the language spoke.

"Could I go play in the snow after supper?" I asked. If I could come up with an excuse to get outside, I knew I would have a better chance of finding Traveler and smuggling him into the loft where I slept when visiting Granddaddy and Granny.

"Boy, have you got cornmeal mush for brains?" Granddaddy said as he raised one of his bushy eyebrows and stared at me like I was a red-headed stepchild.

"Now, Lark, don't be so hard on Skip. He really enjoyed being out there this morning when we went to milk the cow. We even made snow angels out beside the barn," she said.

I was surprised when Granny stopped along the long path to the barn and fell backward into the snow. She had lain still—almost as if she were dead—then slowly moved her arms and legs, bringing them upward toward her ears and back down several times. "Come over here and help your old Granny up," she said after she had finished.

I struggled through the deep snow, stuck out my hand, and pulled with all my might. Granny came up in one motion and let out a big grunt at the same time. She looked back at the outline of the snow angel.

"That's the kind of angel that come to them shepherds in the field when Jesus was born," she said.

I looked carefully at the figure. The angel's wings and robes were cut deeply into the snow. I could clearly see the outline of Granny's head where her gray hair bun had made its mark.

"Boy, quit day dreamin' and bank the Warm Morning Heater for the night."

Granddaddy's voice jolted me out of my daydream. I went over to the coal scuttles behind the stove and selected one with some finer coal in the bottom, carefully tipping the bucket and removing a shovelful of the glistening, black fines. As I opened the stove door, I gingerly placed them on the hot coals so as to not cause them to explode into flame. I kept scooping from the bucket and placing them on the coals until all I could see was a smoldering, yellow smoke rising from a faint, red glow. I closed the door and shut the front draft completely. This would hold the fire until morning when Granddaddy would open the draft and punch it with a poker to get the flame started again.

Granddaddy stood up from his ladder-back chair where he had been reading his Bible, took out his chew, and threw it into one of the coal scuttles. He yawned and stretched his great arms out in a wide circling motion.

"I could stretch a mile, if I didn't have to walk back," he said as he expelled a long breath. He walked over to the well-worn, porcelain double sink, picked out a glass from the drain board, ran it half-full with water, and plopped his false teeth into the bottom. He looked funny without his teeth—his lips rolled inward and his mouth wrinkled and puckered like those on Granny's dried apple dolls. The gray stubble on his chin moved up and down as he raked his upper lip back and forth

across the bristly beard.

I knew he was getting ready to go to bed. He always did the same things. After putting his teeth in to soak, he would cough deeply as if he wanted to clear his entire head and chest before shuffling toward the cannon-ball brass bed in the living room.

"I'll be there directly," Granny said. "I've got a few more things to do. I just have to sew the rickrack along the hem of Sarah's dress."

He didn't look back or answer. I watched him through the doorway as he took off his bibbed overalls and hung them on a 20-penny nail driven into the door facing. His long underwear was dingy from coal dust soaked into every thread. He didn't even take off his socks. He just peeled back the quilts, slipped under, and turned onto his left side.

"Good night, Granddaddy," I yelled from the kitchen.

"Night ..." was all he said. The quilts pulled up to his ears muffled his voice.

I stayed up with Granny while she sewed the rickrack on the gingham dress. When she finished pressing it, she folded it carefully into a brown box she had gotten from the Auburn Ash Commissary Department Store. She tied some white, cotton twine around it in two directions and very simply wrote Mom's name, Sarah, with a stub of a pencil.

"We'd better be off to bed before the

old bearded fellow comes," she said and winked at me. At 10, I had known for a couple of years that the "old bearded fellow" slept in the brass bed in the living room.

Granny took the pins from her bun and let her hair fall. It cascaded down her back, stopping right at the back of her knees. She pulled it forward over her shoulder and brushed it vigorously with long, deliberate strokes.

"I'm going to the loft," I said. Granny turned and held her arms out for a hug. She gave the best hugs. I put my arms around her roundness and squeezed.

"Sleep tight," she said. She patted my head just before I turned to climb the steep wall ladder in the corner of the living room.

I already had a plan. When everyone was in bed and I could hear Granddaddy snoring, I was going to sneak outside and look for Traveler. He would purr like a quiet motor running under my warm quilts. I could put him out my little window onto the porch roof Christmas morning before Granddaddy found him.

I didn't bother to take off anything but my shoes and slipped under the quilts in one swift motion and waited. I must have slept for several hours. Then, for some reason, I woke up suddenly, sat straight up in bed, bumping by head hard on a rafter in the steep roof. The room was dark except for a faint glow from a candle

Granny had lit and placed on a table beside the Christmas tree. She had said she was leaving a light burning for Santa Claus.

I could hear Granddaddy's steady snores, woven with Granny's deep breaths. I listened to make sure I hadn't awakened anyone, and then slid my feet into a pair of lace-up half-boots Mom had mail-ordered from Mason's Shoe Company catalog. My wool coat went on next and right after, my homemade wool gloves. I climbed down the ladder, lightly placing each foot on the rungs so as not to make any noise. I made my way to the back door, and then stepped outside where the wind was swirling fiercely. The temperature had dropped several degrees since we had gone to milk the cow. It was snowing so hard that the flakes stung my cheeks, some sticking to my eyelashes, blinding me almost immediately.

I called out for Traveler. "Here, kitty, kitty, kitty," I said in a muted, high-pitched voice. I searched around the outdoor toilet and the smokehouse, trying to coax him out of hiding with a more high-pitched "kitty, kitty, kitty," but he didn't answer. He didn't appear to be anywhere near the house. He must have gone toward the barn, I thought. The barn was out of sight from the house and sat several hundred yards away on a little ridge by itself. Its location aggravated Granddaddy.

"Why the heck would anybody with half a brain build a barn so far from the house?" he often complained to Granny.

"I don't know why you're so worried about it. You never go out there. I'm the one who feeds and milks the cow," Granny declared.

With every step, my feet broke through the wet snow, causing my legs to sink to mid-calf. My gloves were already wet. The darkness and blowing snow made it difficult for me to see as I struggled up one hill and then another calling Traveler, but he didn't answer. I found myself in a dense pine forest when I heard a faint meow coming from somewhere down below. I stood still and strained to listen. My heartbeat pulsed loudly in my ears, reminding me of the deep, vibrating sound of those big steam locomotives that pulled coal out of Auburn Ash.

I was on the edge of a steep hillside when I heard him again. I tried to run toward the sound but stumbled, lost my balance, and tumbled over the edge of the hill, rolling over and over, striking rocks and limbs littered across the steep bank. My head struck something, creating a terrible explosion of light followed by flashes, much like I had seen when I closed my eyes and pressed against my eyelids with my fingers.

I don't know how long I was unconscious, but when I came to, I was under one of the pine trees and felt what I thought to be a tiny rough piece of sandpaper being raked across my face. As I moved my hand upward, my hand brushed fur.

"Traveler!" I cried. "Where have you been, boy?" I sat up quickly, picking him up and cradling him in my arms. He purred and nuzzled my hand, dipping his head downward over and over and pushing it under my fingers.

The snowstorm lifted some and the wind slackened. A peppering of flakes still fell as I looked around to figure out where we were, but I couldn't make out anything I recognized. An uneasy feeling crept into my heart and stomach. My feet were freezing and turning numb. There was a hill on either side of me. Which way out of here? I asked myself as I began to panic. Traveler tucked his head under my arm as I rose to my feet and began making my way up one of the hills. The snow reflected a little dim light, but I could barely make out the shapes on the ground. Mostly, I felt my way along with my feet and one free hand. More rocks and trees blocked my path.

When I arrived at the top, I still didn't know where we were. The sickening thought of being lost closed in around me like the depths of a cave. I sat down in the snow and began to cry. As I tried to wipe my bleary eyes with my hands, Traveler jumped from my arm, ran about 20 feet, stopped, meowed, and looked back at me.

He moved again, hopping like a rabbit in the deep snow. He paused, craned his head around as if to say, *Come on, Skip, follow me!* Then he disappeared.

I managed to get to my feet and trudge across the snow crust toward where I had last seen him. Periodically, I could see the little pockets of his tracks in the snow, leading down the hill directly toward the opposite side. I lost his signs in the dim light and then suddenly they reappeared.

As I topped the opposite hill, I saw that his tracks made a wide circle and then headed down the ridgeline. Halfway down, they veered off to the right and onto a flat. A small, dark object caught my eye just off to my left and I moved toward it. It was Traveler! He had stopped and sat down in the snow. As I approached him, he rolled onto his side and wiggled like he did when he was around Granny.

It wasn't until I was right upon him that I realized why he had stopped. There, lit by the dim light of a crisp morning breaking over the snowy ridges, was the faint outline of Granny's Christmas snow angel. The darkness within me disappeared like a wisp as Traveler and I moved toward the house.

James B. Goode

JAMES B. GOODE

Santa Claus is Coming to Town

You better watch out,
You better not cry,
Better not pout,
I'm telling you why,
Santa Claus is comin' to town.
He's making a list,
And checking it twice,
Gonna find out,
Who's naughty and nice,
Santa Claus is comin' to town.
He sees you when you're sleepin',
He knows when you're awake,
He knows if you've been bad or good
So be good for goodness sake.
You better watch out,
You better not cry,
Better not pout,
I'm telling you why
Santa Claus is comin' to town.
Santa Claus is comin' to town.

James Lamont "Haven" Gillespie

About The Authors

Tammy Ramsey *is an Associate Professor at Bluegrass Community and Technical College where she teaches English and journalism. She has also been a faculty member at Spalding University, Kentucky State University and Midway College. Ramsey worked for nine years as a freelance copy editor at the* Lexington Herald-Leader. *She holds a master's degree in English from the University of Kentucky and a MFA in writing from Spalding University. Ramsey's poems have been published in* The Louisville Review, The Heartland Review, *and* Arable, *and in the anthology* New Growth: Recent Kentucky Writing. *Because she had an aunt who saw to it that Christmas was breathtakingly beautiful, and because she had parents who made sure the gifts were just right, Ramsey came to think of Christmas as the best time of the year. To this day, it seems to her the season when people cut each other a little more slack, give each other a little more empathy. Ramsey believes this to be a good thing.*

Georgia Green Stamper *is a graduate of Transylvania University with a bachelor's degree in English. She is a former high school English, theater, and speech teacher. She grew up on a tobacco farm in Oldham County, Ky. She and her husband still own her ancestral land at Eagle Creek, Ky. Her essays have been published by the National Public Radio "This I Believe" series;* Kentucky Monthly; Kentucky Humanities Magazine; *and the literary anthologies* New Growth *(Jesse Stuart Foundation);* Tobacco *(Wind Publications);* Daughters of the Land *(in press - Texas Tech U Press);* The Journal of Kentucky Studies *(Northern KY U);* Motif I and Motif II *(Motes Books). Since 2004, she has written a bi-weekly column, "Georgia: On My Mind," for* The Owenton News-Herald *(Owenton, Ky.). Her books include a collection of essays,* You Can Go Anywhere: From the Crossroads of the World *(Wind Publications, 2008). She has been the recipient of many literary awards including the Emma Bell Miles Award for Essay from Lincoln Memorial University's Mountain Heritage Literary Festival, the Carole Pettit Creative Writing Medallion and Legacies Award from the Carnegie Center, and the Leadingham Prose Award from the Frankfort (Ky.) Arts Foundation. In early 2006, she became a regular commentator for NPR member station WUKY. She and her husband reside in Lexington, Ky.*

James B. Goode's *biography can be seen on page 69.*

James Lamont "Haven" Gillespie *is best known for having written the lyrics for "Santa Claus is Comin' to Town" in 1934 during a 15-minute subway ride in New York City. His collaborator was composer J. Fred Coots. The song debuted on Eddie Cantor's Thanksgiving radio special and was soon selling 25,000 copies of sheet music a day. Born in Covington, Ky., Feb. 6, 1888, Gillespie was one of nine children of William and Anna Gillespie, a poor family that lived in the basement of a house on Third Street between Madison Avenue and Russell Street. Gillespie dropped out of school in the fourth grade but eventually found work as a typesetter for the* Cincinnati Times-Star. *As a sideline, he found work as a "plug" man, entertaining audiences at local vaudeville shows by playing and singing songs he had written. He left Cincinnati in his early twenties to move to New York City where he worked for* The New York Times, *continued his interest in music as a song plugger on Tin Pan Alley, and wrote songs for vaudeville acts. His first major hit was "Drifting & Dreaming in 1925 followed by "Breezin' Along With the Breeze" in collaboration with Dick Whiting the following year. His 1949 hit "That Lucky Old Sun" was recorded by such greats as Frank Sinatra, Louis Armstrong, and Jerry Lee Lewis. He was inducted into the Songwriter's Hall of Fame in 1972. He died in 1975 in Las Vegas, Nev. His songs are still being recorded by contemporary artists. George Strait covered Gillespie's 1921 song "Right or Wrong," which earned Gillespie an ASCAP Country Music award in 1985.*

Publication Credits & Reprint Permissions

Arnow, Harriette. "Ode to a Purple Aluminum Christmas Tree." *Selected Kentucky Literature*. Danbury, Conn.: Archer Editions Press, 1980. 115. Print.

Arnow, Harriette. "Chapter 18." *The Dollmaker*. New York: The Macmillan Company, 1954. 246-259. Print.

Berry, Wendell. "VI: Remembering that it happened once." *A Timbered Choir: The Sabbath Poems 1979-1997*. Berkeley, Calif.: Counterpoint, 1999. Print.

Bingham, Sallie. "The Birds' Tree." *The High Cost of Denying Rivers Their Floodplains*. Louisville, Ky.: Crazy Rabbit, 1995. Print. Used with permission of the author.

Caudill, Rebecca. *A Certain Small Shepherd*. New York: Henry Holt, 1965. Print.

Cobb, Irwin Shrewsbury. "The Exit of Anse Dugmore." *The Escape of Mr. Trimm: His Plight and Other Plights*. New York: George H. Doran Company, 1918. Print.

Fox, John Jr. "Christmas Eve on Lonesome." *Christmas Eve on Lonesome and Other Stories*. New York: Charles Scribner's Sons, 1914. 3-9. Print.

Gillespie, James "Haven" and J. Fred Coots. "Santa Claus Is Coming to Town." New York: Leo Feist, Inc., 1934. Print.

Goode, James. "A Change of Heart." *Kentucky Monthly* December 2009/January 2010: 38-41. Print.

Goode, James. "The Christmas Snow Angel." *Kentucky Monthly* December 2001: 26-28. Print.

Goode, James. "Gathering Christmas." *Kentucky Monthly* December 2004: 35-37. Print.

McElmurray, Karen. "Chapter Nine: Maria Milgrosa." *Surrendered Child*. Athens, Ga.: University of Georgia Press, 2004. 183-207. Print.

Merton, Thomas. "Christmas Card Poem: 1947." *Thomas Merton's Marian Poetry*. Web. 4 Nov. 2011. <http://campus.udayton.edu/mary//resources/poetry/merton.html>.

Niles, John Jacob. "Now That it is Christmas." *Brick Dust and Buttermilk*. Frankfort, Ky.: Boone Tolliver Press, 1977. 34. Print.

Ochs, Phil. "No Christmas in Kentucky" Words and Music by Phil Ochs. Copyright © 1964 Barricade Music, Inc. Copyright Renewed. All Rights Controlled and Administered by Almo Music Corp. All Rights Reserved. Used by Permission. *Reprinted by Permission of Hal Leonard Corporation*.

Pruett, Lynn. "Heartichoke." *When the Bough Breaks*. Lexington, Ky.: KaBooM Writing Collective, 2009. Print.

Smith, Dave. "In Memory of Hollis Summers." *The Wick of Memory: New and Selected Poems 1970-2000*. Baton Rouge: Louisiana State University Press, 2000. 26-27. Print.

Smith, Effie Waller. "December." *Songs of the Months*. New York: Broadway Publishing Company, 1904. 25. Print.

Stamper, Georgia Green. "Shepherds in Bathrobes." *Kentucky Monthly* December 2010/January 2011: 28-29. Print.

Stuart, Jane. "New Year." *White Barn*. Frankfort, Ky.: The Whippoorwill Press, 1973. 27-28. Print.

Summers, Hollis. "Christmas Card: For Edward." Web. <www.betweenthecovers.com/btc>.

Tate, Allen. "Ah, Christ, I love you rings to the wild sky ..." *Sonnets At Christmas*. Cummington, Mass.: Cummington Press, 1941. Print.

Tate, Allen. "This is the Day His hour of life draws near ..." *Sonnets At Christmas*. Cummington, Mass.: Cummington Press, 1941. Print.

Toner, Gerald. "Lipstick Like Lindsay's." *Lipstick Like Lindsay's and Other Christmas Stories*. New York: Pelican, 1990. 27-36. Print.

Walker, Frank X. "Elves." *Black Box*. Lexington, Ky.: Old Cove Press, 2006. 21-22. Print.

Warren, Robert Penn. "Christmas Gift." *Virginia Quarterly Review Winter*. Web. 1935: 73-85. <www.vqronline.org/articles/1937/winter/warren-christmas-gift/>.

Whitman, Albery. "One Snowy Night." *Not a Man, Yet a Man*. Springfield, Ohio: Republic Printing Company, 1877. Print.

Wilkinson, Crystal. "Little Bird." *The Birds of Opulence*. Unpublished Manuscript. Print.